Sapalah Shuunka Wanblee win
Grey hound Eagle woman

Freedom – It is Creator's greatest gift. It is what two-legged (Human) seeks, as well as the Wamaskaskan - the four-legged, the finned and the winged. Unfortunately, Two-legged has given away his Freedom to the Blue Man of Black Elk's vision.

Art by Charles Russell

For Sky –
The epitome of
Freedom
Love from
Gluyhound EagleWoman
The Bee
EagleMan

CREATOR'S CODE
Planetary Survival & Beyond

Ed McGaa, J.D., Eagle Man, OST 15287

Editors: Pamela Cosgrove, Diane Elliott,
and Pam Hanway

Cover Artist: Marie Buchfink

 Four Directions Publishing, Minneapolis

Four Directions Publishing

For information, address:
188 Moreland Ave. E.
W. St. Paul, MN 55118
eagleman4@aol.com or delliott@usafamily.net
www.edmcgaa.com

Cover illustration by Marie Buchfink
Art Direction by Kimberlea A. Weeks

ISBN 9645173-5-3

Contents

Acknowledgements

My Teachers and Mentors:

    Chief Fools Crow

    Chief Eagle Feather

    Ben Black Elk

    Hilda Neihardt

    Dr. John Bryde

    My Dad – William Denver McGaa

    My Older Sister – LaVerne Heiter

To all the courageous and the brave who would not give up The Way despite the seemingly hopeless odds against them. To those who came later and supported Chief Eagle Feather and Chief Fools Crow's efforts to begin anew by bringing alive our annual Sun Dance thanksgiving to Creator.

About the Author

Ed (Eagle Man) McGaa, J.D. is a registered Teton Oglala, born on the Pine Ridge reservation. Following his childhood ambition, he became a Marine Fighter Pilot and flew 110 combat missions in Vietnam. He holds a law degree from the University of South Dakota and is the author of eight books; including *Mother Earth Spirituality* (Harper & Row Publishers), *Nature's Way* (Harper/Collins) and *Native Wisdom* (Council Oak Books). Eagle Man participated six times in six years as a sun dancer under the tutelage of the holy men Chief Eagle Feather, Chief Fool's Crow and Ben Black Elk.

Foreword

*Dr. John Bryde, *Modern Indian Psychology,* former Jesuit Missionary, 1940's, Lakota Sioux Reservations.

As a result of their awareness of God's Presence in the world, the Indians had two main drives: to seek and speak the truth, and to be happy with one another. In the old days, it was unheard of that an Indian would tell a lie to another person after smoking the pipe with him. Seeking the truth, which comes from God, was behind all their vision quests called the hanbleceya. People who think that the Indian people didn't have much in the way of religion are astounded upon reading the following words of Black Elk. More profound thoughts cannot be found in any other culture on the face of the earth–and Black Elk is simply saying what his people had believed for centuries:

"We should understand well that all things are the work of the Great Spirit. We should know that He is within all things: the trees, the grasses, the rivers, the moutnains, and all the four legged animals, and the winged people; and even more important, we should understand that He is also above all these things and peoples. When we do understand all this deeply in our hearts, then we will fear, and love, and know the Great Spirit, and then we will be and act and live as He intends.

Unfortunately, as in any group of people or things, there are always some people that are bad and are out to deceive or to trick the good people. In the end, however, the good people will win, just because they are good. This belief is seen again and again in the Indian stories about Iktomi, the spider. He is the tricky fellow who is out to fool, to cheat, and to take advantage of good people but, in the end, Iktomi usually ends up losing, and this reflects the Indian view that the Good Person eventually comes out ahead. In brief, man is made to tell the truth, to be good, and to be happy with this fellow man because all things are one, related, and holy with God in them.

Some people think that the Sioux held the Sun Dance because they worshipped the sun as their god. This is not true at all. The sacred cottonwood tree was at the very center of the dancing circle and it represented Wakan Tanka, to whom they constantly prayed during the dancing.

They were constantly aware of the Presence of God in the world, working through all things and trying to communicate with man. Consequently, they had God constantly on their minds. There was hardly an action that they would do without first praying. On rising in the morning, they would pray. Before eating, they would pray by making a small offering of their food. Whatever they were going to eat, they would first pour or drop a little of it on the ground "woshapi" or "wasna" as an offering to God, returning it to the earth from which it came in a gesture of gratitude. If someone came to visit, before talking, they would pray first by smoking the pipe together. Smoking the pipe was a religious act, binding all who smoked it to tell the truth. The entire universe prays together with the man who offers the pipe to God. Not to speak the truth after smoking the pipe was a great evil because it was an act against the truth and against God.

Back in 1893, the official report of the Bureau of Ethnography wrote: *"The most suprising fact relating to the North American Indians, which until lately had not been realized, is that they habitually lived in and by religion to a degree comparable with the old Israelites of the theocracy.*

Even earlier than 1893, the famous author, Washington Irving wrote in 1837, *"Simply to call these people religious would convey but a faint idea of the deep hue and piety which pervades their whole conduct. Their honesty is immaculate, and their purity of purpose and their observance of the rites of their religion are most uniform and remarkable. They are certainly more like a nation of saints than a horde of savages."*

The famous George Bird Grinnel wrote about the notion of God in the lives of the Indians: *"He is an intangible spirit, omnipotent and beneficent. He pervades the universe and is its supreme ruler. Upon his will depends everything that happens. He can bring good luck or bad; can give success or failure. Everything rests with him. As a natural consequence of this conception of the Deity, they are a very religious people. Nothing is undertaken without prayer to the Father for assistance."*

Dr. Bryde spoke fluent Lakota. Therefore he was able to converse freely within hundreds of interviews beginning in the early forties with experienced warriors and direct descendants of Sioux campaigns against the U.S. Army. The aging warriors took a liking to the Jesuit linguist and readily spoke of their experiences; always with verifying comrades present of battles and their reflections of their leaders, Red Cloud, Crazy Horse and Sitting Bull as well as others. **Early writers did not speak our language.** Father Bryde, S.J. did! This was a tremendous advantage for accuracy and the real truth which early writers such as Marie Sandoz and modern ones as well, continue to distort, dilute and downplay. John Bryde's historical research is a gifted resource within these pages. I respect Bryde's research to such a high degree regarding the Teton Lakota, that I hold his work as far more reliable to the extent that notations will be listed from other writers/researchers only. A goodly portion of the Sioux history and the four major leaders depicted within this work is from his book: *Modern Indian Psychology* and other notes as well. Since the linguist, Dr. Bryde, had such an advantage over the attempts of other writers including his constant reservation presence (along with his scholarship, respectful attitude, devotion and expertise), I have dispensed with notating every historically claimed statement or comments spoken by those warrior's of the past whom all that he interviewed with the exception of several accredited comments from Chief Flying Hawk, Oglala warrior and Chief of that era. John Neihardt of *Black Elk Speaks* set this precedent to some extent in his interviews.

I have twelve brothers and sisters, all of whom attended the reservation mission boarding school where then, Father Bryde, served as teacher besides his historical research. All spoke highly of his ability to derive and instill positive attitudes from the historical leadership and real life track record of their past. These needed facts for young minds are highly evident in *Modern Indian Psychology*, wherein lies **23 years of research with the Sioux**, interviewing those who truly knew our history, leaders, values, culture and our spirituality; and which differs considerably from the white man's portrayals. *Author's Note: Dr. John Bryde is presently 87 years old at the time of this printing and retired as a university professor in Vermillion, SD.*

Introduction

"A tyrant must put on the appearance of uncommon devotion to religion. Subjects are less apprehensive of illegal treatment from a ruler whom they consider god-fearing and pious. On the other hand, they do less easily move against him, believing that he has the gods on his side."

Aristotle

This is not a writing of mythology, fairy tales, 'hocus pocus' or worse - superstition. You will find far more superstitious beliefs, practices and proclamations emanating from the two largest religions upon the planet than you will in the spirituality of the traditional Lakota Sioux. Possibly Creator (God) could finally be tired of Superstition which has caused death and destruction down through the centuries of mankind and even presently. With the forthcoming environmental edicts about to emanate from reacting Nature herself in these suddenly aware times; quite possibly Creator is beginning to show us how disastrous our superstition based (along with accompanying ignorance and wasteful, materialistic appetites) folly and disrespect for Its Creation can become.

It is time that Indigenous speaks up in this hemisphere and it is time that Dominant Society keeps quiet and listens for once, after all these centuries since he first came here. The ongoing Environmental Catastrophe happening at this very moment tells you to Introspect and listen to a people who have lived safely, harmoniously with Nature down through many more centuries on this continent than Dominant Society has. From my observation, the white man is bent on the *appearance of obtaining* personal salvation. The North American Indian is more concerned with planetary salvation. In obvious Truth, it did not take Dominant Society long to un-do the successful environmental pattern the Indigenous employed. We do not believe that we need to be 'saved' from our Benevolent and All-Providing Creator who made us. Such superstitions the white man has placed upon us, even banning our religion and language to force us to comply. Religious extremists hatched a federal built and staffed all-Indian (mostly Sioux and Chippewa) insane asylum built at Canton, S.D. to primarily contain our religious leaders. Thanks to the Martin Luther King civil rights movement our ban was finally lifted in 1978 through the Congressional Freedom of Religion Act. In the meantime, we faithfully served our country beginning in WWI and on into the Iraq wars.

Conversion is not a word in the Sioux (Lakota/Dakota) language. No such attempt is intended herein. Creator's Observable Truth will be the intention, however, and how to respect, live, act and promote what you discover...if you care at all for your own progeny...the generations unborn. There will be no 'sign-up sheet' filled with a litany of false, gilded, man-made religious promises at the end of the last chapter.

Sioux traditionalists believe that one will be greeted by their own progeny in the Spirit World when it becomes their time. What will they say to you if you left them an overpopulated, over-heated, resource-depleted and water-scarce habitat? All Truth is believed to reign in that Beyond. They (your progeny) will discover where you were, what trail you walked, your earthly journey...be it **for or against the planet** - Creator's Creation. Those who suffered from environmental chaos, they may chastise you...for an Eternity. Would they not have a Truthful Right to? You have the choice: to prepare your legacy for good by protecting Mother Earth, or for bad (chosen ignorance) by ignoring Mother Earth. She is your gift, your home given to you from none other than the Ultimate - Creator. Do you not disrespect the Ultimate Maker by not appreciating the great gifts allowed you? You will have a heavy burden if you do not appreciate and worse, chose to ignore/ harm/ *abuse*, Creator's Mother Earth.

Native Americans and Christianity - 19th and 20th Century

A significant percentage of Christianity's faithful maintain that God (Creator, to we Sioux) will come down from the sky and resurrect (save) the faithful. This is what we Indians were taught by reservation missionaries and as well in the off-reservation mission churches located at nearby reservation border towns where many Indian people moved to after leaving their parent or home reservations.

Most North American tribal affiliated Indigenous were forced into Christianity via the 1885 federal banishment of Native religious/spiritual beliefs and the related ceremonies that accompanied or fulfilled Native prayer or beseeching to their concept of a Higher Power (Creator). This un-Constitutional edict was initiated by lobbying Christian missionaries and carried forward by the Grant Administration. It was enacted into federal law and henceforth followed through by succeeding presidential administrations. This blatant disregard for constitutional protections finally ended with the Congressional removal of 'The Ban' formally with the Freedom of Religion Act in 1978.

Missionaries were granted large tracts of reservation land for the building of their churches and boarding schools for Indian youth despite the acclaimed Constitutional declaration that the Federal Government will not support any one particular religion nor diminish rights of others to beseech or to not beseech one's concepts of a Higher Power. To enforce the Ban among the Sioux, who were the last of the large North American tribes to finally submit to the U. S. Government, the insane asylum mentioned previously, was built at Canton, South Dakota at the beginning of the 20th century. Its primary purpose was for incarceration of Sioux Lakota/Dakota medicine men who stubbornly kept to their ancestral spiritual beliefs and practices. The Hiawatha, U. S. Federal Indian Insane Asylum was cast upon a people who historically had very few mental illnesses. Several hundred graves representing these innocent victims yet remain as stark proof between the fairways of the Canton Golf Course. Authors, including Indian authors, never tell of this religious inspired and governmental oppression. In this Indian author's opinion, their cowardly avoidance is akin to those who deny that the Holocaust existed. The extremes of the religious sects do play a deadly game.

Non-believer and Believer Categories within Dominant Society

Group 1: Many folks do not believe in a Higher Power. For them, there is no such thing as this foolish 'God' so many humans have come up with. As to how we got here or how this planet evolved to provide living entities, they have various theories. Their initial defense is that they 'have never seen' this so called 'God'. They might add; "We also have never talked to this supposed entity." From my experience and conversations with these so-called 'non-believers'…which such classification, I am sure they resent…they look down on us 'believers' as a sorry bunch of silly fools, misfits actually, who are now hell-bent on destroying the earth environmentally while we are at it. As a neighbor next door, however, I would expect little trouble from them and would prefer them over many others. Their concept of a life beyond is fairly simple: 'Lights out!' 'The Curtain has dropped.' 'Poof! Blackness! Nothing!'

Group 2: In the middle of the non-believers and the more extreme believers are those fairly peaceful folk who believe in a Higher Power of sorts; They are ethical and moral, have a degree of common sense, are often college educated or at least well read, keep up on current news, often see a movie, are independent, vote, respect Democratic principles and generally appreciate that they live in a free country if they happen to be so blessed. These folks usually will not condemn the non-believers or the extreme believers although politically they worry about where the extreme believers are taking the country. In America, their favorite remark regarding differences is, 'It is a free country!' They remain wary of extremists however. They hold to a life hereafter, at least, but often admit they are not exactly sure as to what it will be.

Group 3: Near the opposite end of the religious spectrum, there are those who are 'hell bent' and determined that God will appear (soon for many who fervently believe it will happen in their life time) to rescue them from the rest of the non-believers. A non-believer to them can be one who does not exactly agree with their express views even though they believe in the existence of God/Creator. They are duty bound to 'convert' you to their beliefs. For practical purposes let us simply term these folks as 'extreme believers'. They are quite adamant as to the life beyond and describe it as 'Heaven or Hell.' One powerful sect within this group has held out for centuries an in-between place called 'Purgatory' wherein one can be cast for some time. They have discovered from the modern masses that this concept is not too popular and now have toned it down somewhat. The concept has become a symbol of ridicule from competing sects who disavow such dogma; hence it has become a serious hindrance for membership competition.

Group 4: A fourth group can be termed extremists. These folks claim to have the one chosen (by God, of course) approach to the higher power. Once in their membership, one is forbidden to ever leave such beliefs. The most extreme of these folks will go so far as to declare that eventually, somewhere in time, a great holy war will have to take place to rid the world of all contrary believers and non-believers and anyone in between. They too have a 'Heaven and Hell' concept except that they will be the only ones allowed to enter the more pleasant and pleasing portion of the Spirit World.

I cannot predict how any one of these two-legged (Native American term for humans) individuals will react to the following happening: **The Lone Cloud Sun Dance**. Many will simply refuse to believe that it happened. No doubt, they will regard me, as a fabricator or a liar with some measure of hocus pocus - even though several hundred Indians and some non-Indians viewed the same experience. Hopefully, if the Group 3 folks will investigate, maybe it will reinforce their holding that a Higher Power (their God) truly does care about us mere humans down upon this planet and quite possibly may or may not take some future environmental action. Some within this group may be a bit miffed that we 'lowly' Indians (to them) should be so blessed and not them. Hopefully, some within this group will be like, I suspect, the Group 2 folks will or may react. "Hmmmm, this is interesting!"

Lone Cloud Sun Dance

On the final day of a Sun Dance in the late 1960's, a lone cloud appeared, in an otherwise clear blue sky, far to the south as eight dancers waited to be pierced.

Chief Eagle Feather and I were the first to be pierced. The large Sichangu Sioux holy man stood next to me urging me to watch what was happening far away to the south. A distant growing puff of white cloud was the only image in the hot August sky. I was honestly too tired to offer it much attention. I was also thirsty and hungry, mostly thirsty from four days, long days of fasting and fulfilling my sun dance pledge along with the other seven pledgers. I have to be honest. At that particular moment in my life, I was simply counting off the final hour of the grueling sun dance. I imagined the relief I would soon be feeling when the ceremony and my four day vow would soon be over.

The cloud seemed to be approaching. It was a vast western sky with no other clouds visible. The dry Badlands air was still, yet the cloud seemed to be moving toward us. I could feel a dull throb where I had been pierced in my chest. I held my rope's weight in one hand to ease off the pain. After a few minutes the pain changed my chest to numbness. I eased my grip on the rope and let it hang freely while shuffling a slow dance step to the drum beat coming from the drummers at the edge of the sun dance arena. We watched each dancer lie on the bed of sage face upward at the base of the sun dance tree and be pierced by the sun dance Intercessor, the Sun Dance Chief. Chief Fools Crow would push his sharp awl in and through the chest skin and back out again, then insert a smooth wooden peg into the first cut and tunneling under the skin he would push the tip back out. Onto this hardwood skewer he would tie the pledger's rope to the peg with a leather thong. The other end of the rope was attached high up on the tree implanted at the center of the sun dance arena.

Surrounding the arena was a pitiful crowd numbering maybe only several hundred or so traditional believing Sioux. This was not a large number coming from the Oglala tribe that numbered at least 25,000 people. The neighboring Sichangu tribe of Sioux - representing some of the pledgers, including Chief Eagle Feather – were also sparsely represented, although they numbered approximately 20,000 in those days. Hiawatha Federal Insane Asylum (Canton, South Dakota) no longer existed but the fear of 'The Ban' lingered. The last embarrassing brick of the asylum had been carefully removed almost overnight by the federal government several decades before.

The numbers of the traditional faithful was pitiful in those days. The reservation missionaries with the unconstitutional help of the federal government had done their job well - from their viewpoint. Little did we know or realize that the return of Native Spirituality would build like a tremendous storm. Thousands would return to the way of their ancestors and our lone Sun Dance would become a hundred in but a few decades. Thousands of new pledgers would arrive. One Sun Dance would not be able to fulfill their four day vows.

"It's coming closer," I remember Eagle Feather's awed tone. The cloud about the size of a football field approached slowly. I should have been in dead earnest awe but I was so weak and tired from the four days fasting. I have to be honest. I simply wanted the ceremony to be over. I was now pierced and all would be over in a matter of minutes.

Fools Crow came toward me after the last dancer was pierced. "Hau, Nephew." Bill Eagle Feather exclaimed. "That cloud is coming right at us!" The cloud was approaching the edge of the campground which was full of teepees, tents, and trailers; all surrounding the circular Sun Dance arena with its lone cottonwood tree at its center, decorated with colored prayer cloths. The drums were throbbing seeming to speed their hypnotic crescendo; that pulsating, haunting tone which one hears only at a Sun Dance. As a Sun Dancer you will hear it for an eternity. It is so powerful; the pain in your chest seems to be carried away with its soothing, magical tone. Fools Crow took me by my sage gauntlet tied around my wrist and walked me inward toward the tree. All the dancers came inward, dancing a slow shuffling gait to the heavy rhythm of the drums, blowing their eagle bone whistles. We touched the tree and blew our shrill whistles. The tree shrilled back!

We danced backward to the end of our ropes. The ropes tightened and our thongs held firm. The drums throbbed as if we were standing before a gigantic, singing waterfall. Fools Crow signaled with a nod and we all danced back toward the tree, our eagle bones shrilly tweeting. Again the tree sang back! Four times in all we would dance inward. After the fourth touching of the tree we danced slowly outward, then leaned backward at the end of our ropes. The silent on-looking crowd would send up their prayers to Wakan Tanka, the Great Spirit whom we assumed was watching from somewhere.

The cloud was directly above as we touched the tree for the final time. It sent down soothing, light rain on the dancers and the praying crowd. We went back to the end of our ropes. Some Sun Dancers would have visions as they leaned back against their bond with Mother Earth. Eventually all would break free and the ceremony would be over.

Was Creator watching over that particular ceremony; the people together? Who controlled that cloud or rather, **What** controlled that moving billowing object of Nature which purposely made such a timely appearance on a windless day? There was no fearsome, rolling thunder or terrifying lightning, no punishing hail stones; just pleasant, soothing, cooling, rewarding light rain. Is that a sign that whatever controlled that cloud, might be somewhat pleased?

What would be your reaction had you seen such a miraculous sight? Indeed, this was a very powerful experience. Would you deny what your own eyes had shown you? Would you be such a coward and never reveal what you had observed? The world is full of such cowards on their life journeys, oblivious to Why they are here. Some folks would find it impossible to believe, would they not? How can some people be so indoctrinated by other humans that they would refuse to believe what their own God-gifted eyes reveal to them? They will actually be lying before God, by denying, will they not? Such is the power of the indoctrination other humans hold over them! Baahing sheep are easily led.

We were beseeching, formally calling, formally acknowledging. Creator acknowledged back, obviously. But modern materialists of today are simply ignoring what they see with their own eyes. They actually do not want God or any power to interfere with their disastrous taking and could care less about the generations unborn. Will Creator (God) intervene someday on our behalf, despite our foolish and irreverent course which has led us to this overpopulated, over-heated, resource-depleted environmental situation we now presently face (and what we two-legged have created)? I hardly think a Creator will rush to our rescue unless we change our attitude. This ceremony was direct observation. It happened!

We will next explore a few more startling spiritual quests. The history and leadership of these planetary and Creator respecting people will be presented as well.

Black Elk and
Joseph Campbell

Dec. 2004, an earthquake struck off Indonesia's Sumatra Island and triggered a devastating tidal wave that cost 230,000 lives. 131,000 lives were lost in Aceh Province alone. The outer island people, those who were first exposed to the deadly onslaught, were mostly not members of organized religion. The island folk were Nature based in their beliefs and readily noticed the unusual actions of the birds and other animals that took to the high ground immediately when the earthquake happened. The outer Island people reacted to Nature's warnings and survived. Thousands of organized religion's adherents did not.

Certain basics are helpful when discussing Indigenous Belief. Sioux Spirituality will be the major base for this work because it is where the majority of my experiences and mentorship took place. I assume the reader is not familiar with these basics, especially so when a book is written with a title such as **Creator's Code**. I would expect that many new readers would be drawn to this subject, readers who are unfamiliar with Sioux Spirituality, Sioux theological concepts, and cultural values not to mention historical and literal guides such as *Black Elk Speaks* or the works of Jack Weatherford, notably *Indian Givers*. Other related and supportive writings will be mentioned later.

We will begin with this brief 'Beginner's' chapter which the 'old guard,' the veteran readers of earlier related works, so to speak, could conveniently skip but I wish to discourage them, if they so choose. The 'old guard,' I consider, are those who have read most of my works as well as those of Neihardt, Vinson Brown, Tom Brown, Weatherford, Ohiyesa, J. Epes Brown to name a few. What I call 'old guard' also have, no doubt, participated in Nature-based ceremony such as sweat lodge. Most of these amiable folks rarely shift back to where they came from; has also been my finding. There exist some new facets that they should not miss out on, however. I myself, along with some valued peers of like mind or like belief, admit that we have repeatedly read *Black Elk Speaks* as well as '*The Sacred Pipe* by J. Epes Brown who lived with the Oglala seer a decade after John Neihardt's recording. It won't hurt to go back over 'Old Ground' especially as the years creep by.

To begin this undertaking, I will readily admit to the premise and an admitted bias that the peoples I am basing my studies upon were highly moral and ethical. Their exemplary track record offers endless examples displaying and demonstrating so, despite a relentless attack from negating Dominant Society. The conquerors had to place these peoples beneath their own non-exemplary conduct within the realm of true humanitarianism reflecting generosity, sharing and a democratic respect for the basic freedoms inherent to man and self-evident...such as one would believe that a Benevolent Creator could appreciate and condone. In regard to these Indigenous people's high regard to live within the borders of harmonious Nature - they absolutely did conduct themselves in a positive environmental manner such that even Dominant Society has a difficult task to deny. What was the condition of this hemisphere when European began to arrive en masse? What condition was the one they were leaving? Why did so many choose to emigrate? Why did the Indigenous of this hemisphere not choose to emigrate? Evidently these folks here, did not misuse their allotted land (from Creator). Iroquois Confederacy Democracy was alive and flourishing here but it was non-existent there. Unfortunately, Democracy's true beginnings, the Dominant Society is completely unaware of; instead they errantly claim Democracy's freedoms as originating from Greece and Rome - which were slave states and were devoid in respect to gender balance. Only a few privileged males could vote. Iroquoian women had voting power before the Pilgrims landed.

Why were the North American Indians so moral and truthful? Is this concept mere romanticism? Were they not really ultra savages as so many Dominant Society historical depictions have claimed?

Throughout this work, there is one word that will reappear consistently. Critics will almost have to insist that it is too overdone, no doubt. That word is - Truth! I believe it is the best one word description for God, Creator, Wakan Tanka, Yah weh, Allah, Higher Power or what have you. Yes -Truth! What God shows us, we are going to follow. I find this concept far, far more advanced from a harmonic, Nature-working point of view. Nature is not going to lie to me nor to you. I can depend on her exactness. With such constant Truth continually before the Indian and their spiritual recognition of such display, I believe this revelation made them a more sincere, honest people. It also led them to discover Democracy! Working with Nature and not against her - brought many values quite contrary to Man-based conceptualized religious pronouncements far removed from Nature's ongoing advice. The Indian has experienced severe dishonesty from the white man. 'He is too separate from Creator's Nature.' Nature has historically brought tremendous benefit, mental, social and spiritual to the tribe as well as to the individual. Take your children out to a broad meadow, a park or wooded area with a serene stream and hopefully still abundant to some degree with the winged, finned and four-legged. Your children will readily appreciate what possibly you yourself can no longer comprehend. Your children understand the Code to some degree: Such a shame that we lose it as we become older and forego such focus.

The original hosts of this North America, the traditional Indians who preserved this Nature-respecting spirituality simply admitted that they did not know who God really is (or Creator to we Sioux). They were too truthful to attempt false, unsupported claims. They have progressed onward in their sheer respect for genuine, unaltered truth, by also stating without reservation, that Wakan Tanka (Great Spirit) is also a Mystery and assumed to be beyond total comprehension by mere humans. Hence another name for the Creator is Great Mystery. They firmly believed IT (not he or she) was kindly, benevolent and were much less afraid of their Creator compared to the fear of God I was taught as a child when I grew up under the Dominant Society belief which of course was Christianity. I do not want to isolate out Christianity alone however. The Islamic faith also is far removed from the teachings of Nature and, in my opinion, much more related to Christianity than it is to Indigenous way of thinking. Surprisingly, I know, I find that some Judaic principles have a degree of commonality with some of what I have learned from the Indigenous.

In summary: from a practical viewpoint, enough evidence exists for such exemplary examples to be a worthy source. In particular, I am basing my studies upon a dependence on the North American Indigenous inhabitants and consequently limit my claims to this group alone. Primarily I depend on the Northeastern tribes, most of whom had to migrate westward due to the European invasion.

The Sioux migrated out of the East. We find them generally in the Piedmont area of the Carolinas in the 1500's and possibly as late as the early 1600's. They were once situated between the Iroquois and the Cherokee, two powerful tribes. They, the Sioux, were by no means a weak tribe themselves. To live between these two adversaries they too had to be able to hold their ground. The Iroquois were to the North and the more peaceful Cherokees were to the South of the Dakota (Later termed Sioux). Their successful exodus to the middle of the continent lends further credit to the theory that they had to be of some numbers to make the journey without serious obstruction from numerous tribal encounters, no doubt, along the way. Quite possibly, there was not as much fighting between the tribes as American history books would like to proclaim.

Trade routes and verifying trade goods from distant locales were scattered throughout the Indian nations. Sea shells were found far inland. Sign language for successful communication was developed to implement such trade. In the North, a universal religion was fairly basic. Ceremonies were similar. Diversity in climate, crops and terrain brought forth the appearance of dissimilar spiritual practice but basically most tribes held to a commonality of belief in a Higher Indescribable Power. I strongly suspect that when a warlike people (the Europeans) (Check their history if you disagree) enter into another's domain and dominate, there is generally a backlash of attempted self-righteousness justifying their historical recording endeavors. Maybe they think they have to please their God and it is most convenient to invent that the conquered were immoral, indecent, savage or what have you, in the realm of human negativity. The conquerors or the 'Takers' were God fearing good, as in 'Onward Christian Soldiers,' so this becomes their perception. Therefore, when history books would be later written, the stories, tales, recollections would be told or altered in accordance with 'They' were bad, 'We' were good (despite being the invaders). Fairly simple and we have seen it, read it and even watched it in the Hollywood movies. This is one area of visual depiction wherein the eyes are deceived. John Wayne takes one shot and five of the Indian actors fall off their horses, or we circle stupidly around the wagon trains and stupider still, let the dust laden Pilgrim progeny take easy pot shots at us.

The people were subsisting well on a wide variety of meats, vegetables and grains. Agricultural crops, namely the potato, corn and beans would soon vanquish the famines constantly plaguing Europe. The Indian was much larger than the European as a result of such a rich diet he and she enjoyed. Go to European museums. Look at the size of the knight's armor. Iron doesn't shrink. Look at the size of American youth in this day and age. A broader and more available diet does make larger progeny in a few generations. A scarcer diet produces smaller folks in time, as well.

Little does America know that the Sioux had a significant higher kill ratio among the soldiers who were also much smaller than the much larger Indigenous warriors, mainly due to diet, down through the centuries. History books will never mention that fact, will they? The average male immigrant stepping from an Ellis Island bound ship was about five foot five or five foot six. The Sioux's were in the six foot range. Chief Red Cloud was over six foot two. Size is an advantage in close quartered combat. Cavalry soldiers were purposely picked for their smaller, lighter and more uniform size, about five foot five and max weight at 145 lbs. For extended marches the Army considered big men as too much of a load for the horses.

The Indian rode his mount with his knees when buffalo hunting or in combat, leaving both hands free: a tremendous advantage for aiming a rifle or in close hand to hand fighting. Strangely The U. S. Army high command refused to adapt to what was obviously a more productive battle tactic. Wouldn't you prefer a trained mount that allowed you both hands free as a large and fierce Sioux warrior was bearing down on you? I certainly would. The horse borne warrior was highly experienced in combat as was his superbly conditioned mount which was quite accustomed to gunfire. He was led by able, battle experienced chiefs who knew their terrain against the protocol, bureaucrat strapped Army leadership. Plains fighting of the 1800's summed up to a tremendous advantage for the Indian which white man history books still will not dare speak truthfully about.

Would you be surprised to know that at the Battle of the Little Big Horn, (The Sioux won this one too.) several hundred Winchester repeating rifles were employed? Guess who was firing them? Guess who was being shot at and complained in later chronicles? (There were survivors from Capt Benteen's and Major Reno's detachments.) How in the world did the Sioux have the Winchester and the U. S. Cavalry had none? Again, American history books have neglected to tell how it really was. The Little Big Horn Battle museum admits this fact in their lectures and display.

Catlin's Creed

An early explorer, George Catlin, appears to strongly disagree with the society he came from. Let us look at the words of George Catlin who lived among the Plains Indians.

Catlin's Creed
I love a people who have always made me welcome to the best they had.
I love a people who are honest without laws, who have no jails and no poorhouses.
I love a people who keep the commandments without ever having read them or heard them preached from the pulpit.
I love a people who never swear, who never take the name of God in vain.
I love a people who love their neighbors as they love themselves.
I love a people who worship God without a bible, for I believe that God loves them also.
I love a people whose religion is all the same, and who are free from religious animosities.
I love a people who have never raised a hand against me, or stolen my property, where there was no law to punish for either.
I love a people who have never fought a battle with white men, except on their own ground.
I love and don't fear mankind where God has made and left them, for there they are children.
I love a people who live and keep what is their own without locks and keys.
I love all people who do the best they can.
And oh, how I love a people who don't live for the love of money!
George Catlin (1796-1872)

George Catlin, Artist, who lived for eight years among Native American tribes, said in 1841: "Nowhere, to my knowledge, have they stolen a six-pence worth of my property, though in their countries there are no laws to punish for theft. I have visited forty-eight different tribes, and I feel authorized to say that the North American Indian in his native state is honest, faithful, brave... and an honorable and religious being."[1.]

Well...George Catlin lived with the Plains Indian. He directly observed their conduct, lifestyle and worldview. I would consider his significant experience as rather credible, would you not also? The victor writes the history however and it is my holding that North American history is in serious error as to its overall portrayal of the North American Indian and in particular the Northeastern tribes and more in particular with the Sioux as they were the last major tribe to finally come into Dominant Society's confines from their cherished freedom on the Great Plains. Because of their late submission and their successful campaigns against American cavalry, there happens to be much more material available as to their lifestyle. The shorter duration under the white man's ruling reservation authorities also allowed them to keep alive their religious/spiritual practice along with their supporting language into these modern times wherein too many American tribes not only lost their ceremonial connections but their language as well.

Indigenous Basics

We have Great Spirit whom we consider as the Maker of all things. It is above, below and all around us. It made Nature, the mountains, the rivers, trees, forests, the animal world, and all that grows or moves upon our planet, even the inhabitants of the mighty oceans. We consider IT as quite vast even beyond total comprehension by these mere mortal minds we possess. We believe we can learn from all that It makes and hold firmly to the premise that all that It creates is made to harmonize with all other life around us except of course, Human. Human is the only creation of Creator's that can and does impede and even destroy the harmonic flow of Nature. With the fast moving results of certain planetary afflictions, primarily Heating of the Planet, Thinning Ozone, Gone Resources and Over-Population presently upon us, that statement holds a high degree of truth - at least for us. I did not mention -Water! That precious item must also be added to the list but this is a probe of the Beyond as well as protection of the environment. You will discover that both subjects intertwine. For those who can cast off their inhibiting ego, this new knowledge will prove rewarding in more ways than just for yourself.

The people and their culture you will be studying did not bring about what may possibly become a planetary breakdown. They deserve accolades in that regard and merit further ecological study for preventive environmental medicine. They also have been able to reach into the area of possible afterlife which we imagine is safe from man's non-harmonic destructive ways. This is the domain of new knowledge which we are intent on exploring; new to Dominant Society expectorations.

Our Spirituality is much more subjective; hence reassuring. For many of the Northern Indians, the idea that the Creator utilizes the Four Directions to work with the planet, Mother Earth and the Sun, which is an integral part of Father Sky, forges for us the Six Powers concept under Wakan Tanka. When we look up at the Big Dipper in the northern Sky we see Creator as the bright North Star and the six following stars are the Six Powers. The dipper portion is the Four Directions or Four Winds which blow upon our lands. You see, we even have an observation, quite a large one, I may add, placed right there above us which supports our viewpoint! It has been there for humans' view for quite some time. Walk outside and look up at it; it is awesome. You will now be utilizing a key word in Native perspectives - observation!

I must ask a question at this point. Does Dominant Society have such a supporting, Creator-made symbol in this hemisphere?

Spiritual Imagery - Creator, Great Mystery, Wakan Tanka

Bill Moyers asked Joseph Campbell, the famed mythologist, in an interview. "You speak of 'Spiritual Imagery' in your world travels, what is the best example that you know of?"

Campbell responded firmly and without pause, "Without question. *Black Elk's Speaks*!"

Here we have a writer, teacher, philosopher and investigator of cultures primarily-Joseph Campbell. He traveled to Indigenous, world wide, and yet he centers back to a Sioux visionary from the Great Plains, the Oglala, Black Elk, who finally told his story, years later in detail to John Neihardt, for the book, *Black Elk Speaks*. The book's narration took place in the early thirties within the very reservation where I was born.

Black Elk came upon a most powerful vision which was attained when he was just evolving into his teens and traveling with his nomadic Oglala Sioux band, following the herds of wandering Great Plains buffalo. It is generally accepted as the year 1874, two years before the Battle of the Little Big Horn would be fought. Strangely, the actual vision took place close to where George Armstrong Custer would soon meet his fate just outside of where the Indian encampment had been pitched for a temporary respite from following the summer buffalo herds. The young lad was yet to view a white man or members of Dominant Society. Nothing of Dominant Society had yet influenced him. His viewpoint of Earth or what little spiritual thoughts young growing youth possess was the natural view surrounding him: a world mainly of tall grass, creeks, vast skies, rivers and of animals. Except for the horses and dogs, all were wild and free upon the rolling plains. After his vision, for decades, he never spoke of it to anyone in great detail.

The Sioux believe that the story of Black Elk and his vision well demonstrates Nature-based imagery of the spiritual forces which govern our planet. Black Elk's vision constitutes the powerful core of our Sioux Nature spirituality today - a visionary teaching that brings to this present time the ancient values of Nature's Way.

Black Elk's vision (in later years he was referred to as Nicholas Black Elk) would take him into the Rainbow Covered Lodge of the Six Powers of the World. West Power, North Power, East Power, and South Power are the Four Directions, and all spoke individually after he entered the lodge. Father Sky and Mother Earth then spoke to the youth. At the end of their speaking, a Blue Man of destruction and corruption appeared down below them. Native Traditionals believe that this Blue Man is now wreaking havoc upon the earth and, unless confronted by human, we will lose the planet. A more detailed presentation and discussion can be found in Native Wisdom. [1]

The Six Powers

West Power (Black). We acknowledge the life-giving rains from the West as the power to make life. Thunder and lightning are power to destroy, but we realize more life than death transpires with each rain. As the sun goes down in the West, darkness comes to the land. The color for the west is black. It is also the time when human must rest for there is less distraction.

North Power (White). We think of endurance, cleanliness, truth, rest, politeness and strength as associated with the North. The cold north has Mother Earth rest beneath the white mantle of snow. She sleeps and gathers up her strength for the bounty of springtime. When the white snows melt, the earth is made clean. When native people wintered over, often confined to a small area for a lengthy time while they waited for the spring thaw, they learned to be extremely polite, to be truthful and honest with each other. They kept clean by using the sweat lodge to take winter baths and to beseech to the Spirit World. They wiped themselves with the pleasing odor of summer picked sage so that they would be more pleasing to others in the crowded confines of the tipis. The power of the cold white north taught them to endure. The cleansing white wing within Black Elk's great vision emphasizes endurance and cleanliness.

East Power (Red). The third power brought him the red pipe of peace. Peace begins with knowledge. To have peace, one must first become aware of knowledge, which comes forth out of the red dawn, the East, with each new day. The sun rises, bringing with it new learning experiences for each new day. When you have knowledge and it is discussed and considered with others who share their thoughts, their observations and their needs; it then can become wisdom. Wisdom mixed with appreciating spirituality can become grace or spiritual power.

The sun rises from the East. Actually, we all know now, that the Earth is turning and the Sun is stationary. Maybe it too is moving in Creator's vast space, but it is a common concept that we two-legged consider the sun as rising daily across our planet. It is a red dawn in the early morning hours. It is not a black dawn or a white dawn. Where some of these tribes reflect these colors as significant for the East is beyond me. Some of them, including members of my own tribe portray the four directions as black for the north and white for the east. In accordance with how the Creator holds Its colors for these directions, they are in serious error and not in harmony with how Mother Earth realistically presents itself. At this point, I wish to point out that the Mayans and the Aztecs, ancient Indigenous civilizations, hold true to the Natural color presentation as does the Mdewakanton Sioux tribe. Red is East, Yellow is South, Black is West and White is North. It does not get light (white) when the sun goes down in the west and I have yet to see Black snow in the White North come winter time. These colors also stand for Creator's created four seasons - Winter is represented as the North in this hemisphere, East is the warming Spring, Yellow is the heating South wind which brings forth the Bounty of Harvest and the summer buffalo hunts for needed golden grains and meat from the growing grasses. Human survives another cycle (circle) as a result. Black is Autumn, the Fall. Tree sap falls in preparation for Winter, furred ones prepare variously, finned begin to hibernate as the ducks and geese, many of the winged, head south.

South Power (Yellow). Medicine from roots, stems, herbs and fruits are associated with the South Power. Today, many species are beginning to disappear and resultant medicines will soon be lost. The sun rises higher and higher as the South Power advances with summer. Eventually plants such as corn and wheat will bring forth yellow or golden kernels that will sustain much life through the long winter. Abundance is the primary gift from this power, for it makes all things grow and we are allowed to take that which grows. During the heat of summer, buffalo hunts provided meat to cure in the hot, blowing wind for long winters. During this time of plenty, gatherings of thanksgiving would happen. To be thankful for what you receive adds strength to your search for sustenance, provisions, shelter and medicine. To be thankful and appreciative toward the Ultimate, the Creator also adds much strength toward one's beseechments, is our belief. Medicine people cannot be successful in their healings if they disregard appreciation.

Thanksgiving is another bolstering value that traditional Sioux people hold reverently.

Sky Power (Blue). Father Sky spoke and said the things of the air would be with Black Elk to help him in his struggle. Could these "things of the air" also be the open space of communication which now can transcend across the globe? Can it also be the satellites - "things of the air," beaming back video and radio waves so we may see and talk directly across the skies? Human is allowed a great range of worldly communication from Creator's designs. I perceive that what the Sky Power said could be closely associated with the advance of more peaceful people upon the earth because the things of the air are helping to promote peace and harmony. It is happening right before us.

One should seriously contemplate what this passage of Black Elk Speaks holds for our present day environmental dilemma now looming before us. The entire planet is in extreme danger of horrendous disaster. We may be focused on the life Beyond but we also need to reach for concepts that will better our lot through our actions or inactions while we are still proceeding here in this spectrum. I believe that if we attempt to become cognizant and endeavor to seriously apply our new knowledge for the well-being of the planet our attempts will not go unrewarded in the Beyond World.

We should not take for granted these 'things of the air'. Whether we know nothing of traditional thought, worldview or philosophy we should at least sit back and realize the immensity of what Creator has allowed regarding a world-wide communication network that now exists. Most of it is truly 'of the air', meaning beamed out into space and back down upon the other side of the world or right next door. It is highly obvious that Creator wants us to communicate with each other. Ignorance can be dispelled if human communicates. Most simply shrug however, and make the blasé reply, "So what. It's an invention. Someone made a few bucks and I don't introspect cell phones. Why should I? My concern is that they work and if I can find a cheaper deal regarding my minutes… well, let me know."

I am amazed at the complexity and uniqueness of communication that this Creator has allowed into our lives and so quickly; from a historical viewpoint. Communication is the key aid in our attempts to help the Earth Mother. It is a long way from Alexander Graham Bell and longer still from cave man drums. Maybe I am but one of few who can state that they deeply appreciate such advancement and optimistically discern it was meant for these times.

Earth Power (Green). Mother Earth, the Sixth Power, is the provider. She is our home. Not long ago it was unfathomable that mere human could actually alter or harm such a powerful Mother. Black Elk's vision was over a century ago yet Mother Earth focused only on the Blue Man, for obviously she visualized the serious threat way back then.

She took Black Elk to the danger that was confronting the earth. In his vision, he was taken to a place by the Sixth Power. Down below at the confluence of three rivers, everything was exhibited to be foul and dying. A powerful Blue Man stood out. It was he who was responsible for the ensuing destruction. The Blue Man of greed and deception was fouling the waters, even the skies and bringing great harm to the living things. This Blue Man symbolizes the corruption, insensitivity, greed and ignorance that are upon the Earth. The Blue Man would wreak great destruction using lies and untruths and would have to be addressed, or else all creatures, including two-leggeds, would perish. Untruth is the Blue Man.

The recent 109th Congress was symbolic of this Blue Man. Every day we observe much deception by those who lobby our political leaders in Washington with disregard for the environment and the ongoing dilemma, human killing human. As the situation worsens, more eyes will be opened and eventually the old ways of real Truth will have to be accepted in order to finally destroy the Blue Man. This nation of ours is and has been in serious need for leadership. The examples we have elected from both parties are pitiful and which present polls agree. The public shows little respect for not only Executive Leadership both past and present and from either political party, but are equally dismayed by the Judicial and especially Congress. Four later chapters purposely will center on four Sioux Leaders who were nature based. It is my strong opinion that their leadership example, morally, ethically, sincerity and ability backed by their spiritual respect is what is desperately needed in this land so besought with deeply serious conflict and problems. Not one of these leaders cared for self gain or promoted greed for his fellow warriors. Contrariwise to modern executives, he would severely chastise or condemn any member who promoted himself over the basic needs of the tribe or nation. To read about their deeds, actions, courage and leadership: you are reading the results of a society that utilizes Creator's Nature as their Earth Journey guide.

Hopefully, it will be in time for the planet to have a chance to regain the old harmony. Maybe however, it will not be arrived at, such is the ongoing power of Dominant Society values; Values that disregard real Truth. Eventually though, Two-legged (Human) will discover that there is no other choice. Religious fundamentalists will no doubt keep on praying, ignoring and waiting for miracles, but the realistic and workable solution will be to turn away from the worship of extreme materialism that is not working. It brings over-consumption, waste and eventually - gone resources. The ozone layer depletion, planetary heating, gone resources and the population spiral (the real Four Horses of the Apocalypse) will not wait for miraculous curing. Water resources; great aquifers deplete as humans increase. Maybe the scarcity of pure waters will become the first casualty. Some tragic consequences are about to happen.

Let us reflect upon these 'Six Powers.'
1. They exist and are readily observable.
2. Each plays a significant role in our lives.
3. They are obviously placed here by the Ultimate (Creator).
4. Each is its own, distinct entity. (North Power is distinctly differentiated from South Power. East Power has little commonality with West Power.)
5. All are essential for human's role upon the planet.
6. All are essential for Mother Earth to provide for our Being upon the planet.
7. None are dependent upon mere human and certainly not influenced by whatever edicts, pronouncements, claims or what have you, mere two-legged attempts to issue forth. Most importantly; they are reflective of Creator!

The Six Powers are all readily observable. They do vary considerably and bear little relationship to each other yet each holds a commonality for each other. For many humans one can say the same. North contrasts with South and East has little in common with West other than that all of the Four Direction powers directly affect and play upon the Earth Power and each has their degree of dependence upon what energy bears down upon them from the Sun. I believe that the Six Power concept brings forth a higher degree of Hunka, (relationship) perspective or the more widely renowned phrase, 'Mitakuye Oyasin', We are all related! We are related to all things! Relationship to Creator's Nature is the important attitude to develop toward an understanding of the major premise within this study. Relationship is a necessary ingredient for you to understand the Code.

Sacralized Nature is another key term to focus upon. Modern society has desacralized Nature. How modern man has allowed his ego to circumvent and remove himself from this divine association, which all of our animal brothers and sisters inherently maintain is the reason for our environmental dilemma we face today! Yes, one animal (Man) was allowed reason. Or was it reason which adapted itself to greed? Anyway, the ways of this particular animal has led to a disastrous turn in what was once a harmonious everyday life of the planet. Planetary Survival! Do not wait for the sheer, disastrous consequences of advancing environmental dilemmas to prove what native traditionalists are trying to tell you, is my utmost advice. I would rather enter the Spirit World with a track record of demonstrated earthly concern, whether I had discovered the Code or not. Relationship and Sacralized Nature are healthy guides to lead us toward a courageous attitude in our stand for Planetary Survival. These two subjects will seriously intertwine for your life's journey, now that modern communication has made us aware.

* * * *

A College Acquaintance

"So Eagle Man, what allows you the 'credibility' to write on such subjects – Creator's Code, the planet and a life beyond, I presume?" A classmate from my Benedictine college past declared. His remark held an air of superiority. It had been some decades from our graduation. He had stalwartly 'kept the faith' not unlike many but not all of my former class mates. I, of course, due mainly to the influence of my tribal lineage, had broken away from church regimen and my early Christian-based upbringing.

I replied boldly. "I believe that I am no less credible than all the other humans, whom I have been told by folks like you, to base my beliefs upon!" I added. "Quite a long list you have, both deceased and otherwise."

"Our way is from the Bible. Those are God's words." His swift reaction was not unexpected.

"Yes, and the Koran claims the same…as does the Talmud. All directly from the Great Spirit Itself, are they not? Spoken specifically to God's one chosen tribe - right? And the results are a continuous fighting, yes, death and destruction down through centuries…which continues to this day. Each one claiming they alone are oh so….Right!" I emphasized a hushed, almost whispered tone, "But now the weapons; cluster bombs, roadside bombs, germ warfare…spread devastation to all these differing 'faiths' but also to differing sects within these 'faiths' as we witness in the ongoing wars – Bosnia and now, Iraq and possibly Iran.

I was afraid my remarks were diverting us from the subject which happens when one becomes involved in sectarian, religious/spiritual discussions. I held up both hands motioning them inward to my chest as if to come back to the issue. "This Life Beyond. We are dealing with Mystery." I paused purposefully. "No one, absolutely no one, including you and me, knows what the hell for sure it is all about…at least I will readily admit it. Can you admit to Mystery?"

He shook his head in disagreement. I added firmly, "God gave me a mind. It also has taught me through Its Nature how truly precious the meaning of the word 'Freedom' is. I cannot give it away to all those claimants whom you believe so adamantly in." I raised both hands with an expression of futility; "Let's conclude that I have chosen to sacralize Nature. I would consider it a denial to my Ultimate Creator were I to let an ulterior-motivated human prioritize his precepts over me, contrary to what I can learn directly from God's Nature."

I received a look as though I needed mental medication. He almost spat the word as if it had some attached evil from his hell attached to it. "Sacralized Nature?"

His no-nonsense Benedictine training boiled up. He was locked on to his rigidity and expressed it. He carried on dependent upon the Talibanesque past of men's teaching, writings, edicts, and pronouncements beginning millennia ago. It is remarkable how most of us raise the limits of toleration to those whom we have gone to school with as I sat and listened calmly. I must admit I have become somewhat hardened toward such dissertations. And then came the fear and control portion of his dire warnings for my spiritual future. Some fiery hell fire complete with pitchfork-wielding super boogey men waited for me (mostly referred to as Devils) (they also have forked tails and even horns) (horns - the bovine type and not to be errantly conceptualized as like band instruments; i.e. Trumpet, Tuba, Trombone, etc).* My adversary heard nary a word I had spoken. It was too much for him to understand or take note of, my opinion.

*[I am compelled to admit that a bit of humor, intentionally or more likely, unintentionally, will be inserted now and then. Creator does endow us with such a pleasantry. Some of us, at least.

Clues

Clue #1. Would an all-providing Creator who has included music, beauty, song, colorful vision, taste, flowers and/or a myriad of other fantastic pleasing gifts bestowed generously upon we humans also create and supernaturally empower these types - the horned, unpleasant ones? Hmmm- I forgot to add Humor to the above.

Clue # 2. Doesn't this scene (the horned ones and also that fiery environment) which I assume as to be more than a bit painful, well, isn't this scene closer to man's imagination or concoction by those men who dearly loved control such as what many of us have witnessed within organized religion? Historically, there is no question that organized religions sought control of the masses.

> *Sub-clue #1.* It worked! Oh how it worked!
> *Sub-clue #2.* The world is loaded with Superstition.

Clue # 3. Does the Creator reflect Itself in what It creates?

Clue #4. It is so obvious that modern human has locked himself into utter darkness when it comes to Direct Observation. I include the two-legged from the Mid-east along with the two-legged from the Western world.

I was asked as to my credibility. Hindsight now tells me I could have, maybe should have remarked that this writing endeavor would be a first as we have all been so suppressed by white man's generally accepted concepts alone. This will be outside his confines regarding a possible Beyond much in contrast to what he has put before us down through the time of our slowly advancing 'civilization'.

I ended the former classmate discussion with a paratrooper's symbolic, 'Pull the rip-cord' and held up both hands accompanied by a serene smile looking upward, pretending to simply float away under a life saving canopy. Had I not done so, his next refrain, the oft used ploy would be: "What are you getting so angry at?" or "Why are you so angry?" Just as often, I am also asked simply, "Why don't you believe in God?" or worse.... "Why don't you believe in God like the rest of us?"

"It takes a lot of courage to write upon such a subject - Spirit World, the Beyond, ...Life Hereafter," a neutral friend remarked.

"Why not?" I answered. A Texas governor candidate was more vivid with his answer to his reasoning to run for office. "Why the hell not?" was his reply. On second thought I ventured a reply in my mind, 'Maybe sheer stupidity!'

I recalled a fortune cookie. It simply stated. 'The eyes observe directly. The ears relay what others tell you.'

Direct Observation

Direct Observation; we do it every day of our lives. It seems so odd that probably 99% of egotistical two-leggeds outside of Indigenous cultures just cannot and will not identify their spiritual or religious thoughts as connected to Creator's Nature. It is odd that religious claiming man so utterly ignores and even denies Creator's very works. 'Ahh a bit blasphemous when you get down to it, wouldn't you say, ehhh Sherlock?' Maybe an astute Englishman on our side of the fence might deduce. Human has utterly divorced himself from what God has made in order for him to exist, let alone attempt to garner any fruitful teachings from said Nature.

"Multiply and subdue the Earth." Is it Genesis that makes this statement? In light of 7 billion people now crowding upon the planet and a billion more approaching in close to a decade and a goodly billion more after that in less than a decade; I find it difficult to believe that this statement is not human's concoction than it is expressly from all-knowing Creator.

Ahhhh, this 'Life Beyond,' such a subject wherein men (mostly white men - my experience) make such commanding all-knowing pronouncements. The Indian expresses himself quite the contrary. He or she uses the word 'Maybe' quite often. 'Maybe this will happen,' or 'maybe the medicine will work or maybe it won't.' 'I don't know for sure.' 'We'll have to wait and see.' 'It is up to the Spirit Helpers now.' These pronouncements are reliable indicators of a valid medicine man than one who would say, 'Now, this is how it is going to work for sure.' 'I know what will happen.' 'If you don't do exactly as I tell you, then something real bad is going to happen to you.' 'What I am telling you, you must follow, you must believe. And above all, do not go to anyone else!'

Nature and Great Spirit

The Indian* has no 'Black Book'- no Koran, Talmud or Bible. The open meadow, the starlit sky, the warming sun, the wind, the calving iceberg from a receding glacier, a mountain stream gurgling it's merry way to the vast ocean is the Indian's so-called Bible and one that bears nary a man-written word or attempted written spiritual teaching. This powerful resonating, continuing echo is our Creator's vast wealth of teaching. Such wisdom is ignored by the white man, even ridiculed as tree-hugging foolishness or worse, associated with some sort of mumbo jumbo or witch craft. The environmental onslaught, the back lash from Nature will eventually convince the naysayers however. Its Force shall be of such magnitude that few fools shall remain unconvinced. White man is loaded with egotistical errant pronouncements from my decades of observation. He thinks he knows everything- yet he actually knows very little. George Bush's renouncement of the obvious - the Kyoto Accords - is an excellent example.

The Indian has a Great Spirit, a Great Holy which to them (the Sioux) is Wakan Tanka; a Great Mystery, Great Unknown, the Indescribable. Yet it exists; most definitely. To them it is also the Great Benevolent Entity which of course is quite obvious, judging from what all that It provides. We have little fear of our All-Providing Creator. Why should we? It made us, allows us, provides for us and most of us also believe that It gives us a Home (Spirit World) when we die (Pass On- is considered a better word). By now the reader will have noticed that It is being used as a non-gendered term for Creator, God or the Higher Power. Makes sense to me since I honestly do not know if It is a He or possibly a She. Maybe it is possibly neither. Since we do not honestly know for sure, the remainder of this text shall remain - It! Sorry if I am hurting the feelings of the majority locked into the He and His wordage. And…the relative few who insist the Higher Power is a Goddess.

*It is my choosing to often utilize the term 'Indian' for the original inhabitants who were in the North American Continent prior to the European arrivals. On occasion, Native American or tribal designation will also be utilized as will the term - Sioux. See dissertation by Dr. Beatrice Medicine Garner, Teton Sihasapa Lakota, regarding Native American naming in Chapter 3.

Credibility

Now for this word credible. A boundless array of observations from my many travels world wide have been received and hence many, many adventures preserved stemming from such variety as the Sioux Sun Dance to blazing speed past Mach at the controls of the versatile Phantom fighter bomber which could take me far, far above Mother Earth for a grandiose view. I have had the Vision Quest experience on Bear Butte Mountain under the direction of two valid, powerful Sioux holy men, Chief Fools Crow and

Chief Eagle Feather. Hahnblaycheeyah - Vision Quest is an incredible teaching/experience. Most all Sioux sun dancers who endure for four long hot summer days will Vision Quest and Sweat Lodge before such a thought-provoking endurance. It is my understanding that the Christ of Christianity went out into the desert, the wilderness, some say. One chooses a lengthy period of isolation while fasting to enhance the attempt to commune with one's Higher Power concept. Did not Moses seek a lone, isolated mountain top for such related communication? Odd, that the leaders of these adherents avoid such similar personal sacrifice. If I were to be on my way down from Spirit Mountain in the Black Hills, I would never expect to encounter an ascending Falwell, Pat Robertson, Billy Graham or his protégé son, rosy cheeked Pastor Bob of the Glass Cathedral and his protégé son nor a host of the intense televised evangelicals. Never would I expect to meet a Pope, Bishop or a Cardinal on their way up a mountain to humble themselves and endure a bit of discomfort despite their constant religious claims to the flocks from their electronic pulpits. I must give credit to a few Jesuit reservation assigned priests however, who have bravely endured what Indians commonly do, to come closer to their God. A later chapter will recount a devout, yet open-minded priest's experience of the Vision Quest.

Most sun dancers, nowadays pledge to return year after year, at least for four long years, to fulfill their vows before on looking Creator. Thousands of adult aged sun dance pledgers now physically/spiritually sacrifice themselves annually on the Sioux reservations. My Sioux reservation alone held over fifty sun dances, this past year alone. Next year this number could increase to 75 or 100. The vast majority of the pledgers also uphold their vows to touch no alcohol or drugs while they are fulfilling their four year vows. Most carry these vows on through a lifetime. White man does not do these things yet exhibits to us that he holds his beliefs far above ours with regard to connection to God and a humanistic track record. Maybe his imagined all-knowing 'knowledge' precludes him from facing Creator for four arduous days beneath God's life giver - the hot July or August sun or up on a chilly, windy Black Hills mountain or hot Badlands butte! It is not difficult for us to exhibit little or no respect for the Falwells, Pastor Bobs, Pat Robertsons, Jimmy Swaggerts, Jesse Jacksons and the rest of the electronic ilk who pose as religious icons. The popes, cardinals, bishops and arch bishops are far more akin to this bunch than our dedicated, non-materialistic, vision questing and healing medicine people we find on our Indian reservations.

It will be ceremony, those that I have experienced personally, wherein I have found my major clues as to the possibility that, 'Yes, a Spirit World Beyond, probably, exists, maybe or it- just- might-be so.' A few of my like-minded peers, I have also asked to contribute wherein they could serve as 'verifiers'. Admittedly, this is a very difficult subject area to present and presumably will bring about a storm of accusations from the all-knowing self-righteous. Had I not had the experience of direct observation along with my fellow peers in this area, I certainly would not have ventured forth with this proceeding.

Nay-sayers

Yes, I expect a raft of nay-sayers : It-just-can not-be-so 'nay-savers'. It is a free country thanks to the white man's welcomed copying what the Iroquois Confederacy had to show him. Democracy! Nature-based Democracy with its beautiful, respecting Freedoms. No way will we attempt to convert the white man although many of the deeper thinking ones are beginning to knock on our reservation doors. We consider these folks as a bit more enlightened in respect to Nature. Nature will make the 'conversion' decisions - they are not for us to do for we understand the Freedom of Respect.

No doubt, my most precious asset to approach such an undertaking is the incredible fact that I was born into a culture that is steeped in spiritual communication. Yes, spiritual communication in the form of ancient ceremony. The nay-sayers cannot truthfully scoff or downplay the results of such communication. Several of these experiences will be vividly portrayed within these pages and bear in mind - the actual results and predictions made. The powerful men I once knew who held this key to a Beyond…I have to believe in what my eyes and ears told me as I looked onward while in such ceremony. Creator gave me my eyes and ears and they have never lied to me! I intend to convince no one, however as to my observations. I really don't care whether one wants to believe, or not to believe, what I viewed; …but I cannot lie or deny what I experienced. Take it from there. I am merely a conveyor. I have too much respect for the term, 'Freedom' to attempt resolutely to convince anyone. I must add however, it is such a spell-binding experience if one is so fortunate to experience such an event. It is indeed refreshing though, that thousands of others across this land have also had similar experiences from devout and respected medicine men and women - mostly from the Northern tribes.

Freedom

Freedom - real Freedom; let us call it; Indian Freedom…is unlike what the European immigrant's past exhibits. American Indian Freedom is strongly bolstered by a deep reverence for God's Nature. The North American Indian mind set, their world view is totally an opposite when relating to European-based values except possibly the Celtics and some of the Germanic tribes. It is my opinion that the early European-based American who 'founded' a new civilization for himself, this westward bound immigrant that turned his back on his own beginnings to walk forever down that Atlantic harbor gangplank did 'pick up' on much of what the Indian, primarily the Northeastern tribes, had to offer to humanity. It was only 'Natural'; so to speak. It (God's Nature) is so powerful it was bound to change his life and on into his progeny. It broke his roots with medieval-steeped Europe. Its power swept back into Europe and changed that continent as well. Organized religion's controlling false fears were finally broken for most; enough so that they could rush to the ships sailing increasingly westward. Thomas Paine, who learned to speak Iroquois, gave his life energies to take freedom spawning Democracy back to convert the French.* Americans, those of European stock altered the value system implanted from their relatives who remained across the waters whether they will admit it or not. They would not totally embrace the Indian's lifestyle, nor their world view and definitely not the Red Man's Nature based Spirituality.

* Jack Weatherford, Indian Givers.

The Planet

While we explore this mysterious realm, or shall we say, 'suppositional possibilities,' we will be studying underneath a gathering cloud of real danger that spans the entire planet. An immense change looms dangerously (for man-kind and unfortunately for the so-termed 'non-reasoning' flora and fauna) on the horizon. The self-spawned danger for human's very existence has to be brought about If Nature over all is to survive the steady onslaught exponentially magnified exceedingly down through Man's inventive, unchecked, unconcerned Industrial Revolution years. It is obviously Creator's built in defense; Creator's design for planetary continuance, a perfected design which overshadows two-legged's survival. Human's Over-population has played its hand as well. Yes, unconcerned, unchecked, even Biblical-enhanced and Church-encouraged Over-population; Self brought on and continuously ignored despite the obvious warnings as human jumped from their first billion in early 1800 to 7 billion in less than two centuries. A one billion increase has been experienced in the last 12 years. Enviro-disaster will not be brought upon us through our own choosing however. Mother Nature will bring this powerful turn to all humans worldwide and that, of course the world populace can no longer ignore for it is happening at this very moment. The deadly alteration of man's environment through his own doing or rather, undoing, will bring forth tremendous adjustments in lifestyle so serious that billions, not millions can be brought to a miserable existence - those that survive. Mother Earth herself shall command the bidding - when, where and how much. It is but a matter of time.

Is this then, a writing of Environmental Warnings?

No, not totally! It is an explanation why there will someday become a tremendous resurgence of what the Indigenous have believed in, held to, and attempted to explain to a non-listening, rejecting, materialistic bound audience called Dominant Society; down through the centuries whom we have been in contact with. Albeit, it will probably be a bit late to command much sympathetic influence from the Earth Mother who will already be set in motion. I merely mention such a forecast to instill in the reader that Nature is and will remain the all-powerful Control of our essential needs and provision to maintain our life upon the planet be it reduced or miraculously maintained at status quo. If she has been allowed with such a disproportionate power compared to any mere entities contrived by man, isn't this a fairly convincing indication that we are most certainly delving into a far richer source should we attempt to relate with her as to any of our mere human speculations regarding the after-world beyond. Would you prefer to continue to warrant or defer to those squabbling, condemning, Talibanesque-styled men of the past who were little different than these modern day ones as your spiritual leaders? Those religious leaders on down into the Dark Ages of medieval Europe were no shining examples of compassion and humanistic concern either. Today, we now have those of the organized religions wildly claiming that the steadily declining environment has nothing to teach us. Everything is just going to be - A-O K!

Plain, simple, sheer reasoning tells me I have to differ. Since Mother Earth (Creator's God made Nature) is so vastly powerful and abundant with tell tale, truthful facts and evidence (and dire warnings) regarding planetary and habitat wise knowledge for ultimate survival, why should we lead ourselves elsewhere for our speculations? Fairly foolish to start out elsewhere, wouldn't you reasonably admit? Nature is Creator. Creator is Nature. She responds to what IT has designed! She reacts according to how IT has planned. Does your past, your training, have you disagree? To ignore Planetary Survival in this day and age is a stupid decision, my opinion, and to put it bluntly.

A Spirit Life Beyond

So. Is there a Spirit Life Beyond? If such an entity does exist, what will it be like for those of us who believe we have a 'Soul' or a "Spirit'? What of this punishment and 'Hell' which so many of Dominant Society believe is a major portion of that entity?

"You, Eagle Man, no doubt, have formulated some clues, many clues maybe, due to your experiences with those holy men as to the Beyond? What is in it for me, Eagle Man, if I were to believe the way you Indigenous folk do? Yes, what is in it for me? What am I going to get out of it?"

"What does the environment have to do with my role in a life beyond? If there is one."

The Code

There exists a Code. It began for me as a child, disappeared and then appeared again when I observed my first ceremony, held some time ago in Chief Fools Crow's cabin. Part of it, the Code, is indeed, even environmental. Our god-made habitat is an essential ingredient as deeply important as one's earthly conduct affects their decisive ending to one journey and on into the new beginning. Mitakuye Oyasin (We are all related), and this means more than just humans. It is new knowledge which we cannot escape from, therefore it is a part of our Spirit (that which goes on) or as the majority holds - the Soul. Chosen ignorance may no longer be an adequate excuse.

Access to the Code is fairly simple, however. We all had it in our innocent (and Truthful) youth. Children seem to 'step in' to Nature's projection yet soon lose that connection. Is it obliterated by such a non-Nature world most all live in? I think back upon the animals who never lose what Nature calls from them. A normal squirrel, in appearance at least, this squirrel plays merrily with the more rare black squirrel or just as equally with an albino, white squirrel, which I have viewed. Color means nothing negative to the Squirrel species when it comes to association. Playing children hold that likewise innocence which is a strong ingredient within the Code.

The existing tribes but a few centuries back displayed that nature-based harmony beginning with an English speaking Samoset holding up a 'Welcome' sign to the Pilgrims and following, when the African slaves were brought to these shores. It was the Southern tribes, namely the Seminoles, who gave them freedom when they ran away from the cruel plantations.

One can even make the search more intricate however through what the Indigenous tribes, some of them, still hold. Few two-legged, it seems however, will reach for it despite what is so obvious in this era. Such a loss to discover, quite possibility, when one finally reaches that Spirit World. Creator gave us a vast mind to use. To not use it is like a flower that never blossoms. In an earlier writing, I referred to the Mind as the 'Disk of Life'. I was borrowing my comparison from the computer age. The more one stores on his infinite 'Disk'; the more he or she takes with them into this supposed Spirit World beyond. Group 3 folks hold that they needn't bother observing and experiencing (or learning) while here. They will be instantly rewarded with 'all-knowledge' once they enter their Spirit World (Heaven to them). I just cannot allow myself to take that chance.

Will tragedy, stark, utter, devastating, deadly disaster finally wake human up? Remember my mentioning that it will be Nature who will make the conversion? When faced with his own death and the sheer diminishment of all around him, modern human may possibly reach in vain for the Code. The inescapable destruction of one's habitat will bring an awakening albeit too late. It will be a time when many...then most...and eventually...all will discard the erroneous beliefs which fostered the ongoing disregard, disrespect and dishonor practiced for centuries. Your new born child or your newly arrived grandchild could experience this dangerous dilemma in their lifetime. Is that the legacy you wish to leave for your own progeny?

I should be more optimistic. Mother Earth, the Sixth Power is at work this very moment and the Things of the Air' the Great Communication is now upon the planet. We shall see.

Encounter with the Spiritual

"The old Lakota was wise. He knew that a man's heart away from nature becomes hard."

Luther Standing Bear, Oglala Sioux

Capt. Jonathan Carver, 18th Century Spirit Ceremony

Capt. Carver's memoirs, *Travels Through the Interior Parts of North America in the Years 1766, 1767 and 1768*, London, C. Dilly, 1781, is the earliest mention of tribal foretelling ceremony that I have discovered. The explorer was two canoe days journey from the Grand Portage area which would later become Minnesota territory. Grand Portage is near the northeast tip of Minnesota, and north east of the Lake Superior port of Duluth, Minnesota. This episode is described following the explorer's comments regarding earlier meetings with the Sioux, so this could place him west of Grand Portage. Capt. Carver mentions the Sioux, the Winnebago, and the Assinpoils. The latter could mean the Assinoboins who headed further west than the Sioux would eventually venture. Chippewa and French guns changed Sioux minds about further exploration north and eastward. These Siouan-speaking tribes, or sub-tribes possibly in that era, were related and part of the grand exodus from what would later be termed the Carolinas. He referred to the Sioux as Nadowessies, Nadewesous or Naddewessiou, which was an early term for the early Dakotas and from this corruption of French and Chippewa came the name that stuck for several centuries-the Sioux. Academics, including Native academics attempting to be politically correct, are presently doing their utmost to send that term the way of the dinosaurs but are having a difficult time with the reservation Lakota, mostly, who don't seem to mind being called Sioux. These three tribes mentioned above eventually migrated westward considerable distances except for the Winnebago who remained in the Wisconsin area. Eventually some were sent southwest to Nebraska after reservations were established by the federal government.

Another tribe Carver mentions, were the Killistinoes. The Killistinoes were more distinctly linked in language with those of the Chippewa and Ottawa tribes. A ceremony was held by a medicine person (referred to as a priest) of this tribe and to such ceremony Capt. Carver found himself invited. The mechanics, so to speak, of the ceremony, to my mind's eye, bear somewhat of a relationship to the Yuwipi spirit calling ceremonies I have observed within my tribe, the Lakota or Sioux.

Let us begin where Capt. Carver was impatiently awaiting a re-supply from Grand Portage for his exploring party. He writes in older English form.

"The traders we expected being later this season than usual, and our numbers very considerable, for there were more than 300 of us, the stock of provisions we had brought with us was nearly exhausted, and we waited with impatience for their arrival.

One day, whilst we were all expressing our wishes for this desirable event, and looking from an eminence (promontory) in seeing them come over the lake, the chief priest belonging to the band of Killistinoes told us, that he would endeavor to have a conference with the Great Spirit, and know from him when the traders would arrive. I paid little attention to this declaration, supposing that it would be productive of some juggling trick, just sufficiently covered to deceive the ignorant Indians. But the king (Chief) of that tribe telling me that this was chiefly undertaken by the priest to alleviate my anxiety, and at the same time to convince me how much interest he had with the Great Spirit, I thought it necessary to refrain my aversions on his design.

The following evening was fixed upon for this spiritual conference. When every thing had been properly prepared, the King came to me and led me to a capricious tent, the covering of which was drawn up, so as to render what was transacting within visible to those who stood without. We found the tent surrounded by a great number of the Indians, but we readily gained admission, and seated ourselves on skins laid on the ground for that purpose.

In the centre I observed that there was a place of an oblong shape, which was composed of stakes stuck in the ground, with intervals in between, so as to form a kind of chest or coffin, large enough to contain the body of a man. These were of a middle size and placed at such a distance from each other, that whatever lay within them was readily to be discerned. The tent was perfectly illuminated by a great number of splinters cut from the pine or birch tree, which the Indians held in their hands.

In a few minutes the priest entered; when an amazing large elk's skin being spread on the ground, just at my feet, he laid himself down upon it, after having stripped himself of every garment except that which he wore close about his middle. Being now prostrate on his back, he first laid hold of one side of the skin, and folded it over him, and then the other; leaving only his head uncovered. This was no sooner done, than two of the young men who stood by took about forty yards of strong cord, made also of an elk's hide, and rolled it tight round his body, so that he was completely swathed within the skin. Being thus bound up like an Egyptian Mummy, one took him by the heels and the other by the head, and lifted him over the pales into the enclosure. I could also now discern him as plain as I had hitherto done, and I took care not to turn my eyes a moment from the object before me, that I might the more readily detect the artifice; for such I doubted not but that it would turn out to be.

The priest had not lain in this situation more than a few seconds, when he began to mutter. This he continued to do for some time, and then by degrees grew louder, till at length he spoke articulately; however what he uttered was in such a mixed jargon of the Chippewa, Ottawa, and Killistinoe languages, that I could understand but very little of it. Having continued in this tone for a considerable while, he at last exerted his voice to its utmost pitch, sometimes raving and sometimes praying, till he had worked himself into such an agitation, that he foamed at his mouth.

After having remained near three quarters of an hour in the place and continued his vociferation with unabated vigor, he seemed to be quite exhausted, and remained speechless. But in an instant he sprung upon his feet, notwithstanding at the time he was put in, it appeared impossible for him to move either his legs or arms, and shaking off his covering, as quick as if the bands with which it had been bound were burned asunder, he began to address those who stood around in a firm and audible voice. "My Brothers," said he, "the Great Spirit has deigned to hold a Talk with his servant at my earnest request. He has not, indeed, told me when the persons we expect will be here, but tomorrow, soon after the sun has reached his highest point in the heavens, a canoe will arrive, and the people in that will inform us when the traders will come." Having said this he stepped out of the enclosure, and after he had put on his robes, dismissed the assembly. I own I was greatly astonished at what I had seen; but as I observed that every eye was fixed on me with a view to discover my sentiments, I carefully concealed every emotion.

The next day the chief took Carver to view the lake. A canoe came into view as the sun was above- 'sun had reached his highest point in the heavens,' a canoe came round a point of land…. "The Indians no sooner beheld it, than they sent up a universal shout, and by their looks seemed to triumph in the interest their priest thus evidently had with the Great Spirit.

When the men came ashore they stated that the trader party had been parted with but a few days before and were to be expected in two more days and in accord with the medicine person's prediction. "They accordingly arrived at that time greatly to our satisfaction, but more particularly so to that of the Indians, who found by this event the importance both of their priest and of their nation, greatly augmented in the sight of a stranger.

"This story I acknowledge appears to carry with it marks of great credulity in the relator. But no one is less tinctured with that weakness than myself. The circumstances of it I own are of a very extraordinary nature; however, as I can vouch for their being free from either exaggeration or misrepresentation, being myself a cool and dispassionate observer of them all, I thought it necessary to give them to the public. And this I do without wishing to mislead the judgment of my Readers, or to make any superstitious impressions on their minds, but leaving them to draw from it what conclusions they please."

Captain J. Carver, Explorer.

* * * *

Chief Fools Crow

Chief Fools Crow, Oglala, (1890? 1891? - 1989) is no doubt, the most famous North American holy man of the latter 20th century. He lived at Kyle in a modest cabin, on the Pine Ridge Reservation. He, along with Chief Eagle Feather, Sichangu Holy Man, and (1914-1979) was responsible for the return of the Sioux Sun Dance in modern times. Thomas Mails wrote an interesting and revealing biography on the venerable and spiritually powerful leader, *Fools Crow.*

First Encounter

My first encounter with the, 'supernatural,' came when I was a young Marine warrior about to go to war. Like Jonathan Carver, I too was a Captain, a Marine pilot home on leave. My mother said to me. "Fools Crow is looking for you." Chief Fools Crow was the chief holy man from my reservation and intercessor or leader for our annual Sun Dance which was barely starting to come back. "He said, he wants you to come down to his cabin. He wants to hold a ceremony for you...for that Vietnam you are going to." My mother had five of my brothers go off to war earlier, mostly W.W. II. She simply accepted it as a regular fact that all of her sons would be involved in combat, one way or another.

My only connection to Chief Fools Crow was that I was but a pow wow dancer and would dance as a social dancer in the evening time, while the Sioux Sun Dance would be held at the same dance grounds in the early mornings when most of the social dancers were yet fast asleep in their tents camped along with those few families who were supporting their relatives in the Sun Dance. My old step-grandmother was there at those early Sun

Chief Fools Crow

Dances. You are not supposed to say step-grandmother in my language. A so called step-grandmother is your grand mother. Your step-mom - if you have one - is your Mom. That is just the way it is. Your "so called" half brother is your brother. Mitakuye Oyasin. It means we are all related. That also is the way it is. There are many differences in our culture and Dominant Society culture that it will not hurt much if some are pointed out.

In those days there was little interest in the return of the Sun Dance, our primary symbol for the return of our Way. There would be no return if the governmental authorities and the proselytizing missionaries had their way. By now they had converted the majority of the reservation - so they thought. They were confident they had destroyed the primary spiritual fires; too confident, they would later discover.

Pow wow Dancing

Pow wow dancing is simply social dancing for relaxation and enjoyment both for the dancers and the on looking crowd as well. Sun dancers are spiritual or religious participants. They did not so much as dance like we did but gathered around a cottonwood tree in the center of an arena and slowly shuffled to the beat of a large drum. Our pow wow dancing was much swifter and faster. We also danced to a drumbeat but various singing/drumming groups would be found at a pow wow. We pow wow dancers would dance long into the night, twirling and turning to the drum beats. It is a magical relaxation. The drums and the singers keep a melodic enchantment. In a way you are a form of fast moving ballerina or whatever the 'male ballerina dancers are called. Our Sioux women also dance. In those days we did not have the contest and prize money dances which are a major part of the reservation social dancing nowadays. We danced for the sheer enjoyment of just dancing. No one got mad or angry at dance judges and went away unhappy as often happens nowadays.

It is utterly hypnotic to wear the plains regalia and whirl and twirl. Tied tightly to your head is a half-foot tall porcupine hair headdress called a pay shah with its two, tall eagle feathers swiveling in bone sockets atop while keeping your bobbing head movements to the drumbeat. Many dancers were bare chested in those days, sporting maybe a necklace of bear, eagle or hawk claws. I wore a bone breast plate which covered my entire front from my neck to my waist. You wear a breechcloth or apron, front and back, fairly elaborate and decorated with sequins, beads; or in my case, a cross stitch of an old Sioux design. At the sides of your breech cloth or apron which is often fringed, you have a pair of fringed buckskin edged, bright, cloth trailers reaching lower, often to your knees. These are weighted toward their bottoms so that they will fly outward as you twirl. Just describing what I used to do offers me a pleasant feeling. At your waist and in back is centered a beautiful eagle feather tail bustle, with high reaching feathers covering your backside and usually centered with a bright matching design or colors of your breech cloth.

In my social dancing time, eagle feathers were not difficult to come by. There were quite a few on the large reservations bearing adequate food for the large golden eagles which are a bit broader and taller than the white headed bald eagles. Goldens feed primarily on the abundant prairie dogs, jack rabbits and cotton tails. Ranchers in western Dakota were allowed to curtail coyotes using cyanide poisoned jackrabbits as bait and unfortunately this procedure would kill many eagles. One could ride horse back into remote areas and most often come across a dead eagle or two. This practice is now outlawed.

Underneath one's eagle feather tail bustle and apron or breech cloth, a swimming suit with a pocket for keeping your money would be worn. You needed some change to buy bottles of cold pop for thirst quenching. Tourists keep you in plenty of money when they come up to you, usually at the pop stand to ask you to pose for pictures, and usually with their children. Mind you, you are all dressed up and with a slight bit of red 'war paint' upon your face and a braided wig; one does look rather fiercely exotic. Usually the little kids often quivered with either awed excitement or maybe from some degree of childish fear of this larger than life human standing behind them. The tourist would often place a fifty cent piece in your hand, or a couple quarters or even a dollar. It sufficed for your next round of cool beverage when you would soon get thirsty again.

The Tourist

One memorable incident happened when a tourist placed a pair of quarters into my hand after a picture was taken with his two children who I remember as standing quite nervously close to me as we faced the camera. He asked if I was from the reservation. I replied politely that I was born on the reservation but no longer lived there. The previous day I had flown a Marine F-9 Grumman Cougar, cross-country training flight into Ellsworth Air Force Base just a few miles outside of my home town of Rapid City, South Dakota. These long flights are essential to your combat training and usually most squadron commanders do not limit one's destination as long as jet engine ground starter units are available at the military base where you land. Most pilots will make at least one flight into their home town area if an approved military field is near by. Rapid was about 100 miles north of the annual reservation pow wow social dance gathering in those days.

I landed my Cougar at Ellsworth, and rented a civilian plane from a friend named Merrill at the local flying service and flew on down to the reservation. I would always have to leave my ejection harness, oxygen mask and helmet in his office when I would rent a plane from him during my hometown forays which he would proudly display on a coat rack while I was gone for a few days. Some times I would 'buzz' his office with a jet fighter or even shoot a touch and go at the municipal field where the flying service was located. He always got a kick out of that and would have a plane waiting for me. Those were the days!

At the reservation graveled air field my sister Mildred and brother-in-law Ralph would usually show up after buzzing the pow wow grounds a few times. They always kept my dance regalia in their shiny Airstream trailer camper. A retired couple, they were avid followers of the pow wow circuit that was just starting to grow in those days. Indian people were just beginning to recapture their identity. At earlier pow wows, when I was quite young and an onlooker, it seemed that only the old danced and very few of the young adults danced or were in attendance. The wahshichu (white man) had all the answers then and was bolstered by the many new inventions constantly coming anew. Even we Indians marveled at the sleeker, fancier models of cars he produced each year. In awe of aviation, I was spellbound by the new military models he produced and the speed and altitude records that were constantly broken. Everyone, it seemed, wanted to be like the white man. My dream was to become a pilot but deep down inside, I realized that it had to be an impossibility. Such was the self-doubt or skepticism held by a young, growing Indian in the white man's world.

My sister danced as well and claimed that the dancing and the drumming had healed what was once a painful back condition she had once suffered from a slick-floored fall while working as a cook's assistant in an Indian Public Health hospital. My brother-in-law, a big strong white man and a former star football player staunchly supported her new-found interest and could always be seen bustling around the trailer making things comfortable for everyone. If his wife was healthy, he was happy, was his attitude. He dearly loved my sister. She never had children, was considerably older than me and treated me like a son which did create a degree of jealousy from her husband. In my teenage days he was not too fond of me, but had to exhibit a degree of restrained toleration because my sister was fairly independent. My Indian dancing had led her to the pow wows where she would hobble to a chair and sit and watch, claiming the drumming soothed her ailing back problem. Once, she simply rose out of her chair and started dancing in the circle. I was startled to see her dancing close by, wearing a shawl. She danced back to her chair after a few circles. Soon she was at it again. In time she was completely healed and even became fairly agile. Her husband credited me for beginning her dance interest and always treated me quite well after her recovery. He did appreciate fully that he had 'gotten his wife back' so to speak. He said to me sincerely on more than one occasion, "It's pretty tough to see your wife in pain. Looks like those days might be gone." As I said earlier, the drum beat, which is in tune with your heart beat, can be very powerful.

Well, that was quite a diversion from the tourist who had just placed a quarter or two in my hand. As an Indian writer, you reflect upon what you consider as a worthy story and you just take off on it. This is a habit of the Sioux storytellers and again makes us different from the wah shee chu. We generally circle back and get on with the beginning however. So let us circle back to the innocent tourist and his family which he brought to the Black Hills and all its natural, beautiful splendor which his children no doubt cherish to this day. He is now on a Sioux reservation watching another splendor-the whirling, decorated dancers, spinning and turning to a hypnotic drumbeat. He asked cordially if I lived in Rapid City and what did I do for a living. Behind my beaded headband over hanging braids, a sweaty face, streaked with a pair of generously daubed, Chinese red lip stick stripes across each cheek bone and wearing a heavy bone breast plate and an eagle bone whistle hanging from my neck, while holding a buffalo horned, black and white horse hair braided, long handled dance tomahawk (was utterly gorgeous), matching beaded arm and wrist bands, buckskin-fringed at that, not to mention the broad eagle feather tail bustle on my back side and matching breech cloth apron or breech cloth covering my front, I guess I did look rather 'Indian', so to speak. I should also mention that small bells like the jingle bells on Christmas horse sleighs, are tied tightly over furred padding at one's ankles and of course, beaded moccasins. All in all, it does give one, especially when you are young and trim, a definite warrior's look. No wonder the two children stared at me in awe as we talked.

I guess I 'brought the house down' so to speak, when I answered calmly. "I am a Marine Captain, a Marine Corps pilot. I just landed a jet fighter at the air base nearby and came down to dance." I thanked him for coming to the reservation and wished him an enjoyable safe journey, shook hands with his two mesmerized children and went back to dancing.

I mentioned that I wore a hair pipe bead, breast plate. These so-called beads are 3 to 4 inches long and lie horizontal upon your chest. The many rows are separated by several pairs of stiff leather strips from the top of the chest trailing down to your waist. Bright, large, French brass beads often decorate the edges of the hair pipe as well as an inner row of shorter hair pipe which is ivory-toned. Many or most dancers in my day were much more bare than what dancers wear nowadays. Back then, mostly full bloods or breeds with considerable Indian blood were the vast majority of dancers so very few of us wore heavy face paint as they do nowadays since we looked fairly much Indian. We considered face paint as a gimmick to hide one's features and as full bloods or half-breeds we felt we had nothing to hide. I have seen some extremely handsome Sioux men in dance regalia as well as the women who were beautiful. Nothing enhances a person as much as a plains dance outfit or costume as we used to call it. Regalia is the term now used. When a handsome or beautiful dancer starts to move, you cannot take your eyes off them, such was my feeling which was shared by many others who looked on.

My sister Mildred had some elaborate beaded dresses for evening dances. For afternoon dancing under much warmer summer conditions she wore less elaborate and much cooler cotton dresses with lighter beadwork. Ralph purchased the Airstream Trailer just for pow wow dancing so I always had a rather plush place to stay, by reservation standards, when I was at the Sun Dance as a social dancer.

At the dance grounds, a sweat lodge for the small numbers of sun dancers participating would be held in the early morning. In those days the advocates for the Sun Dance were attempting to bring it back to the tribe and were facing strong resistance from many tribal members who had been converted to the white man's religion. The strongest resistance came from the missionaries themselves, primarily, on my reservation. Certain Jesuit priests from that order came to convert us in the latter part of the 19th century. Their successors were most adamant in their opposition to us. To draw a crowd, Chief Fools Crow combined the two events, pow wow dancing and the Sun Dance. With the heavy resurgence nowadays of the ceremonies return, this procedure would be unheard of but those were different times and Chief Fools Crow knew what he was doing. Know-it-all detractors will pay dearly in the Spirit World should they criticize him, is my biased opinion.

Fools Crow's Cabin

I picture Fools Crow waiting at the horse gate when we arrived for the yuwipi ('they tie him up' or, 'to be bound') spirit calling which the holy man would conduct. My traditional-leaning grandmother's last request was that I attend a yuwipi ceremony before leaving for war. In the centuries-old calling, Fools Crow would beseech the spirit people for protection. My mother had been with us that clear summer night as we drove from Rapid to the holy man's reservation home. She was considered quite a church goer and volunteer at the local mission but my grandmother's prediction that I wouldn't come back if I failed to attend a yuwipi was enough to dispel the black magic aura drummed into my mother by the missionaries. I wished my father and grandmother were alive to attend with us. My father kept his distance from the missionaries yet advised me to follow my mother's way. "Those priests can make too much trouble for you. Don't be following what I believe," was his practical summation. "It's a white man's world and you have to be part of it if you want less trouble."

The tall, trim holy man held us for a few moments with that mysterious look, the penetrating stare of a hawk or an eagle. Fools Crow was like a Badlands hawk or an eagle - regal, keen, and observant - alone and aloof within his own vast spaciousness, oblivious to the encroaching Wahshichu (white man) world.

The straight-postured man spoke from the gate as they got out of the car, "What took you so long? You should have been here earlier."

On the way down to the reservation, my sister drove and stopped in at a super market to purchase a considerable amount of groceries for Chief Fools Crow as is the custom of our people when you go to visit a medicine person. You do not take them pretty rocks with ribbons attached as some think they have to now days. As I recall, we did not take them a can of pipe tobacco. My mother may have purchased a carton of Camels cigarettes as that is what she smoked and gave them to Fools Crow as he occasionally lit up a cigarette but the intention of 'giving tobacco' as is the custom now days was not the intention of my mother or sister. The large amount of groceries was much more of a custom back then. To this day I wish people would dispel with giving me tobacco when they first come to visit as I am no medicine man and do not intend to be one. I am a writer and a Veteran.

We're sorry, Grandpa," my sister Mildred answered. "We stopped to get groceries." Grandpa is a common and respectful form of address for Sioux holy men.

Chief Fools Crow had no telephone, so how did he know we were coming to see him and even knew we had been delayed to purchase food?' This would be my first taste of the Lakota supernatural, as the holy man led us into his mud-chinked cabin. Kate Fools Crow stood by the wood-burning stove and welcomed us with her warm smile. Speaking in the rich Sioux language, we visited and laughed together as the blue enameled coffee pot was filled, meat was cut and put into boiling water, dried woshapi (berry cakes), were set in a pan of water and fry bread preparations were made. The laughter flowed. My sister, Mildred, my mother, Sonny Larive and his grandparents, and Fools Crow's son-in-law, Amos Lone Hill, exchanged conversation in Lakota Sioux. Blacktop, a bashful eight-year-old, sat fiddling with the damper on the pot-bellied stove near the west wall.

Spirit Calling

When Fools Crow went to the closet for his medicine bundle, it was a signal for the women to push back the furniture and draw the curtains. Sonny helped prepare for the tying ritual that preceded the *yuwipi*, while Mildred unrolled a long string of tiny cloth tobacco offerings. The four directions were represented by red, yellow, black and white flags, which were placed in earth-filled bowls to form a square before an earthen altar in the middle of the cabin. Mildred wrapped a string of tobacco offerings around the bowls, marking the limits of the spirit area. Sage was passed to all participants, who placed some in their hair and over one ear.

The holy man entered the square made by the string of tobacco offerings to place two leather rattles on the floor before raising his peace pipe to offer an opening prayer. Afterwards, he stood ready to be bound. Sonny tied his arms and hands behind his back with bailing twine before draping a blanket over the Oglala's head. An eagle feather hung from the top of the blanket that covered the holy man down to his moccasin tops.

Next, Sonny wrapped Fools Crow with a rawhide rope, beginning with a noose around his neck and then six more times around his body, down to his ankles. Each wrap represented the seven sacred ceremonies or possibly the Six Powers and of course, the Ultimate Power. While the holy man was lowered, face down to the floor, Mildred sat at the place of honor with the peace pipe, behind the dirt altar with her back against the stove. The kerosene lamp was extinguished.

Amos tapped a drum and sang a centuries-old call to the ancestors of the Sioux, the spirit beings. They came quickly from the west, rattling the stovepipe and swishing the rattles through the room, as if they had been close by, waiting for the call. My Mother commanded me to start praying. Would I return from the war? Would I be a prisoner? We knew the spirits would tell if we prayed humbly. If I promised to live for the people, they would try to protect me, is what I learned later but at the time I was so suppressed by the white man's false stereotypes. Startling, tiny blue lights entered through the stove door behind Mildred while I prayed. They flickered and danced with the heartbeat of the drum, then raised to the ceiling, circled the participants and, then, as the song ended, disappeared back through the stove door behind the pipe holder. I sat down in awe at what I had seen. The buckskin rattles that had accompanied Amos Lone Hill's song, now fell to the floor, silent.

The Wotai (woe tye) Stone

A stranger's gruff voice came in and began to speak to Fools Crow. "Changu Tanka." I heard my sister whisper to my mother. I knew enough Sioux from my parents who constantly spoke it, 'Big Road'. The area where Fools Crow was bound emitted a dim haze. The spirit of Big Road, Fools Crow's Spirit Helper, carried on in conversation with the medicine man. I was experiencing what I termed then- my first ghost.

Fools Crow's muffled voice spoke out in the darkness, telling us how a stone had fallen to strike the sacred tree at the summer Sun Dance, while an airplane flew high overhead. The stone bore the image of an eagle within its grain. Later he had a vision. "I saw the airplane land in a far-off place, and a warrior walked away from it without looking back. He walked toward the sacred tree and stood there with a boy. The stone was brought to the Sun Dance lodge. I took the stone from Eagle Feather and put it in my medicine bundle. It remained in the bundle only a short while and then it was gone." The group waited while the holy man took several breaths.

"The stone has returned and is now among us here. Eagle Boy, you must pray hard so it will remain." (My Indian name then would later be changed.)

I answered quickly, blurting out, "Grandfather, ask the stone to stay with us. Tell the spirit people I offer myself for the Sun Dance. I will live for the people and the power of the hoop." A shrill tremolo pierced the darkness, followed by a chorus of "Hau". The cry came from the women to honor a warrior who would go off to battle. It would be repeated when the warrior returned, or at his grave.

Later on, I would alter that pledge, 'I would live for the Way!'

Prediction

Then Fools Crow spoke with uncharacteristic volume and excitement. "The eagle on the stone is for a warrior who will fly with the winged. Eagle Boy, you shall wear this stone as your wotai. When you are across the ocean, you shall carry it. As long as you wear it faithfully, the bullets shall bounce from your airplane. You shall see the enemy many times. You shall not fear battle and shall laugh at danger."

After a long pause, he spoke more cautiously. "There is no guarantee, however, that you shall return and become a new warrior to stand beneath the Sun Dance tree with Blacktop, my grandson."

Fools Crow paused with a cough, weighing what he would reveal. The rattles buzzed. Later I would learn that the old man had envisioned that I would see the enemy 100 times and would vision quest before my Sun Dance….if I returned. The small blue lights flourished one last time. Big Road made his exit. The rattles clashed, each shaking a different rhythm, their discord breaking the stillness.

A concluding song, the untying song was sung. When the lamp was lit, Fools Crow was sitting up untied. His blanket was neatly draped over the stove. The tying rope was wrapped in a tight ball. No one, including Fools Crow had moved during the untying song. The wotai stone, oval and not much larger than a fifty cent piece and twice as thick, waited on the cabin floor and was bound in a buckskin pouch. After the pouch was opened it revealed the small stone; an eagle was clearly discernable in its grain.

Combat

I wrote this memory not long after I had finished law school which began immediately after I left Vietnam. Actually, I was only 8 days out of a combat cockpit and I was sitting in law school. I had missed freshman week. The following is written in 2nd person but is an accurate presentation of what happened after I had attended Fools Crow's Yuwipi.

It was nearly noon when he left the debriefing room at the operations Quonset. A helicopter gun ship buzzed low across the distant row of tin-roofed huts sitting on a sand dune. There was little to do at Chu Lai but wait for the outdoor movie, wash clothes and clean the hut. The endless boredom of shifting sand and dreary shacks made him yearn to go home. He had resigned from the Marines to attend law school, but had first requested a combat assignment. His orders home were due. Any intention of remaining in the service had ended with this war. The Marines had allowed him to rise from enlisted rank, but a warrior's role in a war like this one had proved too frustrating.

His grandmother's advice echoed in his memory, "There will always be a war, Grandson. If they can make a business out of their religion, war can be a collection plate, too." But the war, despite the frustrations, had provided the way to reach for what he must. Even Fools Crow, a pacifist, never objected to his involvement and had helped his warrior's role with the coming of the wotai.

Later, He would learn to contend that the war was mostly political and economic, no different than most, where the poor were rallied for cannon fodder through a sense of patriotism and, especially in this war, the higher realm, those in control, the elected and economic leaders, strove to keep their warrior-age sons out of combat units, taking no share of the direct and deadliest exposure. In but a short time, He would set his course upon another path and would leave the warring to politicians.

Alone with his thoughts for the moment, he rested his head against the ejection seat. Before leaving Vietnam he would fly over one hundred missions. All that had been foretold in the ceremony held at Fools Crow's cabin had come true. Spirit people had entered, predicting that he would see the enemy many times. 'Bullets would bounce from his airplane,' they said.

* * * *

Spiritual Predictions

The high-finned Phantoms circled like a pair of tiger sharks above the South China Sea. Two electronic-laden Grumman A-6 Intruders orbiting off the coast of North Vietnam were contacted by the F-4's. The Grummans took their positions, holding a separated, lengthy, racetrack orbit, their missile surveillance scanners sweeping inland. The mission's target was located in SAM territory. He was getting close to his last mission. He was due for discharge and new pilots were checking into the squadron. The cruising fighter-bombers turned inbound. The thin beachhead giving way to beige landscape, looked little different than South Vietnam, except for monsoon-flooded rice paddies casting mirrored reflections of false tranquility. The late summer storms were saturating North Vietnam, Laos and Cambodia further inland. Meteorology predicted that Chu Lai would receive heavy rains by noon.

He glanced at his watch. His main gyroscope for instrument landing had turned faulty and he didn't want to make an instrument landing at Chu Lai in heavy rain. The pilots had noted the cloud buildups west of Chu Lai. All Laos and Cambodia missions had been cancelled. He hoped to leave Vietnam before the monsoons; emergency missions were launched regardless of weather and more than one crew and their aircraft had disappeared in the torrential downpours.

He unzipped the top of his flight suit, adjusted his pistol shoulder harness and pulled the braided cord at his neck. He tugged to bring the small lump of buckskin from underneath his survival vest. He fondled the buckskin. His orders were due.

"Where are my orders?" he asked as he clutched the wotai pouch.

Square coastal rice fields thinned away to rising piedmont, the rice paddies climbing with the terrain, narrowing to stepped radial bands ending at mountainous, dark green, almost impenetrable jungle. Yet, fifty miles further, somewhere under the thick foliage, a North Vietnamese truck company was hidden and protected by surface to air missiles.

The first warning tone issued by the patrol planes crackled like scrambled eggs across his helmet's receivers. His muscles flexed like a prizefighter circling an opponent. The voiceless tones meant North Vietnamese, or more than likely their Russian advisors, had activated radar sets and were no doubt tracking the Phantoms. Both pilots tensed on their flight controls, their feet poised to jam down the rudder pedals in coordination with a sideways slam of the control stick to full aileron.

Any further warning beginning with the spoken code word for the sector, in which they were flying, he would do an abrupt split "S" maneuver to his right, at the same time igniting both afterburners. Fritz, the section leader, would roll in the opposite direction.

The split "S" maneuver was the most expedient means of losing altitude and changing direction. The plane would roll over on its back like an upside-down turtle before it dropped its nose straight down in a dive. In theory, the launched missiles would be radar locked to a computed destruction point out ahead where target and missile were calculated to converge if evasive action had not been taken. Below, the enemy controller would attempt to alter the missiles' course into the targets. Fortunately, for the fighter pilots, the missiles' smaller steering surfaces made the projectiles awkward and clumsy in comparison to the fighters. Too much correction and the SAMs would tumble and cartwheel futilely. If the early warning surveillance aircraft detected the upward-bound missiles in time, the fighters usually had a high survival rate... if the fired missiles were detected in time.

Pilot error jeopardized the pair of fighter-bombers from Marine Fighter/Attack Squadron 115. The lead A-6 surveillance aircraft, having flown north longer than the uneasy pilot had wanted, suddenly banked seaward before signaling their counterpart. At this point, the surveillance radar was blind and it was now the mission of the second A-6 patrol plane, trailing further south, to scan the enemy areas inland. Precisely at this moment, the experienced Russian missile technicians fired a salvo of three missiles.

Fortunately, an alert radar operator in the second A-6 had anticipated the lead aircraft's turn and was already sweeping his scope inland to locate the Phantoms, while three ascending blips were off the bottom of his screen for a few long seconds. When the three ascending dots appeared, the operator's eyes went wide. He punched the emergency warning indicator without a moment's hesitation.

"Q-B Seven, Q-B Seven!" The code word for fired missiles was shouted out across both pilots' helmets. Q-B was their sector by latitude, Seven by longitude. Both pilots reacted to the code word as instinctively as if their own names had been yelled in alarm. The lead plane rolled left, his wingman rolled right. The inverted pair hung suspended for a long, precarious moment before the black noses dropped, hurtling down, down to the green jungle, miles below.

A flash of gray, like a gigantic telephone pole, roared ahead and past the wingman's window. It was the second missile. The first missile had been directed at the section leader's plane and was now tumbling wildly out of control. Preoccupation with the lead missile caused the enemy controller to err, detonating the second missile too late. The shock waves reached out with a solid thump, but no damage was inflicted to his plane.

His machine was just beginning to scream downward under full afterburner power when the last missile flashed from below like a giant spear, detonating much closer. The vacuum shock from this blast snuffed out his right engine, sending the machine spinning. Around and around the F-4 spiraled down, the dark jungle revealing a glistening silver streak bisecting the whirling circle, the peaks and valleys growing deathly sharper. The 'G' forces paralyzed his leg upon the rudder. He strained to release the pressure upon the rudder and pushed back on the control stick toward a neutral position. Down he whirled and he began to panic. Something told him he could not panic. It was the time to concentrate and believe in the Way. Believe in the prediction in Fools Crow's cabin.

The streak of silver transcended to a discernible river before the pilot managed to neutralize his controls, pushing the stick forward against the centrifugal force with all of his strength and pushing his foot with equal difficulty against the rudder pedal opposite from the spin. The stabilator, rudder and aileron surfaces responded, the spin ceased, the dive shallowed and, finally, the plane came under control. Smoke trailed from hot kerosene in the dead engine. He pressed the aileron and rudder controls to point the machine out to the safety of the South China Sea.

His adrenaline began to subside. He had been too excited to notice the loss of the right engine. The power of just one afterburner, coupled with the supersonic speed accumulated from the dive over ten thousand feet, concealed the loss of the engine. Now, as he brought the throttles out of afterburner, the sudden deceleration warned him of his situation. He checked the dead engine's RPM gage, relieved to find a wind-milling turbine indicating that the engine wasn't frozen, decreasing the chance of battle damage.

At that moment, Fritz called across the radios, "Chief, where are you? Are you okay?"

"Feet wet," He replied.

"C'mon back, Chief," Fritz ordered, disregarding radio formality as he glared down through his canopy at the telltale smoke trails. "I got the bastards spotted." The vindication in his voice flooded through his transmission.

He scanned the left engine instruments, satisfied with their readings. He double-checked the fuel flow, pressing the quantity indicators, calculating his reserve fuel. The Phantom was a flying kerosene tank: fuselage cells, wing cells and two external tanks fed the thirsty machine. Abnormal fuel loss would indicate battle damage. It was against battle regulations to re-light an engine that had been taken out of action if one had adequate power to return to base.

He had adequate power to return to Chu Lai or Da Nang on one engine and could disregard the section leader's order. Another order, considerably higher, from Air Force Command, decreed that the destruction of SAM missile sites within the DMZ area, including the QB sector, required U.S. Air Force clearance. Even if missiles had been fired, a half-hour waiting period was required before attack. Fighter-bomber pilots were at a loss to understand this directive. Was it to allow the Russian crews time to escape? The telltale smoke trail left by the SAM missile did not last a half-hour.

The regulation made his decision for him. He recalled, with disgust, proclamations made by dove senators on college campuses. It was his last mission, unless emergency missions demanded his duties. What would they do? Ground him and send him back to the States? He laughed aloud.

"Let's get the bastards, Chief!" the RIO's vehement voice encouraged across the intercom.

The right engine lit without incident. Satisfied, he pointed the big machine back toward Finger Lakes. Fritz called out his altitude and position, boldly oblivious to enemy radio surveillance. He lit both afterburners to scream back to the section leader, homing on a black orbiting speck. Within minutes, he was joined in formation.

They made only two passes apiece. The leader called for his wingman to bomb several hundred yards short of the napalm drop after Fritz had pulled up from his first pass. A flaming secondary explosion erupted from the jungle when the first load of six bombs detonated. "Right on, Chief," Fritz yelled with exuberance across the radios. The section leader expended his remaining napalms close to the fiery jungle, sending a ricocheting fire streaking a half-mile, obviously igniting a missile, like an errant Fourth of July rocket. The last of his bombs scattered the diminishing fireball below with resultant lesser explosions.

After several victory rolls, the section joined back in formation, departing south across the mountains north of Da Nang. Out ahead of the monsoon, scud clouds were lowering below the mountains to the coastline, moving toward Chu Lai and Da Nang. Within an hour, the rains would be drenching both bases. At a thousand feet, both Phantoms streaked above the landing end of Chu Lai runway, the lead plane peeling away, breaking sharply to arc smoothly back to the touchdown point. The wingman held his course for several seconds more down the runway then rolled ninety degrees to the horizon, following in a wider arc to increase the landing separation from the leader. The drag chutes deployed as each aircraft landed.

The pilots offered little at the debriefing. They reported possible secondary explosions, presumably a minor truck depot. Possible ground fire was alleged; anti-aircraft fire was reported to be negative. The aviators were thankful they were not career men and that they'd both be rotating back to the States soon.

He walked across the sand dunes with his RIO and Fritz, their conversation oblivious to the mission. Instead they laughed and reminisced about two attractive schoolteachers the pilots had met in Okinawa. They stopped at his hut for a rum and coke, despite the time of day.

After Fritz and the RIO left, He sat on his locker beside his bunk and mixed one more rum and coke. It had been a good mission. He languished confidently, assured that there were fewer Russians to fire missiles at the fighter-bombers. He never finished the liquid in his canteen cup. The ever-present heat and the rum made him drowsy. He fell back on his air mattress and was soon asleep. Before he fell backwards, he managed to stand and hang his shoulder holster and pistol on a nail above his mosquito netting and then placed his Wotai pouch across the pistol butt jutting from the holster. While he slept, the maintenance crews checked his aircraft to correct the gyroscope. Despite the engine squelching blast, not a mark was to be found on the huge Phantom. "You will see the enemy over 100 times, and the bullets will bounce from your machine." Fools Crow had told him.

Sioux History – Exodus from the East

'The Dakota/Lakota migrated suddenly out of the East, not long after the first sailing ships. Some claim: 'Our medicine warned us.' It is our communication with Creators Spirit World.

I would consider the study of those who retained the Natural Knowledge, those who lived daily within the Code in this hemisphere as an informative base to begin with. All religions offer their 'Biblical' or 'Koranic history', so to speak. The Jewish folk tell of their Exodus out of Egypt, claiming Creator specifically protected them from Pharaoh's pursuing Army. I find it easy to believe their claim. The Dakota/Lakota (later named Sioux) possibly were warned spiritually to leave their abundant living in what would later be called the Carolina Piedmont area. And they were smart enough to listen. Why else would such a large tribe, living so comfortably; up and suddenly move thousands of miles?

Earliest Mythology

Many Lakota/Dakota, claim that we Sioux evolved from Wind Cave in the Black Hills. The original opening was but a small aperture, smaller than the torso of a human being by far. Wind from the fist-sized opening allegedly blew the hat off a bypassing cowboy; thus, it was discovered. According to a Sioux mythological theory we were confined there, within the void, for quite sometime. Eventually, the early Sioux emerged out of the small opening and therefore the Black Hills is considered by the mythological leaning as our birthplace. I do not consider mythology, when I write about the Sioux, as anything more than passing information. Such information is not offered as a historic happening.

Despite the numerous proven theories of Science, many in this country, those who are indoctrinated by particular sects within Church doctrine, consider the Earth as less than 10 millennia old, 5 to 6 thousand years to be more exact. They dispute scientific data and have their own theory called

Creationism. I am hoping the majority of the open-minded citizens of the land remain on the side of Science, whose measurement data dates us back some millions of years, or is it billions? Science simply measures what Creator has made and estimates when Creator allowed the living entities to evolve, adapt, continue or perish. Creator has even allowed Science specific measurement tools such as carbon dating techniques, laser measurement, telescopes, atomic or optical microscopes and other accurate measurement instruments. I place much more trust in scientific measurement of Creator's wonders than I do a group of fanatics who appear as less than rational. I think it is highly doubtful that the Creationists can squeeze the Age of the Dinosaurs somewhere within those limited 5 to 6 thousand years.

Again, I personally hold these 'faith' concepts as mythology, no matter how many Sioux consider Wind Cave as the birthplace of the Lakota/Dakota people. It is a free country and I have no objection to what people choose to believe, as long as they do not get over zealous and attempt to cast harm on those who will not join in their views. Superstition has killed millions down through time along with fostering unimaginable mental and social suffering against the non-superstitious. When I enter the Spirit World, I want to proudly look back and reflect that I allowed few superstitions to guide my trail. What I can directly observe from my surroundings and/or become influenced from plausible scientific theories is the basis of my beliefs and that includes origin as well. Superstition clutters the mind from accepting real truths based on Direct Observation.

Superstition

Ahhh, Superstition. *Superstition is akin to drugs. If you never let it in, it can not harm you.* Superstition definitely leads one away from the Creator, my opinion. Why? Because I find it difficult to believe that an all-Truthful Creator would originate what is superstitious. What is Superstition? First, it is an insult to Creator, because only Creator allows or makes all things: simple and practical as that. Superstition, however, has to be originated by man, in the first place. Were some tribes superstitious? Definitely, some were and quite considerably, but they never evolved spiritually, obviously, to the degree that the Sioux did!

I believe it is important for the reader to get a feel for or from the people who have been able to maintain their ability to explore the realm of the mysterious. The Scientist prepares him or herself with accumulated data which leads toward accepted knowledge after forms of measurement are set in motion. Most all scientists had former teachers in their earlier preparations. The medicine person likewise has had former mentors which generally follow basic tribal precepts handed down from time and honed by the medicine person. The astute medicine person however, adamantly maintains his own individuality. He has no commanding, unyielding book, (written by men, of course) or established dogma to keep him from realizing his own experiences and direct observations. Had not the Sioux preserved their spiritual precepts, we would have no base from which to begin our study. So let us begin to study the people who preserved what we are about to explore.

Dakota/Lakota

Siouan-speaking tribes that remained in our ancestral home of the Carolina's were the Wacama, the Catawba and the Biloxi. The Biloxi moved as far south as South Carolina, yet never left the East with the main body of migrating Sioux. The Wacama remained in North Carolina.

The history of the Sioux during the past five hundred years can be traced from their origins in the Piedmont area of the Carolinas. To their north were the Iroquois, the most powerful of the North American tribes. The Iroquois were a united confederacy, made up of five organized tribes. We must thank them for giving human's greatest gift to human - Democracy. Democracy was already being practiced by the Iroquois, the Sioux and the Cherokee long before the Pilgrims, who knew nothing about it. The next most powerful tribe in North America was the Cherokee. Their domain lay south and southwesterly of the Piedmont where they enjoyed lush agricultural lands. European ships were passing up and down the Atlantic coast by this time. For it was a century since Columbus and the first newcomers brought their fatal diseases, wiping out or severely decimating many coastal tribes. The Shawnee were most likely already west of the soon-to-be-migrating Sioux. The Sioux were called Lakota or Dakota in those times. They regarded themselves as the Friendly People of the Seven Council Fires. Later, they would pick up their "Sioux" name from the French explorers and Chippewa on their journey westward.

We can imagine the Sioux living quite comfortably in the Piedmont area that provided adequate soil for tilling and planting. Meat supplemented their diet: primarily deer and wild turkeys, even some forest buffalo and elk, which foraged in abundance all the way to the Mississippi River and beyond. Their houses were not the conical buffalo-hide covered dwellings that came later, they were square or rectangular frame structures made of sturdy saplings and covered with bark and thatch from lesser branches, often with leaves for insulation. Winters were milder than the climates of the northern United States. Overall, they were quite peaceful, as were many of the agricultural tribes who had little need or desire for pursuing another tribe's possessions. Their diet consisted of corn, squash, beans, potatoes, tomatoes and the rich array of wild game the land offered. None of the aforementioned protein-rich vegetables were found in Europe in those times. Fish also supplemented their diet. Journeys to the nearby Atlantic coast brought them succulent seafood as well. Truly, they lived in a virtual paradise. It remains a mystery why they would pick up and vacate such choice living conditions and head westward. No one has yet to come up with an adequate explanation for that mystery.

The Westward Move

Some scholars believe it was the constant raids by the powerful Iroquois to the North that caused the Sioux to leave their territory. If this was the case, then why did they continue to move so far away from their adversaries – over two thousand miles in all? The Cherokees to their south were considerably more peaceful than the Iroquois. No doubt, the Cherokees appreciated having the Sioux as a buffer between them and the powerful Iroquois.

The westward move soon became a mass migration, and very few stayed behind. They would soon be swallowed up by the European tide of immigrants fleeing their own homelands. Europe was not a particularly choice land to live in at the time the Sioux were leaving their productive lands in the Carolinas. Europeans were barely removed from serfdom, brutalized by a harsh church that was still in the throes of the Inquisitions. The Europeans had two masters: the church hierarchy and the land-owning nobility of barons and earls. They knew nothing of the Democracy the American Indians were enjoying at the time Columbus was making his journey and even later, when the Pilgrims landed.

By the 1600s, they were already on their great move westward. The Iroquois were mentioned as a possible reason for the Sioux's sudden migration from their comfortable surroundings. One would wonder as to what significant event would drive out an entire tribe. Could it have been the deadly diseases that the early ships had brought to the coastal tribes, as in the fatal cases of the Patuxets, Naragannsetts, Wompanoags and others? Most Atlantic coastal tribes disappeared due to disease.

Exodus

The National Geographic Supplement, September, 2005, 1. suggests the Sioux as being from the Ohio area and negates the possibility of the three remaining tribes staying in the Carolinas, but also negates the added clue offered by the medicine bundles of the Siouan speaking Kansa and Arkansa tribes. In the early 1800s, the chiefs of these two tribes stated that they were from the tciyeta (ocean) which is at 'Nyu Yak' (New York), or "the land where the Sun comes up from the water"; known to us as the Atlantic Ocean. Their medicine bundles were analyzed and the sea shells therein did indeed come from the east coast, precisely the bay that the chiefs described. The Kansa and Arkansa evidence suggests that the Sioux may have once been in Iroquois territory, but were finally driven out once the Iroquois formed their strong confederacy of five tribes. This theory would have the Sioux as once coastal dwellers at one time. This theory is yet another riddle to be solved, possibly for those who believe in a Spirit World, wherein we may all go some day. Any historical puzzles will be answered, hopefully there, should such an entity as the Spirit World exist.

Westward and eventually down the Ohio River Valley, the Sioux moved on. Not in one mass but gradually, band by band and in varied numbers. Possibly, bands joined for security to minimize resistance of the other tribes along the way. The Shawnee were the largest tribe to be confronted. They seemed to have smoked the peace pipe with the Sioux bands, granting them unrestricted passage. As stated earlier, it was not one mass movement. It may have taken the Sioux a century to reach the Mississippi, sometimes settling on their journey, but gradually heading westward and turning upstream when they reached the Mississippi.

When the main body of Sioux reached the Mississippi some bands broke off and crossed the great river. The Mandan eventually crossed to the Missouri to settle far upstream. The Arkansa, and more likely the Kansa, may have crossed the great river near the Missouri confluence. Joe Medicine Crow, tribal historian of the Crow Indians in Montana, states that the Crow broke off from the main body of Sioux on their upstream journey at the mouth of the Wisconsin River. The Crow then wandered for a century toward the shores of Lake Superior and eventually crossed westward over the Great Plains, finally settling in Montana where they remain today. They would scout for the U.S. Army, and in time, against their former relatives, the Sioux.

After the main body of Sioux congregated toward the headwaters of the Mississippi, fierce opposition from the Chippewa sprang forth. Then, as the Sioux moved even further north, the allies of the Chippewa, the Cree, waged battles with the newcomers. Fighting was quite primitive by modern standards. Flint knives, stone axes, bows and arrows were the warrior's tools. At first the Sioux got the best of their foes as they traveled northward against both opponents. It was during this time that the name "Sioux" was first placed upon the invading Lakota/Dakota, allies or friends, which they preferred to call themselves.

Nadowessi

The adventurous Captain Jonathan Carver, the American explorer and writer we met earlier, was instrumental in the naming of the Dakota/Lakota as 'Sioux'. The Sioux, possibly the Santee group, had reached into Wisconsin by as early as the 17th century. Wisconsin and Minnesota were considered the wild, western territories in those times; Ouisconsin and Minne-ahtah. Minne-ahtah means much water. Ouisconsin is not a Dakota/Lakota word. Neighboring tribes primarily to the north - Objibway, Chippewa and Cree - referred to the Dakota/Lakota as Nadowessi, which meant lesser enemies as compared to the bigger enemies to the east; the Iroquois, the powerful confederacy who pushed them westward. Faced with an endless stream of European immigrants, the Iroquois moved west and northwest up the Hudson valley and consequently drove the Chippewa (Ojibwas) out of their ancestral lands surrounding the St. Lawrence Seaway. The newcomers, the Sioux, moving up the Mississippi south and west of the three northern tribes initially proved themselves as deadly and aggressive enemies on the move. The French, as was their custom, came along and added x or ioux (oooh) to the Chippewa/Cree term and we have Nadowessioux (Nah doe wes suks). That term was soon shortened to the word Sioux, a combination of French and Chippewa.

Although the term "Sioux" is a practical name which combines the Lakota/Dakota designation, some college educated Indians and many academics (Indian and non-Indian) in particular disapprove of the term "Sioux". However, a sign on a tribal building wall, back on my home reservation, simply reads "Oglala Sioux Tribal Council." The Tribal Council stationery also reads "Oglala Sioux Tribal Council." On the adjoining reservation less than a hundred miles east, their signs reveal "Rosebud Sioux Tribal Council." If it bothers an academic that we are "incorrect", they should first complain to the tribal councils instead of employing academic circles to change our name, which we have grown quite used to.

Knowledgeable Teachers

Any name can be a source of pride and respect when we have dignity and a proven track record of fighting successfully in many battles. I suppose I can qualify as an academic if degrees are a prime qualification, with which I disagree with of course. I have a Doctorate of Jurisprudence but it was my experience and initial fortitude, and common sense actually, to be with the real old-time holy men and other great teachers, like Ben Black Elk and Hilda Neihardt (daughter of John Neihardt, author of *Black Elk Speaks*). This is where I received a considerable amount of my knowledge, along with Doctor John Bryde's influence, where it pertains to tribal history. Dr. Bryde speaks fluent Lakota. He spent many years among the Oglalas as a Jesuit missionary. Add to this mix another mentor, Dr. James Howard. I flew both men throughout the state of South Dakota as a commercial pilot, while working my way through three years of law school. Both were teachers at the University. Dr. Howard also had two adopted Indian children whom he raised. Long hours in the cockpit sitting close to two knowledgeable scholars revealed much of my tribe's history as the Dakota landscape passed beneath us. Participation in the ceremonies, especially at the time when they were being revived by the old-time medicine people, was a Godsend. I must also credit fate or the Forces for giving me such a remarkable opportunity to acquire such valuable information. A truly traditional Indian would credit the Spirit Forces, who to us still abound upon the land. They placed me in those times, in the moment, and the place, according to my belief system, which was more than coincidental; just my opinion.

Spirit Forces

Christianity seems to shudder and become alarmed when we use the term, Spirit or Spirit Forces. We were always warned by the missionaries that we should never attempt to establish any contact with any spiritual concepts other than what they would recommend. In other words, we would have to follow the white man's instructions with strict obedience. If we didn't we were warned that a fiery hell would await us. What I observed take place in Native ceremonies was a myriad of positive results, however, which did nothing else than to better the innocent well- being of those who sought contact with 'our' Spirit Forces. I have to say 'our' because the Spirit Forces we Indigenous establish contact with are spoken of by the white man in a very derogatory way. These beneficial forces obviously exist because of the Creator's blessing or endowment, and it is no wonder that white men cannot contact them nor will the Spirit Forces work with them. Such a loss his blind ego and false sense of superiority have caused. He has missed out. Such a loss, especially for the perilous times that now lie before all of us. He will continue to waste precious decades of needed change before he is finally brought to his knees by Mother Earth.

Mrs. South Dakota

Bear in mind, this was a time when a majority of Indians, even Siouxs, were brainwashed in the boarding schools to deny their heritage when it came down to the spiritual or religious side. I recall, as a law student about to speak at an event at South Dakota State College. My theme was "Go back to your culture." Russell Means was also a speaker. The then-reigning Mrs. South Dakota, an attractive Yankton Sioux wife of a successful Flandreau basketball coach, both of Yankton Sioux extraction, publicly stated to the news media she would turn down her speaking request because of the presence of myself, and of course, Russ Means. We were "persona non grata" because we advocated our spirituality as worthy of going back to.

Very few Indians back then rallied to support us: we who were bound and determined to bring back the old way, at least for ourselves. Initially, I was off in the military and not at the forefront, but I did join them when they were offered little support and were being shunned by the leading Indian academics of the time. The elite Indian academics sat too comfortably upon their university chairs to risk championing the old medicine men who knew far more about tribal culture than they ever would. An academic just could not bring himself or herself to stand tall for the return of the Indian Way, back in those days. This would "rock the university boat" and Mr. Indian Academic was not going to take that risk. This is the major reason why I have little respect for those individuals. The old traditionalists led then, mainly the holy men, well before others, and – as I note – in the absence of the Indian academics. That is why so few of them (the Academics) can honestly quote the old time medicine people as their close advisors. Look at their books! I look at these academic authors who now brazenly attempt to write about our spirituality and especially our Sun Dance; none of them have ever been in the demanding and grueling but deeply moving event! Only one Academic do I know, a full-fledged academic, if degrees are the requisite, and that is Dr. Chuck Ross. He is a Mdewakanton Sioux, who has been in more sun dances than I have and now conducts the ceremony in the Black Hills. Chuck is also an author. I will take experience any day over Academia when writing of a people's deepest beliefs and their resultant culture. Enough said! Once again, I proudly quote those historical newspaper headlines, "Sioux Wipe Out Custer!" We will not be undermined by the labels of Dominant Society, or anyone else who wants to label us without our express permission.

'Native American'

While we are on the subject of names; what about the term Indian or Native American, which is constantly brought before us? Dr. Beatrice Medicine, a Sihasapa Teton Sioux and a noted anthropologist has this information to pass on to us:

"The term *Native Americans*, the most recent gloss for North American aborigines, is now in disfavor with many tribal groups and individuals. The National Congress of American Indians, a powerful self-interest group, has passed a resolution (1978) opposing its use at their last convention. Throughout the historic Indian-white interface, such names as 'North American Indians,' 'American Indians,' 'Amerindian,' 'Indian American' and 'First Americans' have been in vogue at various times. In this essay I use Native American and American Indian interchangeably. As for the focus of the essay, the Lakota who are often labeled 'Sioux,' 'Teton Sioux,' 'Western Lakota,' and 'Dakota' in the anthropological literature, I use the term 'Lakota,' for I am referring to the Western Sioux who speak the Lakota dialect of the Siouan language. I also use designations such as 'Rosebud Sioux' to indicate the reservation as a social system to which one assigns oneself. This is accepted procedure by most Lakota Sioux." [2]

Dr. Bea, is my "Indian Aunt," another of my teachers and always a strong supporter. Pilamiya Oh Tun win, Pilamiya. (Thank you oh Auntie.) She recently entered the Spirit World where she can now proudly look back at her courage and determination for standing firm for the return of the Way.

Native women are not expected to Sun Dance; therefore my Aunt Bea was never required to pledge. The Indian woman 'gives her pain so that the people may live' when she gives birth to off-spring. Childbirth in the old days was often fatal. She already suffers her pain for the tribe and therefore would never be expected to pledge as a male sun dancer would. Such is the deep respect and recognition that we have for the woman. It is much different than what we know of the white man's two major religions- Islam and Christianity… is it not?

In the summer time on various Sioux reservations, there will usually be some old-timers sitting around discussing yesterday. If you get the chance, ask them what tribe they are from. They will reply that they are Sioux. If you ask them what particular band they are from, one will point to himself and say, "I am an Oglala Sioux." He may point to another and state, "He is a Sichangu Sioux from over there on the Rosebud." Then, ask them if they are Lakotas or Dakotas. They will respond that they are Lakotas. Perhaps one will remark, "We are Lakotas, the Dakotas are far to the east, but, we are all Sioux."

Sioux Held Their Culture – Others Did Not

Indeed, the Dakota were considered enemies by those who came across their path, and offered resistance to the many groups on their westward journey out of the East. I have often made the statement that the Sioux are the last of the large tribes to be reined in from their natural, Creator-given freedom; and hence, this is the major reason why they have kept so much of their culture compared to the other tribes who have spent much longer with the dominating white man and his "melt-all, melting pot" culture and concepts. The Sioux have only been "in" for just a bit more than a mere hundred years. This was a blessing for us and is the major reason why we still speak and retain our language, and why we have kept our religion intact. It is simple math; less time with the dominant culture and you retain more of your own culture. The majority of America's once prolific tribes have lost their language and know nothing of their religion. It is not their fault, however. Time, along with geography, has had a lot to do with their loss. A tribe spending two hundred years with Dominant Society can easily lose their roots. Four hundred years with the white man's destructive methods for rooting out native culture and it is a miracle that some cultural roots manage to survive. The Navajo and Pueblo suffered under the brutal Spanish occupation and, their equally destructive, Spanish Catholic Church, which made slaves of the people, digging for silver and gold in the many mines dotting the southwest. This slave wrought gold and silver now gilds the altars of the Spanish churches in Europe. Geography protected the tribes to some degree (especially the vast spaces of the West); yet, the Pueblo, Zuni and Navajo religious concepts differ considerably from the Northern tribes. In my own opinion, the Spanish Catholic Church influenced their religion over the 400 long years they suffered under brutal rule, until Congress finally passed the freedom of religion act in 1978. To this day, missionary churches still hold the most prominent sites within the Pueblos.

Recently Pope Ratzinger (Pope Benedict VI) made a very foolish and insulting statement on his trip in South America. He declared that the 'Church' brought 'Salvation' to we Indians in the Americas. The horrible slavery conditions placed on the South American and Central American Indians by the Spanish Catholic 'Saviors' to mine silver and gold was never mentioned by the Pontiff. I do not believe one bit that I are my fellow Sioux have to join his beliefs to enter on into the Spirit World beyond.

Physical Comparisons

I have observed that the Sioux and Iroquoians are not similar in looks compared to most of the other tribes, especially those further west. Both tribes are a bit lighter complexioned than most western tribes. The once-bordering Cherokees may be grouped in with the Sioux, since they are certainly the lightest complexioned, Caucasian-featured people of any North American tribe I have ever seen. The Mandans (whose main reservation is far north along the Missouri in North Dakota) are almost as light as many Cherokees, but they have more Indian features than the Cherokee's I have viewed. I am speaking about Mandan individuals whose blood is over half Mandan. As with most Plains Indians, they are fairly to totally without hair on the chest, back and extremities. The Mandans are tall and heavy-boned people like the Northern Europeans, but have a "commonality" in their facial appearance; whereas just about every Cherokee I have met (who was not enrolled from the Oklahoma Cherokee reservation based in Tahlequah, Oklahoma) seemed to have differing, unrelated, Caucasian dominant features.

The Hunkpapa Sioux in areas of central North and South Dakota are large people in general. The Hunkpapa are slightly darker than the Mandans, but similar in appearance and relatively hairless, with little or no facial hair. Most Siouan people have a heavy head of hair where it counts — on top of the head — and do not go bald, even in senior age. Their hair may thin, but I have yet to see a full-blooded Sioux that went bald, unless some sickness caused it. The hair also stays black much longer, it seems.

Mississippi Headwaters and Further West

Before confronting the Chippewa in the 17th century, the Sioux had previously swept through the Shawnees, the related tribes west of the Carolinas and those settled in the lower Ohio River Valley. They quickly gathered a reputation for being fierce fighters. When they came into the Minne-ahtah (Land of much water) region, the Sioux were made up of three groups or divisions: the Tetons, the Yanktons (including the Yanktonai), and the Santees, who were made up of four tribes or bands. The Santees encompassed the Mdewakanton, Wahpeton, Wahpekute and the Sisseton. All Santees spoke the "D" dialect of the tribe's language and referred to themselves as Dakota. The Santee tribes may have been the earliest portion of the great Sioux migration, for they ranged far into Ouisconsin (Wisconsin). A "D" dialect Dakota would say wanbedee for the word; eagle. An "L" dialect Lakota would say; wanblee (wanbli).

Westward

As mentioned earlier, the main body of Sioux explored the headwaters of the Mississippi. Despite some earlier battles, the Yanktonai tribe made peace with the Crees who lived to the north of the Sioux while the Cree allies, the Chippewa, were further east.

Before 1660 the Sioux were winning most of the battles; in 1658 the Sioux won a bloody fight according to Radisson, an early French explorer. In 1670, however, the Crees and their Algonquin-speaking allies traded in their furs for French guns from the Hudson Bay Company. They angrily retaliated against the Sioux for the earlier battles. In 1674 the Crees attacked and killed Sioux envoys at Sault Ste. Marie. The flash of gunpowder and smoke from many yards away — with it's accompanying loud 'bang'- would soon send shivers through even the most stalwart of the Sioux warriors, who were still inexperienced with gun fire. The loud sound accompanying each firing, and resultant death or wound, was a terrible experience to behold. Guns were such superior weapons that the Sioux had little choice but to 'up and move'. For the Chippewa, with their Cree allies and French guns, the tide changed. The Dakota/Nadowessioux advance into what is now Northern Minnesota became a retreat down from the headwaters of the Mississippi to the Minnesota River valley and the area of present day Minneapolis. A Sioux named body of water, Lake Minnetonka (Great Water or Big Water) lies just west of Minneapolis. In a matter of 10 years, an eyewink in historical terms, most of the Chippewa's southern enemies had vacated out of northern Minnesota.

The migrating people realized that the land of Minne-ahtah was also a cold, inhospitable place to live. Far fewer artifacts are found within this region, a fact that suggests that most tribes avoided the area to some extent. Deep snows and cold winters can indeed be fatal. Further southeast, in the Kentucky area for example, numerous artifacts — stone axes, arrowheads and spear points — are still found to this day by collectors. This simple fact illustrates that the more conducive the land was for productive agriculture, the more population the land attracted and sustained. Productive agriculture typically does not grow as abundantly where the winters are long and the summers are short. Being comfortable was another main reason tribes would be drawn to an area. Extreme cold, dangerous deep winter snows and a shorter agricultural season were generally avoided; unless, a smaller tribe was being crowded by potential enemies and did not have a choice. Often these tribe's settlements would be only temporary, until better locales were scouted or they joined together with another smaller tribe for mutual survival and movement onward.

The Sioux would send out scouts and were always looking for what was beyond the next bluff or river. The majority of the Dakota/Lakota were soon heading westward. The Yanktons and Yanktonai were the first to move. They drifted southward and came to the great elbow bend of the Minnesota River in the Swan Lake district. The Yanktons crossed the Minnesota River, separating from their tribal cousins, the Yanktonai, and settling in an area between what is now Blue Earth, Minnesota and the famous Pipestone Quarries near the Western edge of Minnesota. The Yanktonais went up the Minnesota River. Later the Oglalas and Brules (Sichangu), part of the seven-member Teton Lakota Sioux, would cross the same area and occupy the Blue Earth River prairies westward, placing them west of the Yanktons. They would parallel the Yanktons and push on further west, gradually leaving the Yanktons behind them.

The Tetons spoke with an 'L' dialect and hence were referred to as Lakota versus their 'D' dialect cousins, the Dakota. First, the lead tribes - the Oglala and their close associates the Sichangu who would later be called Brules, would have to get past the powerful Arikara. The Arikara were settled comfortably in bastion-like earthen-structured barricades: Indian forts along the Missouri. It was a perplexing situation for the Siouxs. Forty thousand Arikara, split into two groups, northern or upstream and southern or downstream, including four thousand warriors and some mounted, were a bit much for the Oglalas who could not muster more than five hundred warriors, all of whom were on foot. A particular grouping of Teton bands, the Saones, the other five members of the Tetons, would go up the Minnesota River, taking them further north. This group included the Hunkpapas, whose chief would eventually be Sitting Bull. They too, were blocked by the northern Arikara at the Missouri river. It would be a half century (around 1825) before the Saones would reunite again with their Teton relatives to the south, the Oglala and Sichangu, to camp once again together during the annual Lakota Sioux Nation Sun Dance.

Arikara

The southern, or downstream, Arikara along the Missouri, were a formidable obstacle to further expansion. The whole Sioux nation could not muster as many warriors. The Arikaras had log and earthen villages, large villages up and down the Missouri strongly fortified with ditches, earthen walls and cedar log stockades. Some of these forts were tremendous in their size. One great fortress of the upstream Arikara, about seven miles south of Pierre was built on a high plateau. The Arikaras lived mostly by corn planting and raising other vegetables and had hundreds of acres under cultivation growing a variety of crops. Since they had horses, they would also supplement their diet with buffalo hunts. The Sioux who had spent some years near the James River were about to face some troubled times. In the beginning the Sioux were on fairly good terms with the Arikara and would visit with them in their villages. To the rear of the Tetons were the Yanktons. Feeling hemmed in, they feared crossing the Missouri however, for there were too many mounted Arikara warriors carrying Spanish saber blades tipping their long buffalo spears. On the open plains they could easily ride down and kill any bands that were on foot, as the Sioux were. Their westward-drifting movement was essentially stopped for at least 25 years near what is presently Chamberlain, South Dakota. The Tetons balanced this threat by periodically getting up large war parties of several hundred men and driving the Arikaras into their fortified villages, so well-fortified that the attackers could not storm them. After taking a few scalps and maybe a few horses, the Tetons would plunder their corn patches and go back home. Then disaster struck the Arikaras that changed everything. Between 1772 and 1780, three great epidemics of small pox hit the downstream Arikara. Their population was reduced from 20,000 to 4,000. The strong fortified villages on the east bank of the Missouri could no longer hold out and were destroyed. As a result, the surviving southern Arikara withdrew to the west bank and consolidated all of their people in four to five villages just below the mouth of the Cheyenne River.

Horses

The Wahshichu's diseases often wiped out entire villages. Horses are immune to most human disease however, and their availability would not be overlooked by a nearby tribe, such as the Sioux who at that time kept their distance from the disease-bearing steamboats that navigated the Missouri. Not only was the Arikara barrier removed, but a new vehicle would become considerably more available, one that could move entire villages swiftly; the horse would change Sioux lifestyle forever.

The horse was the catalyst that released the tremendous energies of the Sioux. In a few hours now they could travel distances that took them days to travel when they were afoot. For one thing, this meant game and buffalo could be spotted, run down and killed, all within a few hours. Before, when they were afoot, it would take days to organize such a hunt and to bring it off and this only with all the people in the band in on the hunt. Now, a few hunters on horses could do in a few hours that which it took all the people many days to do. As a result of this increase of food, the people grew stronger and more vigorous. Babies that would have lost their lives by the constant travel and shortage of food were now being saved, and the people increased in number. Daring leaders were not lacking to get up exploratory parties and war parties to increase the range of their territories.

Westward Expansion

The way was now open for the southern Tetons, at least, to push westward. To the north, the northern Tetons would be held in place by the northern Arikaras. These Tetons would not cross over until 1825. The Oglalas were the first of the Sioux to cross the Missouri, the first to reach the Black Hills and the first to turn south to reach the Platte River in Nebraska. It was the year 1775. Far to the east a new nation was about to declare its independence. The American colonists were desiring freedom and control of their own destiny. The Declaration of Independence would bring a new era of freedoms unknown in Europe.

After almost three quarters of a century, the glorious life on horseback took the Oglalas and their constant companions the Sichangu/Brule as far west as the Rocky Mountain foothills and northward to the Big Horns. The next 100 years saw an incredible expansion in territory and an explosion in population that would make the Sioux the most powerful tribe on the Great Plains. The strength for this expansion came not only from physical strength and endurance, but also from an inner spiritual strength that gave them supreme confidence and pride in themselves and a conviction that they couldn't lose. It would seem that this inner spiritual strength came from their intense awareness of their union with the Great Spirit, with themselves and with this Creator's Nature. There was a force for the people that made them recognize no odds. This same force gave them the strength to adapt to anything in changing their way of making a living because they were about to change from a food-gathering and planting people to a people constantly on the move, hunting the buffalo for a living. Adaptability was a key word for the success of the Sioux, especially the Oglalas and their almost constant partners, the Sichangu or Brules.

White Settlers

Before the mid-point of the next century, they began to resent the intrusion of the early white settlers, however. Long accustomed to thinking that the supply of buffalo from Mother Earth was inexhaustible, it came as a shock to them, when checking with other bands, to find that there were actually fewer buffalo around, and that bands had to travel farther and farther to find them. Since the earlier Indians had been living on the buffalo for centuries and had apparently never made a dent in the vast herds, the only cause of the decrease was the large number of non-Indians coming through their land and settling near it.

From a small band of foot-traveling rovers that straggled to the Missouri between 1750 and 1775, carrying their belongings mostly on their backs and begging food and horses from the Arikara, in just a few years, they were to be swarming over the plains from the Missouri to the Rocky Mountains and from the northern border of Kansas to the Canadian border. The very name Sioux, not as much the terms Lakota or Dakota, but Sioux, would strike terror in the hearts of other Indians and non-Indians alike. Obviously, the advancing nation retained their identification as Lakota or Dakota but as the Tetons went westward and became more successful, the other tribes, especially those who were in front of them and had to fight or flee from the advancing Oglalas, they were referred to by opposing tribes as Sioux. The name obviously stuck and in time, even the Tetons got used to it.

The last of the Sioux tribes to move would be the Santees, some of them settling down in Eastern Minnesota and the Twin Cities area (the Mdewakanton), where they remain to this day. The Santees were the last to leave the Wisconsin woodlands, and were possibly who Captain Carver wrote of when he projected the new name, Nadowessioux (or Sioux) upon the wandering People of the Seven Campfires. Of the Santees, the Sissetons would move the farthest west, settling in northeast South Dakota.

Tetons

The Tetons were one of the original Seven Council Fires of the Sioux. They increased significantly in population when they discovered the horse and the vast buffalo herds in the Dakotas. They evolved into the seven sub-tribes, or seven bands, of the Teton Lakota speaking Sioux. Chief Sitting Bull, Chief Gall, Chief Red Cloud, Chief Spotted Tail and Chief Crazy Horse would soon become their leaders; all would speak the L dialect. Historically, three of these tribes stand out and are listed first below. If we refer to the Sioux as a Nation, then we can confer tribal status on the seven tribes. If one refers to the Sioux as a Tribe we would name each of the seven as bands. They are:

1. The Oglala (Red Cloud, Black Elk, Crazy Horse).
2. The Sichangu (Spotted Tail).
3. The Hunkpapa (Sitting Bull and Gall).
4. Minicoujou. (High Backbone)
5. Sihasapa (Blackfeet).
6. Oohenumpa (Two Kettles).
7. Itazipco (No Bows).

The last five representatives of the Tetons, including the Hunkpapa, would be referred to as the Saones. The Tetons would soon be the most numerous of the Sioux, more numerous than the other two divisions (Santee and Yanktons) put together.

Four Great Sioux Leaders

Chief Red Cloud
(Makhpia Lutah)
Photograph by David F. Barry.

Crazy Horse
A sketch by Amos Bad Heart Bull

Sitting Bull
Denver Public Library, Western
History Collection
Photograph by D.F. Barry #B-69.

Black Elk
Denver Public Library,
Western History Collection
Photograph by Joseph G.
Masters #X-33351.

Leaders

Four great leaders would come to the fore among the Sioux after the entry of the nineteenth century:

Red Cloud (Makpiyah Luta)
Crazy Horse (Tahshuunka Witko)
Sitting Bull (Tatanka Iyotanka)
Black Elk (Hehaka Sapa)

All were spiritual men. Why should one study Sioux leadership in order to seek the Code? Does the White Man not tell of his leaders back in biblical times? The lives of the Sioux leaders may be found to be just as interesting, and for many readers, more so.

By studying the four leaders, we will immerse ourselves deeper into the 'natural' living and nature blended mind and hence come closer to honing our own abilities. These men demonstrate honor, bravery, self-sacrifice, decision making and always kept a deep spirituality. Example is a powerful teacher. In these perilous environmental times, our country is in dire need of such leaders.

Life is not a pharmaceutical supermarket wherein one can purchase a quick-fix to serenity and happiness. At least not from what I have observed. Nature does not condone or allow the encapsulated, 'ready made' approach to life's journey. Isn't it obvious that we are here to 'prove ourselves' over the long haul for hopefully a higher purpose in a Beyond? This holding is not my exclusive thought, by any means. It seems to be a universally accepted viewpoint. The danger laden attempts through drugs or alcohol and/or over materialism, greed and selfishness demonstrate the futility of human's foolish short-cuts to real happiness, character building, exemplary track record and true confidence. We also have a planet to save!

Warrior Chiefs

Three of the above were warrior chiefs. Their bravery upon the field of battle was unquestioned.

These men sun danced, vision quested, sweat lodged and smoked the sacred pipe to beseech to their Creator and Creator's Six Powers. Chief Red Cloud was known to pull back his troops in the midst of a military engagement and ride away to participate in the annual sun dance. Obviously his commitment to God was more important than fighting with other men. No American or European military leader would ever think of doing such an act. Their culture would not condone it.

Sun Dance

The primary ceremony for the Sioux was the annual Sun Dance which is mentioned by most all past writers in regard to Chief Red Cloud, Chief Crazy Horse and Chief Sitting Bull. I do not believe any of these writers had the depth to explore why this was such an important event to stop fighting their campaigns or at least placing their combat on hold. Something this important would certainly seem to bear some scrutiny, some curiosity, some probing; would not one think? Did not any of these leaders go into the Sun Dance before their Creator concept and ask Wakan Tanka to spare them one more time, one more battle, feed them one more winter, bring the Wahshichu to the treaty table? Would not these issues be heavy on their minds? I have participated as a Sun Dance Pledger in six Sun Dances. Many sun dancers have taken part in many more sun dances than I, but as a writer, I believe I have taken part in at least six more sun dances than most all the rest of the related subject writers of Native extraction, with the exception of my fellow authors, Manny Two Feathers and Dr. Chuck Ross.

Chief Red Cloud was born in 1821 (1821- 1909). He bore the brunt of the major fighting with the Army during the turbulent 1860s. He was the Commander in Chief for five years of constant battle from 1862 to 1867. His superb fighting tactics were dependent upon well conditioned, well trained mounts which repeatedly defeated the U. S. Cavalry culminating in his winning the famous Treaty of 1868. The Army had to submit to the burning down of their three forts on the Bozeman Trail because of Red Cloud's leadership. Sioux horse herds grew significantly under Red Cloud as did their weaponry and ammunition supply which was mostly captured from the U.S. Cavalry. This solid fact, historians are loath to admit. How else could the Sioux mount so many warriors and effectively arm them?

Twenty years after Red Cloud's birth, Crazy Horse, also an Oglala would be born. Crazy Horse was renowned for isolating himself in Creator's Nature for days and nights. I would assume that Crazy Horse was Vision Questing to Creator. He shunned publicity or the public limelight despite his fame and military prowess. During the 60's era fighting with the Army, Crazy Horse would be a young warrior under Red Cloud's command. He counted over eighty coups during the earlier era of tribal combat. His rise to acclamation as one of the greatest of warriors was culminated with his victories in his last three battles with the Army during the spring and summer of 1876.

Sitting Bull of the Teton Saones, (born 1831); the Hunkpapa tribe of the seven tribe Tetons would be far to the north of the Oglalas and

Sichangus during the heavy fighting in the 1860s. He would stay out of the 60's era conflicts in the southern Dakota Territory and North Platte/Powder River battles but he would be fighting his own with the Army, first General Sibley and then General Sully further north. It would be after the signing of the Treaty of 1868 and the breaking of that treaty's agreements that the northern Tetons would rise up with the Oglalas and Sichangus.

Sitting Bull's spirituality is highly exemplary; he prayed almost daily and had powerful prophetic dreams. About a week before the famous Little Big Horn battle, at the huge encampment where the attack would soon take place, Sitting Bull had a powerful dream of soldiers falling into the camp upside down. This vision predicted that enemy soldiers would come and be defeated as the dream symbolized by having them fall upside down.

The Battle of the Little Big Horn was fought. Sitting Bull's powerful dream, the prediction, was quite accurate.

Black Elk (born 1863) was not a military leader but was a powerful visionary. His revealing vision which is applicable to our present day environmental dilemma we have already studied. It took place close to the Little Big Horn River, where Sitting Bull would later receive his vision just prior to the famous Custer Battle. Black Elk out lived all of the leaders mentioned above. He remained basically unknown throughout his life time, except among his own people where he was regarded as a powerful healer. His healing abilities took place while the Sioux were in containment on the reservations after the turn of the century. Since he was a holy man and a leader in is own right, we will center on this person who has brought the power of Creator's Nature up close for millions of readers through the miraculous contact made by Nebraska's poet laureate John Neihardt (*Black Elk Speaks*) and a later writer, Joseph Epes Brown (*The Sacred Pipe*).

4

Chief Red Cloud

They made us many promises, more than I can remember. But they kept but one –They promised to take our land… and they took it.

Red Cloud – Oglala, Teton Lakota

(Chief) Flying Hawk (Oglala) said that Red Cloud was one of their wisest men and knew what was best for his people; he had been their Chief for a long time; he tried to keep peace with the whites but it was 'no use' - they would not stay out of the Indians' country, but came and took their gold and killed off all their game. This started the trouble, and the long bloody war with the soldiers came.[1]

The first of the Four Leaders is Chief Red Cloud (Mahkpiyah Luta) who was born in 1821. Of the war chiefs, he lived the longest. He died in 1909. As mentioned earlier, he was Commander-in-Chief of the Sioux forces for five yrs of fighting successfully against the U. S. Army. Crazy Horse held this position for four months in 1876, March through June.

Lula Red Cloud, Chief Red Cloud's great, great-grand daughter, was told by her Grandfather that Chief Red Cloud was well over six feet, no doubt six foot two or three. There were many photographs of Red Cloud but none were taken when he was in his younger days as a fearless and ferocious warrior. He appears solidly built.

European immigrants were mostly five feet five or six. Western writers are hard pressed to admit this fact. The much heavier protein diet of the Sioux, especially abundant wild game, down through the centuries had much to do with this fact. Europeans had little meat. The nobility owned the forests and enforced severe penalties upon trespassing hunters seeking to supplement meager diets which also lacked such staples as; corn, potatoes, beans, tomatoes and a host of other foods which finally ended the constant famines that plagued Europe. In hand to hand combat and especially the way the Sioux fought on the open plains, and most always commencing from a mounted attack, being taller, with but just a few inches reach on your opponent who also had to devote one hand to holding on to his horse, was a tremendous advantage. Siouxs were generally taller, often a half a foot or so, than the Europeans they fought in the 1800s. Chief Crazy Horse, however, was somewhat smaller than Chief Red Cloud yet larger than the average U. S. soldiers he faced repeatedly. Admittedly, Southwestern Indians are smaller, but the Eastern Indians were considerably larger than the early emigrants from Europe. Diet is the key reason. Modern day Americans are generally much taller than their grandparents and more so compared to their great-grandparents.

First War Party

Red Cloud was an outstanding warrior from the beginning of his warrior's life which began in 1838 on his first war party at the age of 16. On his first trip out, he took his first scalp, the first of many to come (some say eighty). After his first war party, his father gave his own name - Red Cloud, to his son.

To the average reader, the taking of an opponent's scalp in battle must seem bloodcurdling, but it was a common custom among most northern tribes. Some authors claim this method was introduced by the French; others blame the English (probably French authors). Regardless, there existed far more 'bloodcurdling' methods of human cruelty in Europe during the centuries long Great Inquisitions. They were so grisly that I will not go into detail and directed mostly against defenseless women.

Leading a War Party

Against the Pawnees, Red Cloud led his first war party and nearly lost his life to a Pawnee arrow below his ribs. One of the older men broke the arrow, pulled it out, and stopped the flow of blood before Red Cloud bled to death. He spent a bad night, but he was able to eat a little the next morning. His men made a travois and carried him behind a horse. For two months, he was very sick, swinging between life and death but, after that, he gradually began to regain his full strength and vigor.

After his recovery, Red Cloud took to the warpath more vigorously than ever. Some years later, Captain Cook wrote that the old Oglalas who had fought by Red Cloud's side as young men proudly recounted his exploits to anyone who would listen. His size no doubt accounts for his ability to survive over 80 coups and taking of enemy scalps. He was deemed ruthless, but it was a ruthless time. No longer would the counting of coup be practiced once the Army was encountered, at least not in the heat of battle, for attempting to touch a saber-swinging cavalry man or one carrying a pistol, or both, would result in too many losses which a besieged people could not afford.

In the years shortly preceding and following 1850, trouble was brewing in the area above the North Platte. Restlessness and hostility were growing not only among the Sioux, but also among the other tribes, stemming from the decrease of buffalo, the increase of immigrants, death-causing diseases caught from the immigrant non-Indians, and the evil caused in their midst by the non-Indians' liquor.

In 1841, the Sioux curiously watched settlers pass through on their way to California. At that time, there were only around 1 or 2 trains per year traveling through, hardly enough to cause more than a passing glance from the Sioux. However, nine years later, in 1850, there were 50,000 traveling through, and all of them ate the buffalo and other game as they passed. This was too much, and something had to be done. Before they could do anything, however, this was their problem: they had no leadership to unite them. Each band and sub-band went its separate way, and there was no one strong enough to gather warriors and sub-bands into a large and strong force under central leadership. They felt they had to do something and to do it on a large scale, in order to be effective. How could they do it without a strong leader?

Chief Smoke and Bull Bear of the Oglalas

It was during a period of liquor availability from the traders that the trouble between Chief Smoke and Chief Bull Bear came to a head. Chief Smoke was a genial, rather plump and good-natured leader of a band of Oglalas who, because of the chief's name, were called the Smoke people. Chief Smoke was not out to out-rival Bull Bear but, since Bull Bear could not stand any other rival, he regarded Smoke as a danger to his position and was always jealous of him. When the traders suggested to Smoke that he put himself up as the chief of all the Oglalas, Smoke had not the slightest intention of doing so, the very suggestion so enraged Bull Bear, however, that he roared into Smoke's camp and challenged him to come out to fight.

When old Smoke would not come out, Bull Bear stabbed Smoke's favorite horse and stomped back to his camp in a high rage. Although Smoke did nothing about this, the young warriors who followed Smoke, including an up and coming young warrior named Red Cloud, were alerted to the danger threatening their leader.

Fortified by cheap liquor from the traders, Bull Bear gathered some warriors together and again came back into the Bad Face camp. (Bad Faces was another name for the Smoke people.) The invading force shot a Bad Face, and then prepared to wipe out the entire village. Smoke's warriors charged at the Bull Bear group. Young Red Cloud dashed in to kill Bull Bear, shooting him in the head. Since it was Bull Bear who had attacked the Smoke group, Red Cloud's killing him was simply in self-defense. If Bull Bear had not been drinking, the whole thing would probably never have happened.

The followers of Smoke became angry at the followers of Bull Bear and they separated and drifted apart. An imposing bully, Bull Bear had held a number of the bands together and had imposed a unity of action upon them. After his death, the bands wandered around without any strong leadership. At this time, Red Cloud was still too young to take over the leadership, but his time would come.

Red Cloud did not emerge as the uniting leader against the non-Indians until the 1860's. From the 1840's to the 1860's, while Red Cloud's star was rising, several important events happened that caused a stiffening resistance among the Indians which finally found their focus on Red Cloud as the one best qualified to represent all their grievances and anger.

In 1841, as pointed out earlier, the Sioux saw only about one or two wagon trains a year going west through their hunting grounds. This trickle had built up to over 50,000 a year by mid-century. During the middle years of this buildup in traffic, the government felt the restlessness of the tribes and, in 1845, felt that something should be done to pacify them. The first plan was to talk to them nicely, offer them lots of presents, and to ask them to be peaceful.

Col. Kearney - 1845

Thus it was that in 1845, Colonel Stephen Kearney rolled into the American Fur Company's post at Laramie with seventeen wagonloads of presents and provisions, and accompanied by five companies of well-equipped and well-mounted cavalry. Here he met with over a thousand Sioux. He paraded his seventeen wagons full of presents in front of the Sioux, gathered them in close, and delivered the speech that he had come to give.

His main point was that the travels of the immigrants should not be disturbed, and, therefore, the Indians should peacefully allow them to pass through. The Sioux, paying more attention to the wagonloads of gifts than to the words of Kearney's speech and with a growing impatience for him to finish, quickly promised that they would let the travelers go through, suggesting in addition that he get to the business at hand, that is, to the dividing up of the gifts—blankets, cloth, knives, beads, and tobacco. Kearney, pleased with the willingness of the Sioux to cooperate, passed out the gifts, gave them a warm farewell, and rode off highly pleased with him that his mission had been such a great success. There would, he thought, be no more trouble on the immigrant trail.

Fort Laramie - 1849

In 1849, the fur trading post owned by the American Fur Company, and which was so pleasantly familiar to the Sioux, was bought by the Government and staffed with some soldiers. It was now called Fort Laramie. This immediately caused further hostility among the Sioux. Traders were one thing, but soldiers were something else. Soldiers, to their way of thinking, came into a country for one purpose, and that was to fight. When and where they didn't know, but it did mean that a fight was coming and they braced themselves in preparation for it.

Soldiers

The one type of non-Indian that the Indians always liked was the trader. Since he had to make his living from the Indians, he was always pleasant and friendly with them, giving them gifts from time to time and always inviting them to come in. Coming in to the trading post was always like a pleasant holiday for the Sioux - something like "going to town" occasionally for country people. They looked forward to seeing the new articles the traders would have, meeting old friends, receiving gifts and shopping around in what to them would be like a supermarket today. Guns, ammunition, knives, metal pots and kettles for the Indian woman were becoming necessities for the fur bearing warriors. To come in now and to find soldiers in the place of friendship and gifts was a severe shock to them.

Mormon Cow - 1854

An early incident that further stirred up the Sioux was the famous case of the Mormon cow. Just three years after the Fort Laramie Treaty, in 1854, during which time the new Fort was slowly filling up with soldiers, a party of Mormons on their way to Utah was camped near Fort Laramie. Also camped near the Fort was a group of Brule Sioux. Their Chief was Conquering Bear. A cow belonging to the Mormons strayed away while grazing and wandered into the Brule camp. The Brules, with joyful and grateful hearts, immediately fell upon the Mormon cow, and promptly ate it, rejoicing in their good fortune. When the Mormons found out what had happened to their cow, they went immediately into Fort Laramie, only a short distance away, and reported the incident to the commanding officer.

Lt. Grattan

The commanding officer sent a brash, hotheaded, young officer named Lt. Grattan with twenty-nine men out to the Brule camp. Lt. Grattan was only twenty-one years old and just out of West Point Military School. Conquering Bear tried to explain what had happened, but, since Lt. Grattan couldn't speak Sioux and Conquering Bear couldn't speak English, the conversation had to be carried on through an interpreter who was drunk at the time. The impatient young lieutenant withdrew his men from the camp and began to shoot at the chief and his people. During the first round of shots, Conquering Bear was killed. His people returned the fire and wiped out Lt. Grattan and his entire force of twenty-nine men.

Word of this immediately spread through both the Indian and non-Indian sides. The Indians were moved to attack the immigrants on the Platte Valley trail, and the non-Indians were moved to send out more soldiers. Just a year later Brigadier General William S. Harney left Ft. Leavenworth in Kansas with a force of 1200. In August of 1855, General Harney came upon Little Thunder and his band of Brules. Harney immediately engaged the Brules and, with his superior force, killed one hundred and thirty-six of them, put chains on the rest, and dragged them to Ft. Laramie. A month or so later, he set out for Ft. Pierre on the Missouri River, where he spent the winter. Without any government authorization, he gathered together the Sioux camping around Ft. Pierre and forced them to agree to permit immigrant travel along the Platte Valley trail and to allow a military road from Ft. Laramie to Ft. Pierre.

Gold

Although the Oglalas, after Harney, had scattered north and south of the Platte for awhile, something happened about six years later, in 1862, that caused them to begin uniting; not only among themselves, but with other tribes as well. Gold was discovered in Montana in 1862. This meant that a new trail would be made and this new trail, called the Bozeman Trail, went right through the heart of Sioux country. The discovery of gold in California in 1848 had caused the buildup of immigrant traffic on the trail along the Platte. Now that traffic was increased, and a lot of it was going up the new trail through Indian Territory. First, there was the trail through Indian country along the Platte in the 1830's. Secondly, there was the trail demanded by Harney from Fort Laramie to Fort Pierre in 1855 through Teton country. Now, a third trail through the extreme western part of Sioux territory, the Bozeman, made the Indians feel that they were truly surrounded and that they were headed for a last ditch fight for survival.

It was the time for strong leaders to emerge. Red Cloud of the Oglalas would be the first.

Red Cloud's Rise to Leadership

Red Cloud, at twenty-eight years, was little known outside of his own band when General Harney called all the western bands of Sioux together at Fort Laramie, Wyoming, for the purpose of securing an agreement and right of way through their territory. The Oglalas held aloof from this proposal.

Man-Afraid-of-His-Horse, then head chief of the Oglalas, took council with Red Cloud in all important matters, and the young warrior rapidly advanced in authority and influence.

In 1862, the surveyors of the Union Pacific were laying out the proposed road right through the heart of the southern buffalo country, the rendezvous of Oglalas, Brules, Arapahoes, Comanches, and Pawnees, who followed the buffalo as a means of livelihood. To be sure, most of these tribes were at war with one another, yet during the summer months they met often to proclaim a truce and hold joint councils and festivities, which were now largely turned into discussions of the common enemy.

Red Cloud's position was uncompromisingly against submission. He made some noted speeches regarding this issue.

"Friends," said Red Cloud, "it has been our misfortune to welcome the white man. We have been deceived. He brought with him some shining things that pleased our eyes; he brought weapons more effective than our own: above all, he brought the spirit water that makes one forget for a time old age, weakness, and sorrow.

"My countrymen, shall the glittering trinkets of this rich man, his deceitful drink that overcomes the mind, shall these things tempt us to give up our homes, our hunting grounds, and the honorable teaching of our old men? Shall we permit ourselves to be driven to and fro - to be herded like the cattle of the white man?"

His next speech that has been remembered was made in 1866, just before the attack on Fort Phil Kearny. The tension of feeling against the invaders had now reached its height. There was no dissenting voice in the council upon the Powder River, when it was decided to oppose to the uttermost the evident purpose of the government. Red Cloud was not altogether ignorant of the numerical strength and the resourcefulness of the white man, but he was determined to face the odds of those times rather than submit.

"Hear ye, Dakotas!" he exclaimed. "When the Great Father at Washington sent us his chief soldier (General Harney) to ask for a path through our hunting grounds, a way for his iron road to the mountains and the western sea, we were told that they wished merely to pass through our country, not to tarry among us, but to seek for gold in the far west. Our old chiefs thought to show their friendship and good will, when they allowed this dangerous snake in our midst. They promised to protect the wayfarers.

"Yet before the ashes of the council fire are cold, the Great Father is building his forts among us. You have heard the sound of the white soldier's ax upon the Little Piney. His presence here is an insult and a threat. It is an insult to the spirits of our ancestors. Are we then to give up their sacred graves to be plowed for corn? Dakotas, I am for war!"

News of the Minnesota Uprising (1862) and of its disastrous consequences for the Santee Dakota spread immediately throughout the West and caused further fear and tension among all the western tribes. Although the western Sioux refused to join Little Crow in hitting back at the settlers and the army in Minnesota country mainly on the grounds that it was too distant and not their fight, nevertheless, they kept a wary eye to the east for the possible appearance of more soldiers from that direction. It was while they were still looking over their shoulders toward the east that a blow was struck on the far western part of the plains that made not only the Sioux, but all the plains tribes tight with apprehension and more ready than ever to fight at the mere sight of soldiers. This was the Sand Creek Massacre at Sand Creek, Colorado Territory in August of 1864.

The opening of the Bozeman Trail through the heart of Sioux Territory was the final sting that the Sioux needed to engage them in a fight. Like a swarm of angry bees, they and their allies were aroused and they showed it by launching attacks on stage stations, immigrant trains, ranches, and farms all the way from the Little Blue Valley in eastern Nebraska to Denver. Travel in the Platte Valley came to a standstill and recent settlers fled places in eastern Nebraska. The outbreak was so widespread and so mobile that the army could not pin down any one band for effective retaliation. Even during these military strikes, however, the government continued to make constant pleas to individual bands to come in and to be peaceful.

It was during this time that Colonel H. M. Chivington, working out of Denver with the Colorado volunteers, was out looking for hostile Indians to punish for the current trouble along the Platte Valley. He came upon a band of peaceful Cheyennes who had decided to sit out the war raging upon the Plains under the protection of the Army commander at Fort Lyons who had invited them to camp outside the fort. Chivington's forces attacked them without asking any questions, or checking with the army at Fort Lyon. Chief White Antelope, making no effort to fight whatsoever, was one of the first to be killed in the village and over half of the people, men, women, and children, were killed. Their entire horse herd was captured and their village was destroyed. Those who managed to escape on foot made their way in the bitterly cold weather to a Cheyenne camp on the head of the Smoky Hill Fork. Black Kettle, who was one of the survivors, was rejected by his own people for leading them into a trap along with White Antelope. It is difficult to emphasize how much this stirred up all the plains tribes.

In the meantime, the commandant at Fort Lyon, as well as the agent for the Cheyennes, Samuel G. Colley, was in despair over this terrible action of Chivington. They were the ones who had persuaded the Cheyennes to come in. They complained bitterly about Chivington to Washington. As a result, Chivington was investigated and disciplined by army authorities in word only, but the damage had already been done.

The tribes had been pushed to the limit and could no longer be contained. All they needed was leadership, and by now, the leadership was at hand. It was time for Chief Red Cloud -- and Red Cloud was ready.

Right after the end of the Civil War, when the forces of war in the far West were gathering that would bring Red Cloud to the fore, groups of humanitarians, church groups, and idealists gained much influence in Congress to do something about bettering the lot of slaves just freed by the Civil War. This interest in minorities who were having a hard time quickly spread to the Indians, and now, with the war over, more attention could be given to Indian policy in the West. These people decided that the way to deal with the Indians was to treat them kindly.

Peace Commission

Thus it was that in May, 1865, when the military was straining every muscle in preparing for an all-out war against the tribes of the far West, that Senator J. R. Doolittle obtained an order suspending movements of troops against the southern plains tribes, and then had a peace commission appointed to make peace with the Indians. The soldiers in the far West, surrounded by and watching the tribes around the Powder River and the Upper Missouri who were angry as hornets and about to break out in a fight at any moment, could not figure this out, but they had to sit in silent frustration and wait for the peace commission to act.

The peace commission did act, but not in the area of the country that needed it. The trouble was in the far West, and, when the peace commission came out, they went up the Missouri, gathered in all the friendly chiefs, mostly Dakotas (not Teton Lakotas) who had been living along the Missouri, and coaxed them into signing a peace treaty. Six hundred miles to the west were the Tetons where the real trouble was, however. The friendly chiefs along the Missouri River, mostly Dakota Yanktons , were given gifts and they readily signed the peace treaty. In the meantime, 600 miles to the west, Sitting Bull was very influential with about 2,000 lodges of angry Sioux along the Little Missouri. Along the Powder River, there were an additional 2,000 unfriendly and disagreeing Sioux.

The thorn in the treaty was the insistence on the part of the government that it had the right to establish roads and to build forts in the Sioux country, including the touchy Bozeman Trail area.

It finally occurred to someone that a peace treaty involving the land of hostile Tetons should include the assent of these Tetons also. A copy of the treaty was hastily sent to Ft. Laramie. However, things were so touchy that no trader, or even a mixed-blood was willing to take the risk of going out and inviting in the hostile chiefs. Nothing happened until the summer of 1866.

Mr. E. B. Taylor came out from the Indian Office with a document appointing himself and an Army Colonel as peace commissioners to deal with the hostile Sioux. He persuaded messengers to go out promising rich presents and even ammunition, and then sat back to wait. About a month later, the Sioux came down from the Powder River area in full force, and Taylor finally found himself face to face with the real force behind the hostilities; Red Cloud had come. With him were Man Afraid of His Horse, and the other important chiefs of the hostiles.

The first thing that Red Cloud and the other chiefs demanded was that the treaty be read carefully to them. When the treaty reading came to the part about building roads and forts through the Powder River country for the Bozeman Trail, Red Cloud and the other chiefs rose to their feet and emphatically and angrily said "No!" Here they would take a stand and fight to the death, if necessary, and they told Taylor this. Taylor was determined that nothing should prevent the signing of this treaty, and, in his desperate efforts to please the Sioux, he assured them solemnly that no new roads would be opened and no forts built.

It was while Taylor was emphasizing, this very point of no new roads and no forts, those 700 soldiers with 226 wagons of road and fort construction equipment under the command of Colonel H. B. Carrington marched into Ft. Laramie. When the Sioux found out that these approaching men had come to guard the Bozeman Trail and to build new forts - the very thing that Taylor had assured them would not happen, Red Cloud flew into a rage and told Taylor that he was now aware of having been deceived. He angrily stomped out of the meeting. His last words to Taylor were that if anyone set foot on the Bozeman Trail or tried to build forts there, he would battle them to the death.

Taylor did a very foolish thing. He sent word back East that the treaty was a success, that the road was open and that only a few unimportant chiefs such as Red Cloud and Man Afraid of His Horse had not signed - - but they didn't matter anyway. Because of Taylor's announcement, there occurred the shocking spectacle of the government permitting immigrants to go unsuspectingly into what the immigrants thought was peaceful country and which in reality was boiling with angry Sioux, Cheyennes, and Arapahoes.

Col. Carrington

The very first parties on the Trail were instantly attacked. Yet, the government refused to face the fact that a full-scale war was shaping up in the last great hunting grounds of the Sioux. The center of this shaping, full-scale war was Colonel Carrington with his 700 soldiers and 226 wagons of construction equipment - tools, saw-mills, forges, hardware - in short, everything that they needed to build forts. Right after the Laramie meeting, Colonel Carrington pulled out of Laramie with his wagons and soldiers and headed up the Bozeman Trail. From that moment on, he was never out of the sight of the Sioux scouts. Day and night, his movements were watched, as the Sioux waited for their chance to put the promise of Red Cloud to work. Carrington's plan was simple and clear-cut:

a. To keep the Bozeman Trail open, and
b. To build two more forts along it, making a total of three:
   Fort Reno, Fort F. C. Smith and Ft Kearney

Colonel Carrington was not a fighting officer. He was an engineer by training, given to fussing about details, and during the time on the Bozeman Trail, he seemed to regard the Sioux as though they were a bunch of angry bees swarming around who would soon go away. On June 28, 1866, Carrington reached Ft. Reno.

The Sioux immediately began raiding all along the road. Wagon trains barely set out when they were attacked. The Sioux boldly raided close in to the new forts, running off stock and attacking any group of soldiers that they met. Yet, with his nose in his blueprints, Carrington seemed hardly aware of what was going on. During July and August, Carrington was busily building Ft. Kearney. His troops could not go a mile outside of the camp without being attacked. On July 17th, the Sioux coolly dashed up within sight of his soldiers, ran off 174 mules, killed two men, and wounded two others. The same war party killed six non-Indians within a few miles of Carrington's camp. On August 28th, just a month later, he sent in an optimistic report saying that everything was going nicely. In the same report, however, he stated that thirty-three non-Indian men had been killed along the new road in the past five weeks, that the Sioux were making daily attacks, and that seventy head of government animals has been stolen near Ft. Kearney alone.

The Horse

Sioux horses were hunting horses and used to repeated gunfire often close to their ears while buffalo hunting at full speed. Sioux veterans interviewed by Dr. Bryde held that the horses responded to such a dangerous role with relish and vigor, never faltering despite occasional buffalo attacks, deceptive terrain, treacherous footing and the speed at which the hunts occurred. They claimed that most horses were created specially to hunt and gave the task their all as if it was a measure of enjoyable sport despite occasional, often fatal falls within a thundering herd. These well-trained, superbly conditioned mounts went on to carry the finest cavalry upon the Plains underneath the Teton Sioux warrior who could ride with both hands free. Contrariwise, many Army horses were unexposed to gunfire prior to their first combat encounter and would often throw their riders or bolt and run from the battleground. After a battle, these horses were easily rounded up and often carried valuable ammunition.

A favorite ploy the Sioux used against the army was to utilize the strength of their horses which were daily exercised and well conditioned, most often by obliging Sioux youth, in contrast to the Cavalry horses which were enclosed within hastily built and confining stockades. A select group of Sioux riders would ride before the forts just out of rifle range and tantalize the troops inside. The Army would often respond by saddling up their horses and weighing them down with rations and ammunition. Out the gates the Army troops would charge, bugles blowing on poorly conditioned horses. The Indians would flee down a pre-designated route where the main band of warriors would be concealed in gullies and draws close to where their leaders would estimate that the Army horses would become winded. The Sioux would hit the army with spirited mounts at the time the cavalry horses were too winded to maneuver effectively. 'They could never catch us... but we could always catch them!' Historians may argue otherwise, but how else could the Sioux capture so many weapons and an abundance of ammunition? They were well-armed when they defeated Colonel Custer at the Little Big Horn. Metal detectors in recent times have proven how well armed the Sioux really were.

Red Cloud had his camp of over 500 on the Powder River. The more hostile bands of Cheyennes had joined Red Cloud, and Medicine Man, an Arapaho chief, who brought his whole group in.

Toward the end of that summer of 1866, Red Cloud eased up a bit for two reasons:

1. He wanted to get in a supply of meat by way of the annual buffalo hunt, and
2. It was time to retire for the annual Sun Dance.

With their tipis filled with dried meat from the buffalo hunt and their spirits renewed by the celebration of the Sun Dance, Red Cloud and his warriors returned to the fighting in earnest. To show how determined Red Cloud was, consider that he decided to fight during the winter. Plains tribes usually let up on their warring during the wintertime. To risk sudden blizzards, to risk losing their precious horses by way of starvation on snow-covered, grassless prairies, and to risk the easy detection of their tracks in the snow - all were too much when added to the already great risks of war in itself. The fact that he was able to stir up the other bands and tribes and to get them out of their warm, winter lodges in order to fight indicates the force of his leadership.

Fetterman

Just before winter officially began, a brash Civil War veteran, Capt. Fetterman, made the statement, "Give me eighty men and I'll ride through the whole Sioux nation." He came upon the Indians who were riding in circles around the wood train and he charged straight at them. The Indians held their ground until Fetterman and his men came within rifle range, then turned, and to Fetterman's way of thinking, ran like rabbits. Fetterman was delighted and was surer than ever that the Sioux were pushovers. The small Sioux war party that he was happily chasing swung around a large hill and immediately obliged Fetterman by standing still and fighting. The reason that they stopped and turned to fight was that there was a large body of Sioux warriors waiting for them to lead Fetterman into the trap. Both groups of Sioux, now outnumbering Fetterman, turned and charged him. Fetterman, with only twenty-five men, dug in to fight. Just when it seemed that Fetterman would be overrun and wiped out, his luck held out, and Colonel Carrington suddenly appeared with his men, causing the Sioux to withdraw.

On returning to camp, Fetterman didn't seem to realize that he had had a very close call. Delighted by the memory of the running Sioux (not yet realizing that he had fallen for the decoy trick they often employed), he loudly boasted, "Give me eighty men and I'll ride through the whole Sioux nation." It was just two weeks later that Fetterman had his second chance to tangle with the Sioux.

On December 20, 1866, just a few miles from the fort at the mouth of Prairie Dog Creek, a large force came drifting in as silently as the recently fallen snow. Red Cloud and his Bad Faces were there. The Minicoujous with their great war chief, High Back Bone, were there. Crazy Horse, at this time about twenty-four years old, was there with his Oglala sub-band, his Wazhashas (Wha zha zhas) along with He Dog and Short Bull who were also famous fighters. Old Two Moon of the Northern Cheyennes was there and, to complete the picture, the Arapahoes were there in force.

Two weeks after his boast, around eleven o'clock in the morning, the word came to the fort that the wood train was again under attack. Colonel Carrington gave Captain Fetterman two strict orders: 1.) rescue the wood train, and 2.) don't chase the Indians beyond Lodge Trail Ridge. As

Fetterman rode out of the fort, a strange thing was happening. Whether Fetterman was aware of it or not, he had exactly eighty men.

Right on the top of Lodge Trail Ridge, he ran into a band of ten warriors. As in an earlier skirmish when he had almost lost his life a decoy group led by the then young Crazy Horse, immediately turned and ran and Fetterman thought again how they resembled rabbits as, without hesitation, he spurred his men after the ten warriors. Fetterman didn't know it, but just beyond Lodge Trail Ridge, there awaited two thousand Sioux, Arapaho, and Cheyenne warriors.

It was all over rather quickly, Fetterman realized his mistake too late. Seeing his men quickly wiped out, he kept firing his revolver until he had one shot left. As the swarming Indians closed in on him, some historians claim he placed the revolver with its one remaining shot against his temple, pulled the trigger, and took his own life. Others name a lieutenant for doing the act. Regardless, his entire command of eighty men was wiped out. Red Cloud was showing that he meant business.

When news of the loss of Fetterman and his eighty men got to army headquarters and to the newspapers back East, the public began screaming for blood and demanding to know who was responsible for this loss. They had to blame somebody. We already know that the one to blame was Fetterman himself for disobeying orders, but there always has to be a scapegoat. The scapegoat in this case was Colonel Carrington. He was relieved of his command. Colonel H. W. Wessles was sent out to take his place.

Peace Commissions

The anger of the settlers in the formerly peaceful country south of the Platte moved the government to send out several peace commissions. The Sioux were always delighted to see peace commissions come out because this always meant presents and supplies for them. This time the commission was made up of J. B. Sanborn, General W. S. Harney, and N. G. Taylor.

The commission sent out word that a great council was to be held at Ft. Laramie on September 13th and that the richest presents that the Indians had ever seen would be handed out. At this time, North Platte marked the end of the new Union Pacific Railroad. Here the commission got off and found Spotted Tail and Man Afraid of His Horse waiting for them, eager to talk. The commission noted in its report that a difference of opinion had arisen for awhile but that the meeting ended in perfect agreement. The difference of opinion was that the chiefs had angrily demanded ammunition and, after displaying some very bad humor at the prospect of not getting it, the commission gave in and let them have the ammunition over the loud protests of the military. It was well known to the military that the Indians used their bows and arrows for hunting and saved their ammunition to shoot back at them, the military.

From this 'victory' at North Platte, the commission hurried to Ft. Laramie fully expecting Red Cloud and all his hostiles to be waiting for them. They found no Indians there, but a message from Red Cloud was waiting for them. Red Cloud said that he was too busy to come down at present, but that he might be able to see them later, possibly next year. When Red Cloud said he was too busy to come down just then, he meant that he was so busy attacking the three forts and everything that moved on the Bozeman Trail that he couldn't afford to take a day off and come down.

By now, during the summer of 1867, the forts were so closely and constantly blockaded that even the wood trains frequently had to fight their way out of the forts and anyone who dared to move along the Bozeman Trail had to do so under heavy guard. As early as May of this summer, word had come in that Ft. F. C. Smith was in desperate straits. There were only 200 men at the fort and all of the horses were either dead or run off by the Sioux. They needed food and provisions right away. It was fortunate for these people at the fort that the Sioux withdrew for their annual Sun Dance at this time. A relief party was able to sneak through unmolested.

It is a strange fact that the government was still insisting that there was no war. Yet, by now, the Bozeman Trail had been abandoned for use by both immigrants and freighters. The only ones using it were military supply groups who had to fight their way to the forts. The posts protected themselves and nothing more. The road that they were supposed to be protecting had been deserted by the public.

After the Sun Dance, Red Cloud's Sioux and their Cheyenne allies began to lay plans for attacking the forts, but they could not agree. As so often happened in Indian discussions like this, the group split up as a result and each group went where it wanted to go. Most of the Cheyennes headed north to attack Ft. F. C. Smith, while Red Cloud and about 1,000 of his warriors went down to attack Ft. Kearney. This was to be the occasion of the famous Wagon Box Fight.

Springfield-Allen Rifle

On August 2, 1867, Captain Powell, was assigned to guard the wood-cutting detail going out from Fort Kearney. For some time, Powell had been trying to figure out a way to surprise the Indians. His chance came when, the government sent out a new 'secret weapon.' These were the new breech loading rifles, the 1866 Springfield-Allen model, with a cartridge shell which could be ejected after firing and hence reloaded much faster. The old musket rifles that they had been using and which the Indians were using took about a minute to reload by way of a four-stage operation. A firing cap would be dropped down the barrel of the musket. Next, powder would be added and tamped down: Finally, the musket ball with a wad to hold it in the barrel. The weapon would be cocked and ready to shoot again. The Springfield rifle cartridge dispensed with this procedure by simply ejecting the spent shell and was quickly reloaded with a fresh one. It would jam however, after a second firing, especially on a hot day. This was a characteristic of the earlier models which were converted from the vast amount of Civil War muskets.

In a battle, the ones attacking knew of this time lag for the muskets of course. The usual strategy was to provoke the enemy to fire and then, before he could reload, to rush him. Captain Powell knew that the Indians would be expecting this time lag and, with his new rapid-firing rifles, he felt he would surprise them and do great damage. Since a wood-gathering party always attracted Indians as certain as honey attracts bees, he felt reasonably certain that the Sioux would show up. On arriving at the tree cutting spot, Powell had some of his soldiers surround the woodcutters to protect them and ordered the others to take the wagon beds off and to prop them up on their sides in the shape of a small fort. He then settled down to wait.

He didn't have to wait long because about 1,000 Sioux were slipping silently toward him. They were mainly Oglalas, Minicoujous, and Sans Arcs under Red Cloud, High Back Bone, and other young chiefs, as well as young Crazy Horse. The Sioux had planned to use the old decoy trick but, as so often happened, some of the young warriors, more eager for glory than team action, rushed out ahead of them and stampeded the herd of horses and mules belonging to the fort. Crazy Horse's party swung around to attack the wood-cutting camp and the rest of the warriors joined them. The Sioux rushed in, expecting the first firing to be followed by the long pause which would be the time to over run the little fort. As they rushed in during what they thought would be the pause, the new breech-loading rifles kept on firing, causing losses among the Sioux. They began circling the wagon box fort for another rush and again lost heavily. Next, they abandoned their horses and tried to work in on foot, but the steady firing was too much for them. The chiefs ordered a withdrawal and the fight was over.

'Body Counts'

Much has been written about the Wagon Box Fight because of early rumors that had gotten into the newspapers. Actually, the Sioux rode away regarding this fight as a victory. They had captured a great many horses and mules and admitted losing only six warriors killed and six wounded.

According to George Hyde, they had inflicted heavier losses on the non-Indians, killing several workmen, one officer, and five men in Powell's force. White Bull, a Lakota, stated that his people rarely tolerated losses over 1 or 2 per cent if given the time or chance to withdraw from an unfavorable fight. His people could not afford high casualties. What appeared in the newspapers, though, and in early books were wild stories of every variety. One early account said that 3,000 Indians attacked and that 1,137 were killed. Another account was supposed to have quoted Red Cloud saying that he lost over 600 men. Still another account said that Red Cloud went into battle with 3,000 men and lost over half of them. Such exaggeration in favor of the Army was typically reported almost a decade later when General Crook lost to Crazy Horse and had to retreat. Even Captain Powell who was the one who was under attack didn't report as wild figures as the above. He estimated Indian losses around 60 dead and 120 severely wounded, but these figures are too high, if we consider the Indian's estimates. No doubt the Springfields were of the converted Civil War vintage and not as effective as the newspapers claimed.

It is interesting to note that in his old age, Red Cloud, when asked about the losses: he had been in so many fights that he said he didn't even remember it!

Springfield-Allen Arms Company

What is little known about the Springfield-Allen rifle was that it was a converted Civil War musket in order to save the government money, or a more reliable prognosis is that it was another ploy of the Springfield-Allen Arms Company to continue their monopoly with the federal government, namely the War Department. The Military Industrial Complex was very much alive and well way back then. The much more efficient and deadly Winchester rifle had been invented almost a decade before the end of the Civil War but was never purchased by the Army, not even for the Civil War unless purchased by private individuals. The Springfield-Allen company (later Springfield Arms) prevailed in their collusion with the War Department to provide their conversion process to the arsenal of thousands of muskets available toward the end of the Civil War. The musket had a thinner powder chamber than what was effectively required for rifle cartridges. This chamber would heat up when a self-contained cartridge, such as the large 45.70 size was fired, especially on a hot day. Upon a second, immediately successive firing, the second cartridge would remain jammed in the chamber for a period of time until the thin chamber cooled somewhat. This may have been the real reason why the casualty count may have been closer to what the more truthful Indians (by reputation, at least) recounted. In ensuing battles, the Sioux captured more and more of these weapons. Their tactic was altered just a bit from the one they used earlier against the old muzzle loaders. They would wait for the Army to fire two successive rounds on a hot day before rushing in, often sporting their own Springfields captured in earlier forays. With jammed rifles, the Army would often provide more rifles and horses plus needed ammunition to Red Cloud's warriors. It is not too difficult to deduce that the many Springfields in the hands of the Sioux warriors were wrested from Army control simply by winning the rest of their battles including the last major battle at the Little Big Horn. White historians will tell you otherwise, but the iron clad fact remains...at that last battle...the Sioux and the Cheyenne allies were well-armed with Springfields and also possessed the Winchester repeating rifle.

The important aftermath of the Wagon Box Fight was that the government finally opened its eyes and realized that Red Cloud was not merely a chief of a small group of discontented Indians, but that he was the leading force behind several thousand highly skilled fighters who were constantly besieging the western forts. After the Wagon Box Fight, Superintendent H. B. Denman of the Indian Office reported that the display of strength shown by Red Cloud indicated that the government must make peace with the Indians, or else flood their country with troops and fight a long and costly war. The long and costly war was out and only one other alternative faced them: agree to Red Cloud's original demands - abandon the forts, the Trail, and get out. This they finally decided to do. Red Cloud had won his war.

Ft. Laramie Treaty of 1868

Toward the end of 1867, the officials in Washington decided to offer the Indians a new treaty. This was the famous treaty of 1868. As far as the Tetons were concerned, this treaty specified that all of the State of South Dakota west of the Missouri would be Indian land and that the Powder River and Big Horn countries would be recognized as Indian Territory into which no non-Indian person could go. Thus, after two years of struggle, Red Cloud and his allies had won their fight. It took the rest of 1867 to draw up the treaty and during the first part of that year the leaders of the new peace commission came out to gather up the chiefs again for the grand signing.

A great council was held at Ft. Rice for the Upper Missouri Sioux on July 2nd. It took an entire day just to distribute the presents to the assembled chiefs. Red Cloud and his comrades, other warrior chiefs, refused to attend. These chiefs stubbornly held to their demands: get the troops out and abandon the forts and the trail first, then they would sign.

The government finally gave in and toward the end of the summer of 1868 orders came to the military in the three forts to withdraw and abandon them. While company after company marched out of the gates of Ft Kearney, Red Cloud and his warriors sat on their ponies not far off and watched in grim satisfaction. When the last soldier had left the fort, the Sioux swarmed down upon it and burned it to the ground. Forts F. C. Smith and Reno were also abandoned, and now Red Cloud had truly won his war.

At the beginning of November, he rode to Ft. Laramie. On November 6th, he finally signed and a new era of relationships with the government began. The Senate ratified the Treaty in early1869.

As we travel on, Chief Red Cloud will walk the political trail and be condemned by the whites and his own people as well, because of a deep inner code which championed a regard for Natural Truth. He simply would not go back on an oath he had taken that; "he would no longer touch the sword" meaning he would no longer fight the soldiers. This oath he believed would bind the U S Government to keep the treaty intact. His main goal was to keep the Treaty of 1868, the treaty his warriors and leadership had won for 'as long as the grass will grow, as long as the rivers will flow and as long as our dead lie buried.'

George Hyde Summary:

Chief Red Cloud is summed up in the words of Author, George Hyde, *Red Cloud's Folk*:

"In recent years, a tendency has developed among some authors of books on Indians to deprive Red Cloud of all credit for having led in the war of 1866-1867. If he did not lead, who did? Neither Sitting Bull nor any of the chiefs of his northern group of Sioux hostiles appear to have taken much interest in this struggle; indeed, Sitting Bull, who is supposed to have been so wise and far-seeing, had no thought of uniting with Red Cloud, but waited placidly until his own hunting grounds were invaded before he took any real action. Red Cloud put himself at the head of the opposition to white encroachments on the Sioux lands at the Ft. Laramie council in the spring of 1866 and he held firmly to his position until the last soldier had left Powder River. The years 1866 and 1867 were Red Cloud's day and the struggle that took place in the Powder River country in those years will always be known as Red Cloud's War."

Generals Sibley and Sully

In respect to Chief Sitting Bull, he did engage the Army, however during Red Cloud's War. Because of drought conditions, he had to hunt east of the Missouri in 1863. After being fired upon, he engaged Sibley at Appel Creek.

In 1864, the Hunkpapa again faced the U. S. Army under General Sully who was all the way into Wyoming attempting to run down a large group of Yanktonai and Santee Sioux fleeing from Minnesota. Sitting Bull lost his camp to cannon fire for this engagement. The following summer, Sitting Bull made General Sully pay dearly by chasing him all the way across Wyoming, to the Yellowstone River where steamboat supplies saved the retreating troops.

Oklahoma Territory

During the federal government's drive to acquire the Black Hills in 1875, Red Cloud stalled the Black Hills cession until it was forced upon the Lakotas as a result of their defeat in the Great Sioux War, mainly between 1869 and 1877. When that conflict ended, he effectively opposed President Grant's specific intention to remove the Sioux to Indian Territory in present-day Oklahoma. Red Cloud, on his own volition, successfully lobbied sympathetic senators against Grant's dead set intentions. I shudder to think that at one time, my people could have been sent to Oklahoma and I shudder again when I think that the Sioux Culture, language and Earth-respecting Spirituality could have died there. Every Teton Lakota should be grateful to Chief Red Cloud for keeping us out of Oklahoma where our culture would surely have died.

Legacy

At a Washington church reception in 1889, Chief Red Cloud had this to say. "When I fought the whites, I fought with all my might. When I made a treaty of peace in 1869 - I meant it, and risked my life in keeping my covenant."

No one collected more arms, ammunition and horses than did the warriors under his command. This weaponry and battle strategy helped the collection of more weaponry and ammunition from the Army by the later leaders. His horses began the increase of the horse herds found at the Little Big Horn battle where the entire camp vanished the next afternoon on horseback or travois. His role in the Fetterman and Wagon Box fights should never be forgotten, nor should his reputation as the most feared Oglala warrior before Crazy Horse and Sitting Bull. He was a man of honor. He kept his word and shrewdly, by doing so, did not give an inch toward the government's treachery and greed as portrayed by those in Washington who specifically wanted the Black Hills gold and the Bozeman Trail for more gold. They now have it and the Homestake mine in the Black Hills has finally played out. It was once the largest in North America. It is the one resource the Sioux people surely will not miss!

5

Chief Crazy Horse

"My lands are where my dead lie buried".
Chief Crazy Horse - Oglala/Mnicoujou, Teton Lakota

Crazy Horse's birth is widely disputed by most writers; all the way from 1840 to 1845. 1841 is as good a guess as any. He was fatally stabbed in his mid-thirties at Ft. Robinson, Nebraska Territory 1877. His birth place, near the confluence of Rapid Creek where it enters the Cheyenne River, is the holding of Dr. Charles Ross, Mdewakanton Sioux, noted Author and Sun Dance leader.

Mitakuye Oyasin

Crazy Horse's father (Oglala) married a Minicoujou (Mnicoujou, Mniconjou) woman. She was Crazy Horse's biological mother and died when he was quite young. Hence that branch of the Tetons or Tetonwan Sioux rightfully claim him as from their own. Crazy Horse's father later married a sister of the respected Sichangu leader, Chief Spotted Tail. She was in actuality, the only mother 'Curly' ever knew. 'Curly' was Crazy Horse's boyhood name. He was light complexioned, had lighter and wavier hair than most.

According to Sioux custom, the terms 'step-mother', 'step-child', 'half-brother', etc. were ill-advised terms and did not promote harmony, familial love, togetherness or true 'Mitakuye Oyasin' ('We are all related. We are all relatives. I am related to all things!'). Children usually do not want to be 'half' of anything. An honorable parent would never consider treating any child within his household as less than his or her own. Even in referring to them it was, "This is my son or daughter." This would also include adopted children of no blood connection. Generally, Crazy Horse is regarded as an Oglala according to tribal designation, but from a cultural stand point, Crazy Horse could be considered Sichangu and Oglala. "A Sichangu and an Oglala raised him, therefore he is both," would be what Indian society back then would say. The Minicoujou cannot be denied their claim as well, if we remain truthful. Mitakuye Oyasin is a very powerful and guiding statement.

A story is told of a winter time when food was scarce. Crazy Horse's band was snowed in and the buffalo, their main source of food, were not to be found. Crazy Horse's father was a tireless hunter. He was out in the storm and cold every day and finally brought in two antelope. The little boy of 6 or 7 rode his pony through the camp and invited the old to come to his teepee to eat. As a result, the mother had to distribute all of it. When it was gone the young child asked for food. His mother told him that the old folks had taken it all, and added: "Remember, my son, they went home singing praises in your name, not my name or your father's. You must be brave. You must live up to your reputation."

Crazy Horse loved horses, and his father gave him a pony of his own when he was very young. He became a fine horseman and accompanied his father on buffalo hunts, holding the pack horses while the men chased the buffalo and thus gradually learning the art. It was usual for Sioux boys of his day to wait in the field after a buffalo hunt until sundown when the young calves would come out in the open, hungrily seeking their mothers. Then these children would enjoy a mimic hunt, and lasso the calves or drive them into camp.

At sixteen, Crazy Horse joined a war party against the Gros Ventres. He was well in the front of the charge, closely following Hump, one of the foremost Sioux warriors. Suddenly Hump's horse was shot from under him and enemy warriors rushed to kill. Amidst a shower of arrows the youth leaped from his horse, helped his friend into his own saddle, sprang up behind him, and, hotly pursued by the enemy carried him to safety. Thus, in his maiden battle, he allied himself with a wizard of Indian warfare. Hump, who was then at the height of his own career, pronounced Crazy Horse the coming warrior of the Teton Sioux.

Crazy horse and Hump (High Backbone), that peerless warrior, became close friends, in spite of the difference in age. Men called them "the grizzly and his cub." Again and again the pair saved the day for the Sioux in a skirmish with some neighboring tribe. But one day they undertook a losing battle against the Snakes. The Sioux were in full retreat and were fast being overwhelmed by superior numbers. The old warrior fell in a last desperate charge. Crazy Horse and his younger brother, though dismounted, killed two of the enemy and were able to escape.

Crazy Horse chose to spend much time in prayer and solitude. Just what happened in these days of his fasting in the wilderness and upon the crown of bald buttes are known only to Crazy Horse. A natural leader, we know that he was much sought after by his youthful associates, reserved and modest, yet rising above them all in the moment of danger.

It is said that when Crazy Horse pursued the enemy into their stronghold he often refrained from killing, and simply struck them with a switch, showing that he did not fear their weapons nor care to waste his upon them. It is an act of great courage and his only brother, who emulated him closely, died attempting this feat. A party of young warriors, led by Crazy Horse, had dashed upon a frontier post, killed one of the sentinels, stampeded the horses, and pursued the herder to the very gate of the stockade, thus drawing upon themselves the fire of the garrison. Though Crazy Horse escaped without a scratch, his young brother was brought down from his horse and killed.

Once, before he was twenty, there was a great winter buffalo hunt. Crazy Horse killed ten buffalo cows with his bow and arrows and came back with ten tongues which he sent to the council lodge for the councilors' feast. Crazy Horse knew that his father was an expert hunter and had a good horse, so he himself took no meat home, but instead put in practice the spirit of his early teaching. The unsuccessful hunters or those who had no swift ponies came home chanting songs of thanks.

Big-heartedness, generosity, courage, and self-denial are the qualifications of a public servant, and the average Native American was keen to follow these ideals. Unfortunately, these traits become a weakness when outnumbered by a culture that is founded upon commerce and gain.

Crazy Horse came into his own at the peak of the difficulties between the United States and the Sioux Nation. He had already proved his worth to his people in warfare against other Native tribes. He had risked his life again and again, and had saved the lives of others. He was no orator nor was he the son of a chief. His success and influence was purely a matter of his personality, courage and success.

Young Crazy Horse was twenty-one years old when all the Teton Sioux chiefs met in council to determine their future policy toward the invader. Their former agreements had been by individual bands. Each had reasoned that the country was wide, and that the white traders should be made welcome. Up to this time they had anticipated no conflict. They had permitted the Oregon Trail, but now to their astonishment forts were built and garrisoned in their territory.

The attack on Fort Phil Kearny was the first noted victory of Chief Red Cloud's leadership. Young Crazy Horse was hand picked to decoy the attack on the woodchoppers, a move designed to draw the soldiers out of the fort to where an army of hundreds lay in wait for them. Crazy Horse's masterful handling of his men insured the success of this strategy. This was the beginning of Red Cloud's war. As a masterful rising lieutenant he was depended upon to put into action the decisions of the war councils, and was frequently consulted by the older chiefs. Even the Cheyenne chiefs, allies of the Sioux, acknowledged his leadership. Yet during the following years of Red Cloud's defensive war, though his teepee was the rendezvous of the young men, he was never known to make a speech. Other prominent young braves were Sword, the younger Hump, Charging Bear, Spotted Elk, Crow King, No Water, Big Road, Red Cloud's nephew, He Dog, and Red Cloud's close friend, Touch-the-Cloud. Because of his fighting abilities,

Crazy Horse was installed as an Ogle Tanka Un (Shirt Wearer or war leader) in 1865.

"There are no pictures of Crazy Horse. There is no truth to how white people write about him. Only his people know the truth - that his spirit is alive through how he spoke through his heart." Bernard Ice, Lakota

Crazy Horse had a relative short life-time (1841-1877) and there exist very few valid accounts regarding his exploits primarily because he refused to be interviewed and shunned any communication with the wahshichu (white man - pronounced; wah she chew). Considerable interview material and early photos exist of Red Cloud, Sitting Bull and Black Elk however, but no reliable photo has ever been discovered of Crazy Horse. One supposed photo, taken of a posed warrior in a photographer's studio has been passed as Crazy Horse. The great Chief, however, was not one to ride in from his freedom on the Plains to ever submit to some photo gallery. Up to the time of his death, combat, was his only contact with the white man. He was a young man in his twenties under Chief Red Cloud's command and was hand-picked by the venerable leader to engage the cavalry in several daring missions. This was during the heavy fighting in the 1860's. Crazy Horse was reputed to always wear a protective wotai stone tied behind his ear when he took the battlefield or served on a dangerous decoy mission. The wahshichu's bullets were predicted to never harm him in combat as long as he faithfully wore the protective stone.

I wore such a protective stone, when I flew 110 combat missions in Vietnam. It first came into Fools Crow's ceremony. Our customs still live and they often spiritually work. The white man holds out certain man made items as bearing a protective or reflective spiritual power. Our items are most often natural entities and not man made but designed by Creator. A wotai stone is a special stone that comes to the bearer in a special way.

By 1868, the many battles with the U.S. Army drew to a victorious close (for the Sioux) with the signing of the Treaty of 1868. As mentioned previously, this treaty, ratified by the U. S. Senate spelled out explicitly that much of present day South Dakota, including the Black Hills would remain with the Sioux tribes forever. After making his mark upon the document, Chief Red Cloud vowed he would never 'take up the sword' upon the battlefield as an obvious measure to hold the government to their word upon the treaty. For almost 8 years afterwards there existed a sporadic peace between the Army and the Teton Lakota and their allies as well.

Six years is nothing in the life of an Indian nation. It was in 1874, only six years after the signing of the treaty of 1868, that the Sioux were again stirred up like a swarm of angry bees. Word got around immediately to the bands that a large group of soldiers, complete with a brass band, was headed straight for their sacred grounds, the Black Hills, and led by the notorious Pehin Zizi or Yellow Hair, the name that the Sioux used for Custer as well as Long Hair. The major culprit resulting in the breaking of the treaty by the U. S. Government was the discovery of gold by the Custer expedition. 'Wahshichu mazazizi, lelah ahtah witkokolah.' (The yellow metal (gold) that drove the white man crazy.) Frenzied miners began to swarm into the Black Hills. Truth! It soon vanishes when a materialistic society discovers material gain, be it gold, oil, bananas, tea, beaver pelts, slaves, cotton, cheaper labor or what have you. The Homestake mining company in the Black Hills, once the largest gold operation in the Northern hemisphere, has finally shut down and moved on, after taking billions in gold and leaving behind Cyanide Creek.

Whenever the Indians heard of soldiers in their country, it meant only one thing: trouble and fighting. The fighting might not come tomorrow or next month, but it would come. The Sioux began to prepare in their minds for another major encounter with the military.

In the meantime, since the signing of the treaty of 1868, two other factors were happening that were steering the Indians toward another showdown. Because of the agencies and the established reservation areas, the government was insisting more and more that the bands stay within the area assigned them. These areas would be soon termed reservations. At the same time, rations were frequently not enough and the Indians solved this by simply leaving the assigned area or reservation and going off to hunt in order to add to their food supply. This wandering off to hunt became more frequent until the government finally laid down the law - that any time they were off their areas out of the assigned hunting times, they would be regarded as hostile, and the soldiers would be sent out after them to bring them in by fighting and force.

Drifting to Hunt

Thus it was that toward the end of 1875, a number of bands had left their reservation areas and had drifted north and west into the Powder River territory to hunt. On December 3, 1875, the government, therefore, issued an order to all Sioux out of their areas that unless they returned by January 31, 1876, they would be regarded as hostile, and that military force would be used on them. We have already referred to this and we have seen that it was impossible for the Indians to comply with the order. First of all, with the bands spread out as they were, getting word to them by messengers was almost impossible. Secondly, even if the bands had gotten the word, winter traveling conditions made it impossible to get back by the assigned time. On February 7, 1876, therefore, the Secretary of the Interior ordered the military against what they regarded as the hostile Sioux. One of the commanders assigned was Lt. Colonel George Custer, who was about to make his last military trip. Custer had been a Major General during the Civil War but, like most of the officers with wartime promotions, had been reduced in rank after the war.

Crazy Horse – Warrior Chief

Crazy Horse was now in his thirties and a full fledged chief of several bands who remained aloof from the agencies; staying out upon the Great Plains to mainly subsist upon the dwindling herds of buffalo, elk, mountain sheep and deer. Occasionally, after Custer's gold discovery he was reputed to have led several retaliatory raids against over-eager gold miners which most often ended grimly for the lustful miners. The Army 'hostile' declaration angered the hunting bands to such an extent that they elected to defy the order and remain hunting. Three major battles were to be successfully fought by Chief Crazy Horse and his warriors in but a short duration lasting only 4 months in the spring and summer of 1876. After the Chief Sitting Bull chapter, these battles will be described in detail.

As mentioned earlier, little material of accurate substance is available regarding Crazy Horse's personal life. The young Chief had more than enough reasons not to trust the white man and it would have been suicidal for any writer to go out upon the Great Plains, in those days of deception and treaty breaking for the foolish purpose of seeking an interview with a man who disdained attention. There does exist, however, a multitude of writings, of what I consider 'mostly erroneous fiction', by scores of writers on Crazy Horse. The past decade, a brand new Crazy Horse fiction work seems to appear almost annually.

Mari Sandoz was the original fiction writer on Crazy Horse which brought public interest and of course, lured other writers. Larry McMurtry, *Lonesome Dove* Author, states that writers or historians on Chief Crazy Horse "have convinced many readers and certainly not this reader - that they have an accurate grip on the deeds, much less on the soul, of the Sioux warrior we call Crazy Horse." [1]

McMurtry goes further, "historians often chide the writers - Mari Sandoz, Evan S. Connell Jr., John G. Neihardt - for producing good writing but bad history." [2] I may agree on his first two examples, especially Sandoz but to include Neihardt with her is a bit in error, my opinion. John Neihardt spent days on end with his source, (old Black Elk) face to face, and with the old man's son as interpreter and the confirming presence of Black Elk's life long friend, Standing Bear, verifying every word for the book, *Black Elk Speaks*. (Verification by others was a customary prerequisite when interviewing the old-time warriors.) There exists too much exculpating proof on the contrary. Neihardt repeatedly returned, as well, to visit his source (old Black Elk) as did the interpreter, Ben, who would in turn, visit Neihardt occasionally. Sandoz, however never had a minute with her source and greatly expanded upon what little information she did arrive at from those who knew Crazy Horse and of course, did not speak her language. Neihardt's 'problem' was that he put down too clearly, the Indian's version, loyally projected by Ben the son. Black Elk's material did not coincide with the way or what the white man, especially the controlling missionaries wanted to hear from the Indian. The Lakota language, especially when shifted to serious revelation in ultra serious discourse, becomes spiritually poetic, an ingredient lacking in the white man's vernacular and therefore foreign and hence Euro-centrically branded as suspect.

Now, let us return to more from Mr. McMurtry. "It is well to say firmly at the outset that any study of Crazy Horse will be, of necessity, an exercise in assumption, conjecture, and surmise. We have more verifiable facts about another young warrior, Alexander, called the Great, who lived more than two thousand years earlier than Crazy Horse and whose career is also richly encrusted with legend, than we do about the strange man of the Oglalas (to adopt Mari Sandoz's phrase)…For most of his life he (Crazy Horse) not only avoided white people, he avoided people, spending many days alone on the prairies, dreaming, drifting, hunting. According to Short Buffalo, a fellow Sioux who knew him well, he was "not very tall and not very short, neither broad nor thin. His hair was very light... Crazy Horse had a very light complexion, much lighter than other Indians. His face was not broad, and he had a high, sharp nose. He had black eyes that hardly ever looked straight at a man, but they didn't miss much that was going on, all the same..." [3.]

"He came into Fort Robinson, in northwestern Nebraska, with the nine hundred people who, in desperation, had chosen to follow him, only four months before he was killed, and those four months were the only period in his life when he was in contact with the record keeping, letter writing whites; and even then, he camped six miles from the fort, rather than the prescribed three, and saw whites only when he could not avoid them. For almost the whole of his life he did avoid all parleys, councils, treaty sessions, and any meeting of an administrative or political nature, not merely with whites but with his own people as well." [4.]

"He was a loner - now, in many respects, he is a blank. Professional writers and amateur historians, professional historians and amateur writers, have all written about him extensively and have not scrupled to put words in his mouth and even to report his dreams - or, at least, one dream that was of great significance in shaping the way he lived his life." [5.]

"If the word "record" is to mean anything, one would have to say that for much of Crazy Horse's life - there is no record." [6.]

I accept Larry's statements as vividly truthful. The writers he speaks of wrote primarily for entertainment, my opinion, and cannot be considered as genuine, truthful representations. To extol Crazy Horse, all the writers found or chose to put down other chiefs, mainly Chief Red Cloud who was in command of more successful battles than all the Sioux chiefs put together. No doubt this is what rankled early white writers especially Sandoz. If they could not defeat the great chief on the open field of combat they surely were going to diminish him by their prejudiced and willfully errant writings. Several Indian writers have fallen into this trap as well. Truth is too important within this work for this author to trade it for entertainment's sake. From a military perspective we will view Crazy Horse's accomplishment upon the battlefield following the Chief Sitting Bull chapter. It will expand upon the young chief's battle prowess and resulting success which I believe he learned well from his older chief.

Let us now go to these modern times and hear the words of a man who dedicated his life to immortalize this great chief in stone which would be the largest carving in the world. Korzcak Ziolkowski has these words which he related to a young Boy Scout named Tom at Crazy Horse Mountain.

"When Chief Henry Standing Bear (Oglala) spoke about Crazy Horse, it was with great reverence. Henry was a direct descendent of Crazy Horse, a distant cousin. Although Crazy Horse had no children who lived to maturity, Henry was descended from one of Crazy Horse's uncles. When Henry told me this, he also told me of an Indian tradition that had a great influence on my decision to carve that mountain.

"Standing Bear explained that the Indian has a concept of honoring their great that's totally different from the white man's. It was difficult for me to understand at first. It seems with the Indians only a relative of a great man has the right to honor that man or build a memorial to him. Other people who are not relatives have no right to honor that great man because those people might have evil motives, want to get something out of it.

"It is a rather beautiful way. We white people do it the opposite. Relatives do not seek to build a memorial to a great man. We get a group of citizens together and have them do it. We go through the back door. The Indian uses the direct approach. He says: 'that man was my ancestor, and he was a great man. We should honor him—I would not lie or cheat because I am his blood.'

"You know, Tom, I bought that. Isn't that the right way? No politics."

"So Standing Bear could ask to honor Crazy Horse because he was related to him?" said Tom with a serious expression.

"That's it. Oh, that had a lot of impact on me. I always had been a sucker for a left, but something about that concept of honoring your own hit home to me."

"Did Standing Bear know Crazy Horse?" Tom asked.

"No, but Standing Bear's father had known Crazy Horse. Thus Henry knew a great deal about his great ancestor, Tashuunka Witko (Tah shuunk ah Wit gko). That's Crazy Horse's name in Lakota. I remember him telling me how the Indians called Crazy Horse the 'silent one' or 'strange one' because Crazy Horse was a very quiet man. He never said much. He didn't participate in camp activities or the councils. He always wanted to stay apart by himself.

"As Standing Bear described him, he wasn't a very tall man. Only about 5' 7"or 5'8", rather slight. He only weighed about 160 pounds. Sioux Indians were usually much larger in stature. As I told you, he was lighter than most Indians and was called Curly because of his wavy hair. Well, it seemed this boy, Curly would distinguish himself in everything he would do. Hunting, fishing and all the things Indian boys did.

"Standing Bear confirmed the story I'd read in the encyclopedia about Crazy Horse's father giving the son his own name. He told the story with great conviction.

"When he was older, Crazy Horse always could go out and bring back food for his tribe in the winter when no one else could find food. He could always get deer or a buffalo. He always would go out alone, but often others would follow. This was how he became a chief, although he was very young.

"As Standing Bear explained it, a chief was not elected as we pick our leaders. A man became a chief if he was the most skilled at whatever he did. If you were the best hunter or the best warrior or the best medicine man, others would follow you. As long as you could produce for the tribe, you would be chief. You see, the Plains Indians were nomads. They didn't live in one place, but they roamed the plains following the food and water supplies and the seasons. They lived from day to day, and those who could provide for them were their leaders.

"Crazy Horse was so skilled at so many things, he became a chief even though he didn't want to be one. He was just a natural leader, and the other Indians wanted to follow him. Since he was such a young man, I don't suppose some of the older Indians much liked the idea of following someone his age, but he was the most skilled, so his people wanted to follow him.

"He was not a council chief, but a war chief. Crazy Horse was a natural military leader. Standing Bear told how he would plan military strategy using decoys to lure his enemies into a trap where he could take them by surprise. Crazy Horse is the first Indian we know of to use the decoy system. It was very successful, although Standing Bear didn't talk much about the battles. He and the others would never mention the Battle of the Little Big Horn, I guess because they won the battle but lost the war.

"He talked with great admiration about Crazy Horse's bravery. He would be at the front of his warriors and enter battle crying, Hoke a heyyy, Hoke a heyyy! 'It's a good day to die.' It was a curious thing, but he never wore a war bonnet; Didn't own one; Only a single feather in his hair. He did become a hair shirt warrior, the Indians' highest honor, but it was taken from him.

"Crazy Horse had another brilliant military idea. He never wanted warriors over about the age of 22 years. From about 15 years to 22 years was perfect. They would obey orders without question. Older men had their own ideas.

"Also, Crazy Horse never abandoned his wounded.

"Standing Bear talked so much about Crazy Horse's great military abilities I could hardly believe my ears, Tom. Remember this was a whole new world to me in 1940 on Pine Ridge. Years later I read that President Dwight Eisenhower, a five-star general, said Crazy Horse was the greatest cavalry leader since the Greeks. That's what they teach at the West Point Military Academy. Since the Greeks! That's something for Eisenhower to say.

"During those weeks I was in Pine Ridge, Standing Bear told me this story in bits and pieces. As I mentioned, he spoke very slowly and deliberately. There would be long pauses when he seemed to be in a trance. I would wait and wait. Finally, he would continue. We would talk day after day, and besides telling about Crazy Horse he talked about the traditional Indian way of life.

"He spoke very reverently about the Great Spirit, although I didn't understand much about that concept at the time. He did say all Indians everywhere in this nation worshiped the Great Spirit, and he said there never had been a religious war among the Indian tribes.

"To the Indian, the Earth was the Mother, and the sun, moon and stars—all relatives. Everything was a circle. A circle of life. He told how the Indians took care of Nature, taking from it only what was needed for their existence. One thing I remember so well was his telling about the buffalo. Without the buffalo the Plains Indians could not live. Of course, when the white man came, he slaughtered all the buffalo. Buffalo Bill alone killed about 2,800 in one eight-month period.

"The Indian killed only what buffalo he needed. Standing Bear told how when the Indian took a buffalo, he would turn its head to the east and thank the buffalo for its meat. Every part of the animal was used. Nothing was wasted. The meat was for food, the bones for utensils, jewelry and weapons, the hide was for shelter and clothing. Some parts were for medicine.

"Standing Bear also talked about the craftsmanship of the Indians. How they made the beautiful things you saw in that museum out there: Wonderfully beaded and quilled clothing and moccasins, intricately woven baskets and blankets: Tools and practical items for the household: So many things: All by hand: All from Nature.

"Henry spoke passionately about the Paha Sapa, the Black Hills. They were sacred to the Sioux Indians. To them the Hills were like a cathedral, a sanctuary, their sacred ground. They never lived in the Hills, but would come here only to worship, to hunt and gather berries and edible plants or to get tipi poles.

"Standing Bear grew very angry when he spoke of the broken treaty of 1868. That was the one I'd read about in which the President promised the Black Hills would belong to the Indians forever. I remember how his old eyes flashed out of that dark mahogany face, then he would shake his head and fall silent for a long while.

"After a couple of weeks, I understood why Crazy Horse was a heroic figure to Standing Bear and the others. He had fought valiantly to defend his people and their way of life in the only manner he knew. He never surrendered, never signed a treaty, he had never gone on the reservation. I realized, also, Crazy Horse was a symbol of everything the Indian had stood for and lost, his whole way of life. Most of it was already gone in 1939. Oh, you wouldn't believe how desolate the reservation was: Poverty stricken in every way. It hasn't changed much in these years since.

"Of all the stories Standing Bear told me, one seemed to sum up the whole character of this remarkable man called Crazy Horse: the year after the Battle of Little Big Horn and after all his followers had gone on the reservation, Crazy Horse remained free. The soldiers were searching for him everywhere, but they couldn't catch him.

"One day on the prairie Crazy Horse met a white trader who spoke Lakota. This trader mocked Crazy Horse and made fun of him, saying, 'Where are your lands now, Crazy Horse? All your people are captured and put on reservations. Where are your lands you fought for?' Korczak's voice grew much softer and very emotional.

"It was a beautiful September morning. The sun wasn't too high in a clear sky. It was still and rather warm, just a touch of autumn in the air. Crazy Horse sitting on his pony, said nothing for awhile. He just stared at this white trader. Then, he slowly raised his arm and pointed out over his horse's head to the east, and said proudly, "My lands are where my dead lie buried."

Korczak's voice broke. A small tear slid down his furrowed cheek and trickled into his beard. He continued very softly, "I can hardly tell that story. I get all choked up. Every time. What a story that is!"

"That's why he's pointing over the horse's head?"

"That's why he's pointing. To his lands. Of course, they were all taken when he said that, but as far as you could see in every direction those had been the lands of the Indians. 'My lands are where my dead lie buried,' that's the tragic story of the American Indian in one sentence. It marked the end of Crazy Horse and the end of a beautiful way of life for a proud race of people that had lived here for untold centuries.

"That same day Crazy Horse went to Fort Robinson in Nebraska under a flag of truce to talk about provisions for his people. He was stabbed in the back by a white soldier, and he died early the next morning, September 6, 1877. Crazy Horse was only 33 or 34 years old."

Coming In

In July, 1877, Chief Crazy Horse was finally prevailed upon to come in to Fort Robinson, Nebraska, with his band. Most say less than a thousand. General Crook had now proclaimed Spotted Tail, who had rendered service to the army, 'Head Chief of the Sioux', which was resented by many, including Chief Red Cloud.

Crazy Horse's wife was critically ill at the time, and he decided to take her to her parents at Spotted Tail Agency. After he had left the sick woman with her people he went to call on Captain Lee, the agent for the Brules, accompanied by warriors of the Minicoujou band.

Captain Lee urged him to report at army headquarters at Fort Robinson and furnished him with a wagon and escort. When he reached the military camp, Little Big Man walked arm-in-arm with him, and his cousin and friend, Touch-the-Cloud, walked ahead. After they passed the Army sentinel, an officer approached them and walked on his other side. He was unarmed but for the knife which was commonly carried for ordinary use by women as well as men. Unsuspectingly he walked toward the guardhouse; when Touch-the-Cloud suddenly turned back exclaiming: "Cousin, they will put you in prison!"

"Another white man's trick! Let me go! Let me die fighting!" cried Crazy Horse. He stopped and tried to free himself and draw his knife, but both arms were held fast by Little Big Man and the officer. While he struggled thus, a soldier thrust him through with his bayonet from behind. The wound was mortal, and he died that night, his old father singing the death song over him and afterward carrying away the body, which they said must not be further polluted by the touch of a white man. It is claimed they hid it somewhere in the Badlands, his resting place to this day.

My grandfather, William Denver McGaa was interviewed by Eli S. Ricker, *"The Indian Interviews of Eli Ricker, 1903 – 1909."* He was the first child born (1859) in the then settlement of Denver. His father and Adams founded Denver. A former scout, interpreter hired to General Brooke, and also a government boss farmer, he left General Brooke when he found out what happened at Wounded Knee. He is quoted: – "Crazy Horse was purposely killed."[8.]

6

Chief Sitting Bull

"That my people may live."

Chief Sitting Bull, Hunkpapa, Teton Lakota.

'Slow'

'Slow' was born on the south bank of the Grand River in March 1831, about 10 years after Red Cloud was born. His boyhood was spent in hunting, practicing shooting, and riding on his gray fast pony. Not long after 'Slow' had turned fourteen, he learned that a war party under the leadership of Good Voice Elk, was shaping up to go out against the Crows. Whenever Good Voice Elk went out on a war party, he was usually successful, and, for that reason, others would often come to him and ask him to lead them in a war party. 'Slow' itched to get into the party, but knew from past experience that, if he asked, he would be turned down by his parents and by Good Voice Elk.

Shortly after the last of the warriors had left the camp, 'Slow' quietly slipped away, caught his gray, and followed the trail of the warriors. In time, he rode quietly into a little draw to find twenty warriors staring at him in stony silence. He had not been invited and he could feel the silent disapproval of the warriors as they waited for him to explain his uninvited presence. Warriors on war parties were particular about with whom they rode. 'Slow' felt deeply embarrassed at crashing their party but, without a flicker of emotion on his face to hide his embarrassment, he rode impassively up to his father and slipped off his horse. He threw one arm over his pony's neck and said slowly and deliberately, "We are going too."

As 'Slow' looked around the assembled warriors, quietly planning their battle, and saw the mighty weapons that they had brought, his embarrassment grew even deeper. He stole a glance at his own small quiver, full of shorter, blunt headed arrows, and realized that they were good only for shooting birds. He realized that the enemy itself would laugh at him if he attacked them with such a light weapon. He knew that he was not going along just for the ride, but how could he take part in the fighting? It was at this point that his father, probably sensing his embarrassment at his lack of weapons by watching him eyeing the warriors' weapons, solved his whole problem for him. He silently handed him a coup stick - a long stick with the bark peeled off and a feather tied to the curved end. 'Slow' knew that to strike an enemy was an even greater act of bravery than killing one, and he was grateful to his father for getting him out of his difficulty. He realized also, with somewhat of a start, that possessing a coup stick meant that he had to get close to an enemy in order to strike him. He suddenly realized that he was really committed now because no one with a coup stick could hang around on the rear end of a battle and have others think that he was expecting to use it. To strike or touch an enemy - dead or alive - was the main goal of every warrior. This, as we said, was even braver than killing an enemy.

Several days passed before the Crows were confronted. Young 'Slow,' armed only with a feathered coup stick, bore down on a Crow warrior who had drawn his bow and was taking a bead on the advancing Hunkpapa. Heedless of the drawn arrow pointed straight at him, Slow galloped straight at his enemy and, just as the arrow was about to be released, struck the arm holding the bow and spoiled his aim. The arrow missed, but Slow's horse didn't. The fast galloping little gray knocked the enemy flat and before he could regain his feet, the Sioux warriors following 'Slow' killed him almost instantly.

'Slow' had struck the first coup in the battle and he almost fell off his horse from the excitement of the deed and from the thought of the honors that would come to him now that he had proven himself as a full fledged warrior. He joined the others as the running fight with the Crows continued, but the memory of his first coup was the high point of the day for him. When the battle was over, the Sioux gathered up their prizes of war, the horses, weapons, and scalps they had taken, and started back toward home.

Naming

On returning home, a great victory dance was held. 'Slow's' father was the proudest man in the camp. He mounted the boy on a fine bay horse and led him around the camp circle, loudly reciting his brave deed. That night at the victory dance, 'Slow's' father gave away four fine horses in honor of his son, and then shouted for silence because he wanted to make an important announcement. Leaping into the center of the circle, he proclaimed in a loud voice, "My son is brave. He has struck the enemy. I now name him Sitting Bull" The name 'Slow' would never be used again and, from that night on, the new name, Sitting Bull, would gradually become known as that of one of the greatest men in the west.

Sitting Bull took his new name gratefully as the most serious responsibility of his young life. Unlike non-Indians whose names are more like numbers, Indian names express a descriptive idea about the one bearing the name and an Indian took his name as his most serious responsibility, because the name expressed the true idea or inner essence of himself. It expressed him. A person had to live up to his name. Indians believed that God was in everything and expressed Its powers in everything by giving everything that existed some special power. Everything, from the blade of grass, with its gentle, nourishing power, to the massive grizzly and buffalo with their awesome, ruling powers expressed God in their respective ways.

Bull Buffalo

Sitting Bull, walking or sitting alone, would meditate for hours on the real meaning and responsibility of his name. He realized that the buffalo bull was a stubborn, powerful creature that was afraid of nothing and would fight to the death to protect his territory and the ones in it. Once a buffalo bull had set his head in a given direction, he would never turn back. He never turned from danger. He always turned toward it and moved toward it. Even in a blizzard, when domestic cattle will turn their tails to the wind and walk in the same direction that the blizzard is blowing, the bull buffalo will turn his head into the wind and walk toward the blizzard. They seemed to welcome opposition and it was danger or opposition that got the best response from them. Finally, the full fighting and protective powers of the buffalo bull were directed not to protect himself, but for others.

Warrior Society

One of the most important organizations in old Indian life was the warrior society. These were like exclusive clubs made up of certain warriors. Each warrior society or "warrior club" was very proud of itself and the only way one could get into a warrior society was to be invited.

Each warrior society dressed in a certain way or wore a certain emblem or badge to show that the warrior belonged to that society. Enemy tribes had warrior societies also, and, because of these special signs or emblems they wore, such as a certain kind of feathers or dress, when one tribe would fight another, they could see instantly just what warrior society that they were going to go against. Sometimes, a warrior society would be so great that the very sight of their particular dress on a battle field would send the enemy running before the battle began.

There was great rivalry among the various warrior societies, and every time the warrior societies would go on the war path, they would compete with one another to see who could get the greatest number of coups, scalps, and horses. On returning, all the members of a given society would add up their coups and trophies of war to see which society had the most.

Horse-Stealing

Not long after Sitting Bull received his sash from the Strong Heart Warrior society, he joined a group of about a hundred Hunkpapa warrior for a horse-stealing raid against their old enemies the Crows. They were camped this time west of the Powder River in what is now Wyoming. They were low on horses and many had to walk. Sitting Bull had a fast black horse with a white face and stocking feet which had been a gift from his brother-in-law Makes Room.

After crossing the Yellowstone and arriving in Crow country, it was not long before the scouts brought back word of a large Crow village on Porcupine Creek. The party immediately went into hiding to wait until nightfall because that was the best time to drive off the Crow horses. When night came, only a few of the best and bravest were chosen to sneak near the Crow village and to drive off as many horses as possible because it would be very difficult for a hundred men to approach the Crow camp undetected. Sitting Bull was one of the few chosen and he and his comrades quickly and silently disappeared into the night in the direction of the Crow camp. To be detected was almost certain death because they were afoot, but Sitting Bull and his warrior comrades faced death almost daily and this kind of danger was nothing new. It was simply a man's job and he did it without running from it.

After Sitting Bull and his few companions left, the other hidden warriors waited nervously for several hours. Suddenly the night silence was shattered by the sound of many hooves galloping hard, right toward them, and they had no way of knowing right away whether these would be the stolen horses being driven in their direction by Sitting Bull and his friends, or whether it would be the Crows themselves on horseback trying to run down Sitting Bull and his friends. As the horses came into their dim night view, they saw with relief that the horses had no one on them and they knew that Sitting Bull and the others would be bringing up the rear, mounted on the horses they had grabbed. Coming out of their hiding places, they quickly milled the herd and divided the horses among them. They knew that they had to make tracks as fast as possible, because the Crows would be following them in the morning and they couldn't make real fast time while driving a herd of horses.

By sunrise, they had put many miles between themselves and the Crow camp, but the daylight had hardly broken when a huge party of Crow warriors came charging into view. Some of the younger men were immediately assigned to bunch and hold the horses, while the rest fell back to meet the oncoming Crows. When the Crows came over the final rise in the ground and saw the whole Sioux force lined up to meet them, they slowed down and then stopped completely. They had tangled with the Sioux many times before and usually came off the worse for it. Now, they were having second thoughts when they saw how many Hunkpapas were lined up to meet them.

Suddenly, three of the Crows, braver than the rest, broke from their lines and came charging straight at the Sioux. As they approached, they spread out whooping their war cries. The first one to reach the Sioux lines, charging right in among them, struck two of the Hunkpapas with this coup stick and then wheeled to make his getaway. Almost miraculously he escaped amid a shower of arrows. The second Crow to reach the Sioux lines charged in and killed a Hunkpapa named Paints Brown. Before the third Crow could reach the Sioux lines, Sitting Bull himself, among all the Sioux there rode out to meet him. As he approached the oncoming Crow, Sitting Bull suddenly leaped off his horse. Leaving his horse in battle, dragging his dog strap, was always a sign that the sash wearer was going to stake himself down to fight to the death, if necessary. Sitting Bull, however, didn't have time to stake himself down to the ground with his sash or dog strap, because the Crow was coming at him fast and leveling his flintlock gun which was capable of only one shot. As the Crow ran forward, Sitting Bull could see that he wore a red shirt trimmed with ermine. Sitting Bull knew that this was the sign of a chief, which also meant that this Crow was a very brave man to have risen to this position. Chief or no chief, Sitting Bull continued running toward the Crow and shouted, "I am Sitting Bull. I'll fight you. Come on!" Sitting Bull was also carrying an old fashioned, one shot muzzle-loading gun and he knew that he had to make that one shot count. When the Crow chief saw that Sitting Bull was so close, he threw up his gun to shoot. Sitting Bull dropped to one knee, threw up his round shield with one hand and leveled his gun at the Crow with the other. The two shots were almost together, but the Crow got his shot off a split second sooner. His bullet went right through Sitting Bull's shield and creased the bottom of his left foot. A second later, when the smoke cleared, Sitting Bull saw that he had shot his enemy through the body and the Crow chief had fallen backwards, mortally wounded. Hopping forward on his one good foot, Sitting Bull finished his enemy with his knife.

When the Crows saw that their chief had fallen, they all turned and fled, with the Sioux in hot pursuit. They counted a large number of coups and took a number of war trophies before they gave up the chase and turned homeward with their captured herd. On returning home, Sitting Bull found out that the Crow chief's bullet had hit his left foot just beneath the toes and had dug a neat furrow straight through the sole right back to the heel. It hurt fiercely, but he did not dare show his pain as they treated the foot with their medicines. He hobbled around for some days waiting for the wound to heal so that he could walk normally again, but that day would never come. For the rest of his life, he walked with a limp and was proud of it because he had received the wound in battle. No one ever dreamed of calling him 'Limpy' because everyone knew that that limp was a badge of his courage and greatness.

Strong Heart Society

Because of his outstanding act of bravery, it was not long before Sitting Bull was proposed by his comrades as the chief of the Strong Heart warrior society. Then, his responsibilities to his people really began. The Strong Heart warrior society was not only the most influential fighting group of his band, but it was also responsible for the tribal hunting. This meant that, as chief of the Strong Hearts, Sitting Bull had the responsibility of feeding his people and keeping them strong. From now on, he was finally in the position to live up to his name and he fell to the task with all his great energy. As his people were to say of him later, "He fed the whole nation." Sitting Bull's response was; "That my people may live."

As Sitting Bull gradually rose to the position of the most influential man in his band, burdened with the double responsibility of fighting to protect his people and of hunting to feed them, he began spending more time alone, thinking and praying for his people. All his people were naturally religious but a chief had to be even more so. Part of his job in caring for his people was to pray for them, which he did every morning, frequently during the day, and at night. Many an hour he spent alone on a nearby hill with his arms raised in prayer for his people: "That my people may live." Even when he hunted he prayed, because like all Indians, he felt a relationship to the animals he had to kill. He had a standard prayer that he prayed before he killed any animal:

"Grandfather, my children are hungry. You were created for this, so I must kill you." When an animal was butchered, a part was always offered to Wakan Tanka, the Great Spirit, who had given it. Once, when riding across the prairie with his young men he came upon the white bones of a number of buffalo that he and his warriors had killed some time before. He got down from his horse, turned the bleached skulls to face the sun and said: "My relatives, we must give honor to these bones. These are the bones of those who gave their flesh to keep us alive last winter."

Itanchan – the Leader

Spending time alone as he pondered and prayed over the problems of his people did not mean that he was aloof from them or apart from the people. On the contrary, he loved to be among them and they were always glad to see him coming. He had a very winning and pleasant way about him that made everyone like him. Although he was a powerful, well-built man, somewhat shorter than the average, he was not a handsome man in the ordinary sense of the word. Children were not afraid of him and would come running up for his customary pat on the head. His smile was winning and charming and he laughed easily and was usually in a good and confident mood.

Sitting Bull was a good husband, a good father, and an excellent provider for his family. At a time when Indian men did not pay much public attention to women, Sitting Bull was an outstanding exception. He was very considerate of the women, talked to them in public, and was very popular with them. They liked him because, as they said, he was always kind to their families. He frequently used his position to patch up quarrels within their families and to help them out in other ways.

Another reason that he was so popular with the men as well as the women was that he was a fine singer with a high, melodious singing voice. The Sioux were great singers and would make up songs for every imaginable event, from killing a buffalo to the birth of a baby

Among the old-time Sioux, there were two kinds of chiefs. The Nacha was a war chief who was in command of the group of warriors only when they were outside the camp on a war party. While in the camp, he was just one of the boys like anyone else. The other kind of chief was the Itanchan, or camp chief who ruled in the camp and was responsible for the welfare of the people. Sitting Bull was both kinds of chiefs in one. A chief, Itanchan, or camp chief, had to have a great heart. He had to be generous, always understanding, and above all spite or selfishness. He had to keep his temper always and had to constantly share with those who, he knew, could never repay him. Sitting Bull was all of this and more.

The famous Cheyenne warrior, Wooden Leg, said, "I am not ashamed to tell that I was a follower of Sitting Bull. I have no ears for hearing anybody say that he was not a brave man. He had a big brain and a good one, a strong heart and a generous one. In the old times, I never heard of any Indian having spoken otherwise of him."

Stanley Vestal said Sitting Bull was "A man who was a peacemaker in the camps, and never quarreled. A generous man, who was always capturing horses from the enemy and giving them away, a man who constantly shared his kill with the poor and helpless when hunting, a man who could not bear to see one of the Hunkpapa unhappy. An affable, jocular, pleasant man, always making jokes and telling stories, keeping the people in a good humor, a sociable man who had tried to please everybody all his life, and was not in the least haughty or arrogant—in spite of his many honors. A man who . . . was devoutly religious, whose prayers were strong, and who generally got what he prayed for."

During these years, a frequent song on his lips was: "My relatives, hardships pursue me. Fearless of them, I live." Also:

"All over the earth I roam, all alone I have wandered. I am doing this for love of my land." He also sang a song that he would sing to the end of his days: "My father has given me this nation. In protecting them I have a hard time." Later on, toward the end of his days, he was to write in a letter one of his convictions that he had carried all his life, ". . . all Indians pray to God for life, and try to find a good road, and do nothing wrong in their life. This is what we want, and to pray to God . . . who made us all."

We have seen that Sitting Bull's one great problem was to make his people live. The first necessary means to this was to acquire more hunting grounds and he did this with dispassionate efficiency. Warfare was directed completely toward one target; other Indian tribes.

In the beginning, the idea of making war against the non-Indians and the non-Indian soldiers never entered his mind. It was only later when the military became a threat to the land he had fought to take and a threat to his people that he did turn his fighting forces against the soldiers, and this was out of sheer self- defense. It was, to his way of thinking, the only way to solve his problem of protecting his people and his country. In the beginning, he had only other enemy tribes to fight. The time would come when he would have not only his traditional Indian enemies to hold off, but strong military forces of soldiers. He knew that dark days would eventually come and he knew that he could handle it in the only way fitting to his name and to himself--turn to the danger and move toward it.

General Sibley

In 1863 Sitting Bull had his first skirmish with the Army. After the Mormon Cow incident the Hunkpapas usually gave the Army troops a wide berth and fought only in self-defense. The chief ranged from northern Wyoming across northern South Dakota to the Missouri River and had been relatively free of contacts with the emigrants and military. Because of drought conditions, he had to hunt east of the Missouri in 1863. General Sibley who had put down the Dakota in the Minnesota uprising was out patrolling the same area. Sibley, without warning, opened fire on a Hunkpapa hunting party. In retaliation, Sitting Bull attacked Sibley's wagon train at Appel Creek. To show Sibley he was unafraid of him, Sitting Bull rode in within easy range of the Army rifle fire and returned with a government mule.

General Sully

In 1864, the Hunkpapa again faced the U. S. Army under General Sully who was all the way into Wyoming attempting to run down a large group of Yanktonai and Santee Sioux who were fleeing Minnesota. This group attached themselves to Sitting Bull's warriors and attracted a running battle wherein the Hunkpapa had their first taste of cannon fire. They wound up having their camp, including the tipis and winter's supply of meat, destroyed. The soldiers then turned back eastward leaving the Hunkpapa the task of working extra hard to get in a new supply of meat, clothing and make new tipis for the coming winter.

The following year, Sitting Bull made General Sully pay dearly by chasing him all the way across Wyoming, this time westward from the Little Missouri River crossing clear to the Yellowstone River. Sully lost hundreds of horses and mules due to the extreme drought and grasshoppers destroying the grass at the time. It came out later that the soldiers had thought that none of them would survive the hunger, thirst and attacking Sioux. They barely survived by reaching the Yellowstone where steamboat supplies saved them. Sitting Bull broke off his attack and went home feeling some retaliation against Sully for destroying his tipis the year before.

Sitting Bull's skeptical, wait-and-see attitude after the Laramie treaty in 1868 was fully justified only four years later. In 1872 Colonel O. S. Stanley commanded a military escort for a surveying party of the Northern Pacific Railroad. The survey placed the railroad on the south bank of the Yellowstone River, in clear violation of the Laramie Treaty. Stanley promptly had a run-in with Chief Gall and his warriors, and when word of this reached Sitting Bull at his camp on the Powder River, he immediately rode out with a large party of his Hunkpapas, accompanied by Oglala, Minicoujou, Sans Arc, and Blackfeet Sioux warriors. He tangled with Major E. M. Baker and his four hundred men in the valley of the Yellowstone below Pryor Creek on August 14, 1872. Losses were relatively light on both sides, but Sitting Bull had made his point that no one was to come into his territory without being hit. The most notable feature of this battle occurred when Sitting Bull got off his horse, gathered together his war pipe and smoking equipment, and calmly walked up to within easy rifle range of the soldiers. Here he sat down, lit his pipe, and smoked the tobacco all the way down to the bottom of the pipe, with the bullets of the soldiers whizzing past his ears and kicking up dust all around him. When he had finished, he quietly cleaned the pipe, put it back into its bag, and sauntered back to his own lines. Having shown his lack of fear of the soldiers, he called his men together and went home.

Custer

The years of 1873 and 1874 were relatively quiet, as far as fighting was concerned, but Sitting Bull was busy, hunting and supplying food for his people. He kept a wary eye toward the east, however, because he still had his wait-and-see attitude. Again, his suspicions were justified when Lt. Col. George Custer led a large force of over 1,100 men and 110 wagons to explore the Black Hills in 1874. This was in clear violation of all the treaties and resulted in large numbers of non-Indians filtering into the Black Hills area - many of them lured there by the reports of gold that Custer had brought out. Sitting Bull knew that the non-Indians were closing in around him and that a showdown would have to be coming soon. He didn't know how he was going to preserve his people against such superior numbers and superior weapons, but he knew that he had to find a way.

The Unrealistic Order

The next year, 1875, found Sitting Bull and his people in their winter camp at the mouth of the Powder River. He and his Hunkpapas had camped here for years during the winter, but further treaty modifications had placed the western boundaries of Indian Territory just east of the Black Hills. For this reason, Sitting Bull and his people, in the eyes of the military, were off reservation boundaries and were, therefore, 'hostile." The government had long been annoyed that the various tribes would wander off reservation boundaries in order to hunt. On the basis of a report filed with the Commissioner of Indian Affairs by a U. S. Indian Inspector named E. C. Watkins, in the fall of that very year, November 1875, the Secretary of the Interior issued an order that all the bands had to return to their respective reservations by the end of January 31, 1876 or the Army would come after them.

This was an unrealistic order. No one including the Army could move during that very brutal winter. Most bands never received the message because no one dared travel or rather could not travel once the winter snows came fiercely in December and way into March. General Crook attempted to march his troops out of Ft. Laramie in that month and barely made it back by eating his mules and horses let alone receiving a severe mauling from Crazy horse and Cheyenne allies.

Little Big Horn

The Battle of the Little Big Horn was fought. This battle will be the main subject within the next chapter. Sitting Bull's powerful dream - the soldiers falling into camp upside down - was quite accurate. After that battle, Sitting Bull and many of his Hunkpapas finally ended up in Canada in 1877, but they were very unhappy there. The Canadian Mounted Police (the red coats) watched them too closely and, in 1881, after four years there, Sitting Bull decided to return to his reservation. He became a friend of Buffalo Bill Cody and even joined his wild west show that toured the East for a period of time.

Ghost Dance

Because of the Ghost Dance craze, which reached its peak in 1890, Sitting Bull was shot by Indian police sent out by an over- reacting Indian agent, Charles McLaughlin. Sitting Bull took no part in the craze that had swept the desperate Indian world, mostly Plains tribes, now confined from their former freedom to barren reservations. Wovoka, a Paiute, Christian-influenced half-breed initiated the craze but a year earlier.

Sitting Bull's legacy was of a man that set the supreme example of being the Truthful man. Bravery, courage, sharing and generosity…he was the epitome of the four cardinal virtues proclaimed by the Teton Lakota-the Sioux. All aspiring children can cast him as their shining example of what a two-legged can set forth to become. We adults can take heart and hope that this good man did so live. In the Spirit World, I would expect this great leader to be well advanced in that realm. From what I have learned regarding truthful fulfillment, he will have few equals.

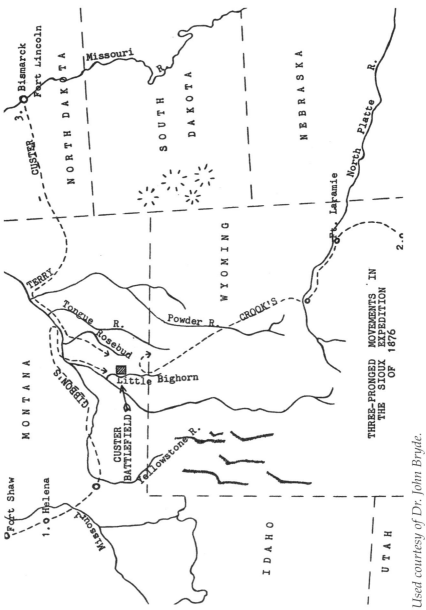

Used courtesy of Dr. John Bryde.

Battle of the Little Big Horn

Three Pronged Plan

Early in the year 1876, Crazy Horse's runners brought word from Sitting Bull that all the roving bands would converge upon the upper Tongue River in Montana for summer feasts and conferences. At the time rumors were circulating that the army would fight the Sioux to a finish but conflicting reports said that another commission would be sent out to treaty with them. To discuss these matters, the Indians planned to meet in early June along the banks of the Tongue River.

The Army high command knew that these bands that had been disappearing from the reservations would be in the last great hunting area of the Sioux which meant Red Cloud's old country around the Powder River area. These last great hunting grounds, would have enough game to support such a large concentration of people. Since the army knew approximately where they were, they decided to approach them from three different directions at once.

This was to be a massive operation. Thousands of men would be involved, and they would have to travel hundreds of miles moving toward the same spot, the Powder River country, and arrive precisely at the same time from three different directions. General Crook would come up from the South, from Ft. Laramie territory. From up in Montana, Col. Gibbon would come down from Ft. Shaw. From near the present location of Bismarck, North Dakota, General Terry would come down from Ft. Lincoln with Lieutenant Colonel Custer in his command.

All three of these small armies wanted to set out as soon as possible. They wanted to find the Indians in the spring or early summer, so that if they had to chase them, they would have the entire summer to do so. General Crook set out from Fort Laramie in early March, 1876. Since the northern two forces were situated so much farther north, the winter weather held them up. These forces didn't get away until later, Col. Gibbon in April and General Terry and Custer in May. In the meantime, General Crook was going to have his hands full as a result of his early start.

General Crook

When General Crook set out from Ft. Laramie early in March, 1876, the weather was bitterly cold, sometimes reaching thirty below zero. After traveling slowly for a couple of weeks, his scouts brought back word of the first sign of Indians on March 16. This was at Clear Creek, a branch of the Powder River. The village was identified as that of Crazy Horse's and some Cheyenne allies consisting of about a hundred lodges. This meant that there were about six to seven hundred people and, among these, about two hundred warriors. They seemed unaware of Crook's presence, and he decided to surprise them with an attack at dawn.

The surprise was a complete success. One military group was assigned to run off the horse herd, another group to attack, and a third group to cut off any escape. About to run off the pony herd, the soldiers ran into a fifteen year old boy who was taking the horses to water. The boy let out a loud war whoop, and the battle was on.

Crook had about 1,400 soldiers, and the Indians had about 200 warriors. Gathering around Crazy Horse, they launched a furious counterattack from the rocks outside the village. As the battle raged on furiously, Colonel Reynolds, who was commanding the attack, was slowly beaten down. Despite their superior number, Colonel Reynolds and his men were driven several miles back down the valley. The Indians retrieved their scattered herd of ponies that night and rode off shouting taunts at the soldiers. I have read a few history books that claim the Indians had bows and arrows mostly. These authors were obviously reluctant to admit that the Army lost a considerable amount of their logistics, namely ammunition and rifles, to the Sioux under Red Cloud who had the better conditioned horses and able riders. Crazy Horse's mounts were fresh compared to the cavalry horses already two weeks under the bitter cold and he fought none other than how he had skillfully learned under the highly successful older chief. If Col. Reynolds was beaten back, it was not by bows and arrows.

Sioux horses were constantly mounted by the youth when the camp was in garrison (not on the move) and the superbly conditioned horses could easily outlast and outclass cavalry horses especially for endurance and combat performance; let alone overall speed when needed.

Weather was also a factor. An army on the move in early spring could find some desperate conditions; bitter cold and snowed-over grass can fatigue the horses as well as fatiguing the men who have to, at times, do their share of walking to get through heavy snow. 'Torrid heat and arctic cold' is a common term for the Great Plains weather. I know; I have lived there a good share of my life. Several accounts hold that Crook had to eat his horses to get back out of the severe weather and looking back in fear that Crazy Horse would attack.

When General Crook found out how badly his men had been beaten, he was so angry that he had Colonel Reynolds and several other officers court-martialed. If the Colonel was not beaten back then why was he court-martialed?

Crook had to go all the way back to Fort Laramie to get his command back in shape again. For this reason it was not until late in May that he finally got his column moving again to keep his meeting date in the Powder River country with the other two columns coming down from the northwest and the northeast. This time Crook had 1,200 soldiers, 86 Shoshones, and 176 Crows in his group - a total of 1,462 men.

The Mounted Horsemen of the Plains

The Sioux rider guided his horse by his knees and weight-shifting when in combat allowing both hands to be free. On the trail, when not in combat or at close quarters on a buffalo hunt, he guided the horse by one rope, a light hackamore arrangement. The Army cavalry horse was directed by bit and reins, requiring one arm for the horse and the other arm free to carry a weapon, but one would have to also aim that weapon with one arm. Try this on a moving horse and see how accurate you are, especially with a heavy, old fashioned military rifle. Try fighting a larger, taller opponent who is coming at you with both hands bearing a rifle or a shield and a weapon, arms free. Maybe it is understandable how two hundred freshly mounted can defeat 1,000. An American army in the field back then did not field all its men as well, not unlike the combat unit of today. Among the Sioux, 200 warriors were just that, all in the field, mounted on superb personally trained horses and no one held back as a support unit. And only a few months away from the Little Big Horn, surely some had Winchester repeating rifles.

Vietnam Revisited!

The cavalryman's horse was always loaded down as well with plenty of ammunition, water and even food on a heavy saddle. An oft used ploy which worked over and over, not unlike the disappearing strategy of the Vietcong and the NVA back into their tunnels throughout the Vietnam War which the American generals never seemed to get wise to; the Sioux would decoy out a baiting troop of warriors before a stockade or fort. Barely out of rifle range, the warriors would tantalize and wait. Finally charging from the opened gates, bugles blaring and the garrison cheering, the fearless cavalry would give chase. The Red Clouds, Crazy Horses and Sitting Bulls would be waiting in force, back beyond hidden buttes, winding, wooded dry creeks, cedar-covered river breaks; concealing nature. It worked over and over. Even bows and arrows were effective at close range once the Army's horse would become too-soon winded. Is it no small wonder why the Sioux had so many guns and ammunition after an encounter? This information has been mentioned before. It is worth repeating.

How could a small force hold its own against such as what Crooks had in the field? The primary answer is – 'in the Horses!' And of course the attitude, experience, belief and command of the smaller force. Again I say, 'give credit where credit is due.' Chief Red Cloud started these tactics when he came upon an enemy who disdained the word – 'Coup'. It was no longer a game of chivalry which the old style warriors adhered to when fighting the enemy tribes. Oddly, as it was, American reaction to a so-called 'inferior enemy' was repeated to a degree in Vietnam. The military commanders ignored or just did not realize what were basically common sense tactics.

Tongue River

In early June, scouts reported the advance of a large body of troops under General Crook. The council sent Crazy Horse with seven hundred men to meet and attack him. These were nearly all young men, many in their teens because young warriors were what Crazy Horse preferred for combat engagements. "Unlike older warriors, they did what they were told." He also considered his smaller force as more than adequate to meet General Crook. He had fought him before and had extreme confidence in his conditioned mounts as well as his warriors. They set out at night so as to steal a march upon the enemy, but within three or four miles of his camp they came unexpectedly upon some of his Crow scouts. After a hurried exchange of shots, the Sioux pursued the Crows back to Crook's camp. With the soldiers forewarned, it became impossible for the Sioux warriors to enter the well-protected camp. Again and again Crazy Horse charged with his bravest men in the attempt to bring the troops into the open, but he succeeded only in drawing their fire. Toward afternoon he returned to his own camp disappointed.

Later, General Crook again ran into Crazy Horse. This time it was on the east bank of the Tongue River on June 9. A lone Indian appeared on the other side of the Tongue with a message from Crazy Horse: "Don't cross the Tongue, or we will fight." Crook sent back word that he was going to cross the Tongue.

That evening, even before Crook could cross the Tongue, gunfire broke out across the river from the Indian side. The soldiers fought back, but when they tried to attack the Sioux, the latter faded away.

They had made their point, and Crook saw it, because he didn't move from the spot for four days. He spent the time drilling his men and preparing for the invasion across the Tongue. He had 200 mules from the pack train broken to saddle and 200 of the infantry broken to riding the mules in order that they could have as many men as possible traveling as fast as possible.

On June 16, he crossed the river and camped on the Rosebud Creek that night. The next day, at the lower end of the Rosebud Valley, he ran into a well-prepared Crazy Horse with his estimated 700 warriors plus his Cheyenne Allies. The battle was on and it continued throughout most of the day, the conflict alternating in favor between both sides. Even General Crook had a horse shot out from under him. In a desperate effort to force the Indians back to their camp, General Crook sent Capt. Anson Mills to circle around and to find and capture Crazy Horse's village. Captain Mills was only five minutes from the village when he received word from General Crook to return immediately or his entire command would be doomed. Captain Mills returned in time to help save the command from complete defeat. At dark, the battle ended, both sides withdrew, and Crook camped under triple guard right on the battlefield. The next day, Crook was so weakened that he had to turn back. Thus it was that the southern thrust of the three pronged approach to the Indians was beaten back and would not make its meeting with the other two columns coming down from the northwest and the northeast. Had Crook been able to meet Terry with his one thousand plus regulars and two hundred Crow and Shoshone scouts as ordered, he would inevitably have intercepted Custer in his advance and saved the day for him. Instead, he retreated, eating his horses on the way in a country swarming with game, for fear of Crazy Horse and his braves and of course the Winchester!

Time-Life editors hold that General Crook lost only 10 men and 21 wounded at the Tongue River/Rosebud battle! He had specific orders to be the major force in the three pronged battle plan. Out of a force of over 1,000 men (some estimates claim the General had 1420 men including his Indian scouts) he loses **less than one percent** and turns back? They also offer that Crooks was low on ammunition and rations after the encounter.1. I am surprised that they did not include that grass is green and water is wet, as well.

Once again, Dominant Society's writers reflect their gross egotism and resultant error regarding accurate reporting of Indian history or is it that most academic based writers have little experience or knowledge of troops in the field and the needed logistics for their support as well as combat operations? They mention that Crooks had superior fire power. Evidently he frantically used most of his ammunition when fighting off the efficient attack by the Indians. Army troops never ventured upon a pre-planned campaign without an adequate supply of ammunition.

The Indians now crossed the divide between the Tongue and the Little Big Horn, where they felt safe from immediate pursuit. On the twenty-fifth of June, 1876, five large circles of teepees, stretched along the level river bottom just back of the thin line of cottonwoods. Here and there a larger teepee stood out. These were the lodges or "clubs" of the young men. They were the often referred to as the 'dog soldiers'. These younger warriors were the initial force for surprise attack.

As was mentioned earlier, Colonel Gibbon had started down from Ft. Shaw in April in order to meet General Terry and Custer at the spot where the Rosebud Creek flowed into the Yellowstone River. General Terry and Lt. Col. Custer set out from Ft. Lincoln in May, and the forces of Gibbon and Terry finally met at the Rosebud and Yellowstone. Here they made a simple plan. Colonel Gibbon would go back and march up the Big Horn River (it flows north), and then, if he didn't find the Indians, come back and march up the Little Big Horn. At the same time, Custer would march up the Rosebud Creek also looking for the Indians. If the Indians tried to run south, General Crook would be there with his 1,462 men to catch them - they thought. The closing in date was June 26. Custer met his fate on the 25th.

Gibbon's force started out on June 21, and Custer's force started out on June 22. During the very days that Custer and Gibbon were moving southward, Crazy Horse and his Cheyenne allies, after whipping Crook, were moving up north to join the main body of all the gathered bands and tribes, and what a gathering it was. Today, it is impossible to know exactly how many Indians were gathered together in the valley between the Little Big Horn and the Rosebud Creek toward which Gibbon and Custer were moving. Most books say that between 12,000 to 15,000 Indians were there, and about 5,000 of them were seasoned warriors. All were mounted and well-armed. Actually, no one really knows for sure as to the real number of Indians there. The huge camp extended for several miles along the west bank of the Little Big Horn. Each band was camped in a circle. On the south end of the camp were the Hunkpapas with Chiefs Sitting Bull, Gall, and Black Moon. On the north end of the camp were the northern Cheyennes under chiefs Two Moon and White Bull. In between, each in its circle, were Minicoujous under Chief Hump, Sans Arcs under Chief Spotted Eagle, and Oglalas under Chiefs Crazy Horse, Low Dog, and Big Road. Bands of Brule and Blackfoot Sioux were there, along with some Arapahos. It was toward this huge gathering that Custer was confidently making his way.

Custer

Custer started slowly up the Rosebud on June 22. He had about 600 soldiers, 44 Indian scouts - mostly Crows, and 20 or more packers, guides, and civilians. On June 24, the scouts reported the tracks of a large Indian group moving west toward the Little Big Horn valley. Custer didn't know it, but he was only about 8 miles from where Crazy Horse had beaten General Crook on June 17. Custer rested awhile and decided to follow the trail at night in order to be as close as possible to the Indians at dawn.

At daybreak on June 25, the smoke from many Indian lodges could be seen in the Little Big Horn Valley, and Custer knew when he had found his Indians. He itched for action. From this point on, accounts differ as to why Custer went into action so fast. For many years, the explanation given was that a report received by Custer mentioned that the presence of the troops had been discovered by the Indians, and that Custer thought if he didn't move right in the Indians would escape.

Most recent historians, however, hold a different version of why Custer didn't wait another day and attack as planned with Colonel Gibbon hitting from the other side on the 26th. Custer was fundamentally a "glory hound" and wanted to grab all the credit for himself; he was simply following his long habit of acting suddenly without sufficient planning. They critically point out that he didn't even bother to scout ahead of time to find out just how many Indians he was about to engage and that, if he had, he most certainly would have waited until the next day when Colonel Gibbon would be in position. Custer was also a Fetterman. He errantly thought he could ride through a thousand Indians if chance could ever place that many in his way. And like Fetterman, Fate granted him that chance! An author named Evan Connel, *Son of the Morning Star*, suggested that Custer had dreams of becoming president and that his 'victory' was all he needed. Mari Sandoz, though writing 'fiction,' holds the same view. As to the real reason, however, why Custer did not wait, no one really knows for sure.

All-Night March

At any rate, Custer decided to move at once after an all-night march. He divided his tired men (600) into three groups, one under Major Reno, another under Captain Benteen, and the third group was to go in with him. A fourth smaller group was not to fight, but to guard the pack train and follow as closely as possible. Custer's last movements began as he stood with his group on a high spot facing west toward the Little Big Horn camp. He was about twelve miles from the huge Indian camp which was on the other side of the river from him. As he moved westward toward the camp, he sent Captain Benteen's group about two miles south to make a scout in that direction and to cover any Indian movements in that area. Custer himself and Reno moved directly toward the Indian camp, each group on opposite sides of the small creek that flowed toward the Little Big Horn and the Indian camp.

When Custer and Reno came within about two miles of the Little Big Horn, they could see part of the huge village across the river. If they had been able to see the whole village, they most certainly would not have charged it. At any rate, on seeing the village, Custer ordered Reno to continue moving straight ahead, across the river, and to attack the village. Custer himself decided to swing north and catch the village at one end. In this way, he apparently hoped that, by starting at one end of the village, he could drive everyone who ran, right into the hands of Reno and Benteen, since Benteen was even farther south than Reno.

Three Distinct Fights

A popular misunderstanding of the battle of the Little Big Horn is that Custer alone rushed in and was defeated by the Indians. The truth of the matter is that there were three distinct fights and, for a clear understanding of the whole day's activity, it is necessary to understand the sequence of the fights which is as follows: Reno was hit first, then Custer was downed, and then the attack swung back to Reno, who by now had been joined by Benteen.

Reno did just as he was told. At about 2:30 p.m., he advanced straight toward that part of the village he could see and crossed the river. It was only then that his blood froze, as he saw for the first time the huge size of the Indians gathering. Up to this time, the bluffs along the river and the trees along the banks had hidden the complete village from view. Reno knew that he was in for it. So outnumbered was he, that a cavalry charge was out of the question. He ordered his men to dismount, dig in, and fight from cover. This sharp shooting defense slowed the Indians down at first, but so many more Indians kept appearing and moving in, that Reno ordered his men to get back across the river that they had just crossed. Across the river, there were higher bluffs from which they could defend themselves better, if they could reach them. Reno lost about one third of his men in the retreat across the river. Once they crossed the river, the Indians stopped attacking and turned their attention to the north and to Custer. In the meantime, Reno's men reached the bluffs and dug in for their lives, expecting the Indians to return at any moment. At this moment, Custer was about 5 miles to the north of Reno.

Custer's Final Hour

As Reno crossed the river to attack the part of the village that he could see, Custer swung north to catch the village at its northern end. Just as Reno was meeting the Indian charge for the first time, Custer was seen on the bluffs from his position, waving his hat to Reno in encouragement right before he swung down from the bluffs to invade the river bottom and catch the Indians at the northern end of their village.

Just as Reno had gotten the surprise of his life when he saw the size of the village for the first time, so now Custer was to get the surprise of his life. Instead of coming out on the north end of the village, Custer rode down from the bluffs right into the main part of the Indian village. It was on this northern end, that the northern Cheyennes were camped, and right next to them were the Oglalas under Crazy Horse, Low Dog and Big Road.

Crazy Horse was a member of the "Strong Hearts" and the "Tokala" or Fox lodge. He was watching a game of ring-toss when the warning came from the southern end of the camp of the approach of troops. The Sioux and the Cheyennes were "minute men", and although taken by surprise, they instantly responded while the women and children were thrown into confusion. Dogs were howling, ponies running hither and thither, pursued by their owners, while many of the old men were singing their lodge songs to encourage the warriors.

Crazy Horse had quickly saddled his favorite war horse and was starting with his young men for the south end of the camp when a fresh alarm came from the opposite direction. Looking up, he saw Custer's force upon the top of the bluff directly across the river. He took in the situation - the enemy had planned to attack the camp at both ends at once. Knowing that Custer could not ford the river at that point, he instantly led his men north to the ford to cut him off. The Cheyennes followed closely. Custer must have seen that wonderful dash up the sage-bush plain and one wonders whether he realized its meaning. In a very few minutes, this wild general of the plains had outwitted one of the most brilliant leaders of the Civil War and ended at once his military career and his life. In this dashing charge, Crazy Horse snatched his most famous victory out of what must have seemed frightful peril for the Sioux, who could not know how many were behind Custer.

As soon as he was sighted by the Indians, they came boiling after him. Custer had about 225 men, and the number of Indian warriors then present has been estimated as high as 5,000 by the white and modern Indian authors. So mixed up by now were the various bands, that the first warriors to hit Custer were the Hunkpapas led by Chief Gall, who originally had been camped on the southern end of the large village. From the first contact, however, all the bands merged together and, like a huge, never ending wave, they moved in on Custer. Custer's men were spread out over a battle line of about three-quarters of a mile on the first considerable ridge back to the river. A few hundred yards from this line on the ridge was another, lower ridge, and it was from behind this ridge that Crazy Horse, along with other bands appeared, cutting off Custer from any possible retreat. It was on this upper ridge that one of the bloodiest battles in the history of the west was fought.

Fighting on horseback was impossible due to the large number of Indians. Many of the soldiers had to leap from their horses and shoot them in order to make a breastwork against the bullets and arrows of the Sioux and Cheyennes who were creeping steadily forward. Most of the battle was fought on foot by both sides. Custer tried to gain a little higher ground, turning left toward the village and fighting on foot. The soldiers were increasingly spreading out as they sought higher ground and gullies for protection, but the Indians were appearing and pressing forward, not only from down below the ridges, but over the top of them as well.

No one knows exactly how long the battle lasted, but many estimate its length to have been a little more than an hour. The horses which were not shot for protection were stampeded by the Indians and many were caught by the Indian women in the village. Without horses as a means of escape, it was only a matter of time as the superior number of Indians pressed forward in a concerted charge that could not be stopped. There was not, as one sees in the movies, the final, dramatic charge with the soldiers finally standing up and swinging their empty rifles. There was just the steady creeping forward and firing by the Indians, with the firing from the soldiers becoming less and less, until it suddenly occurred to the Indians that they were the only ones doing any shooting. Not one of the original 225 soldiers was left alive.

At what point Custer was killed, no one knows. Later on, Custer's body was found and, although it was stripped of its clothing as were most of the bodies of the soldiers, he had not been scalped nor mutilated. He had been struck twice by bullets, either one of which could have been fatal. Although perhaps reckless, this much must be said about Custer: he did not kill himself when he saw that his end was near. He went down fighting.

It was complete annihilation, and not one of the Custer-commanded soldiers remained alive after the battle. The only living thing left after the battle was Captain Keogh's horse, a well-built bay named Comanche. The horse had strayed from the battle and had not been discovered by the Indians in the roundup of the other horses. Eventually, the horse strayed back to the scene of the battle, and when found, it was noted he had suffered seven wounds. He was taken back to Ft. Lincoln, nursed back to health, and put on the retired list. Every time the regiment paraded, the horse was saddled, bridled, and led in the parade, but no one was ever allowed to ride him again. He died at the age of thirty years and was mounted and placed in the museum at the University of Kansas, where he can be seen to this very day.

Major Reno

Let us now return to Major Reno. We left him after he had retreated back across the river to the higher bluffs on the east side, at which point, the Indians withdrew and gave their attention to Custer. Digging in on the eastern bluffs, Reno had 40 men left, 3 officers, and a few civilians. He had started out with 140 men. Although he could hear the firing of the Custer engagement in the distance, he did not dare venture out of his position, because he thought the Indians might come back at any moment and finish off his weakened command.

In the meantime, Captain Benteen had been scouting farther south, as Custer had ordered him. He had seen no action, of course, and when he found the bluffs farther south were almost impassable, he swung back north again to find Custer for new orders. As he was making his way north again, still about eight miles from where Custer was last seen, he met a messenger from Custer with a hastily scrawled note which said, "Benteen—come on—Big Village—Be quick—Bring packs. P.S. Bring packs." It was signed by W. W. Cooke, Custer's adjutant. Since this was about 3:30 in the afternoon, Custer was probably already dead when Benteen got his message for help.

Benteen pushed north at a rapid rate, looking for Custer. He found Reno dug in on the eastern bluffs with over two-thirds of his men gone and expecting another attack at any moment. Benteen, Reno and the other officers conferred for a while as to what to do. They couldn't decide whether to dig in with Reno and thereby have a strong defensive position, or to go on up and relieve Custer. Finally, it was decided to send Captain Weir with one company of soldiers, and Captain Benteen was to follow them. When Captain Weir came to a high spot about several miles where they thought Custer was, they could see Indians moving around and looking at the ground. Because of the distance, they could not make things out clearly, but this scene took place just after the battle when Custer and all of his men were already dead.

Holding Out

As soon as the Indians saw the soldiers, however, they swarmed up at them in order to cut them off. The soldiers dismounted to fight on foot, and this they did for a while. When they saw how many Indians there were and the impossibility of holding their present line, they decided to go back to Reno's original defensive position in order to have a more fortified place from which to defend themselves and also to form a single concentration of men. No sooner had they dug themselves in at Reno's old position than Indians appeared from everywhere. It looked like Custer all over again, and the heavy fighting continued until dark when the Indians withdrew to their camp for the night.

All during the night, the soldiers of Benteen and Reno dug rifle pits and trenches with shovels, knives, tin cups, and mess kits, anything to make holes big enough to protect themselves. Ammunition cases and hardtack boxes were piled up for barricades. Meanwhile, down in the huge village, the sounds of a wild celebration could be heard. Great fires lighted the sky, and the sounds of singing and dancing could be heard most of the night.

At dawn of the next day, the fighting resumed in earnest. The Indians were back in force. Together, Reno and Benteen's men made up a force of about half the entire command that had started out. They had dug in well during the night, and they had all the ammunition from the pack train. The battle continued all morning and into the afternoon, but from their strong defense position, the soldiers were able to hold off the Indians. It was about the middle of the afternoon that the Indians began to withdraw, leaving only a small force to keep up occasional firing to force the soldiers to remain in their place. Gall and his men held the survivors there until word from scouts reported the approach of another army, compelling the Sioux to break camp and scatter in different directions.

Chief Flying Hawk's Observation

The Oglala warrior and later a chief who was there had a much lower estimate of the number of warriors who took part in the battle.

"The Indians were camped along the west side of the Big Horn in a flat valley. We saw a dust but did not know what caused it. Some Indians said it was the soldiers coming. The Chief saw a flag on a pole on the hill.

"The soldiers made a long line and fired into our teepees among our women and children. That was the first we knew of any trouble. The women got their children by the hand and caught up their babies and ran in every direction.

"The Indian men got their horses and guns as quick as they could and went after the soldiers. Kicking Bear and Crazy Horse were in the lead. There was the thick timber and when they got out of the timber there was where the first of the fight was.

"The dust was thick and we could hardly see. We got right among the soldiers and killed a lot with our bows and arrows and tomahawks. Crazy

Horse was ahead of all, and he killed a lot of them with his war-club; he pulled them off their horses when they tried to get across the river where the bank was steep. Kicking Bear was right beside him and killed many too in the water.

"This fight was in the upper part of the valley where most of the Indians were camped.

It was some of the Reno soldiers that came after us there. It was in the day just before dinner when the soldiers attacked us. When we went after them they tried to run into the timber and get over the water where they had left their wagons. The bank was about this high [twelve feet indicated] and steep, and they got off their horses and tried to climb out of the water on their hands and knees, but we killed nearly all of them when they were running through the woods and in the water. The ones that got across the river and up the hill dug holes and stayed in them.

"The soldiers that were on the hill with the pack-horses began to fire on us. About this time all the Indians had got their horses and guns and bows and arrows and war-clubs and they charged the soldiers in the east and north on top of the hill. Custer was farther north than these soldiers were then. He was going to attack the lower end of the village. We drove nearly all that got away from us down the hill along the ridge where another lot of soldiers were trying to make a stand.

"Crazy Horse and I left the crowd and rode down along the river. We came to a ravine; then we followed up the gulch to a place in the rear of the soldiers that were making the stand on the hill. Crazy Horse gave his horse to me to hold along with my horse. He crawled up the ravine to where he could see the soldiers. He shot them as fast as he could load his gun. They fell off their horses as fast as he could shoot. When they found they were being killed so fast, the ones that were left broke and ran as fast as their horses could go to some other soldiers that were further along the ridge toward Custer. Here they tried to make another stand and fired some shots, but we rushed them on along the ridge to where Custer was. Then they made another stand (the third) and rallied a few minutes. Then they went along the ridge and got with Custer's men.

"Other Indians came to us after we got most of the men at the ravine. We all kept after them until they got to where Custer was. There was only a few of them left then.

"By that time all the Indians in the village had got their horses and guns and watched Custer. When Custer got nearly to the lower end of the camp, he started to go down a gulch, but the Indians were surrounding him, and he tried to fight. They got off their horses and made a stand but it was no use. Their horses ran down the ravine right into the village. The women caught them as fast as they came. One of them was a sorrel with white stocking. Long time after some of our relatives told us they had seen Custer on that kind of a horse when he was on the way to the Big Horn.

"When we got them surrounded the fight was over in one hour. There was so much dust we could not see much, but the Indians rode around and yelled the war-whoop and shot into the soldiers as fast as they could until they were all dead. One soldier was running away to the east but Crazy Horse saw him and jumped on his pony and went after him. He got him about half a mile from the place where the others were lying dead. The smoke was lifted so we could see a little. We got off our horses and went and took the rings and money and watches from the soldiers. We took some clothes off too, and all the guns and pistols. We got seven hundred guns and pistols. Then we went back to the women and children and got them together that were not killed or hurt.

"It was hard to hear the women singing the death-song for the men killed and for the wailing because their children were shot while they played in the camp. It was a big fight; the soldiers got just what they deserved this time. No good soldiers would shoot into the Indian's teepee where there were women and children. These soldiers did, and we fought for our women and children. White men would do the same if they were men.

"We did not mutilate the bodies, but just took the valuable things we wanted and then left. We got a lot of money but it was of no use.

"We got our things packed up and took care of the wounded the best we could, and left there the next day. We could have killed all the men that got into the holes on the hill, but they were glad to let us alone, and so we let them alone too. Rain-in-the-Face was with me in the fight. There were twelve hundred of us. Might be no more than one thousand in the fight. Many of our Indians were out on a hunt.

"There was more than one Chief in the fight, but Crazy Horse was leader and did most to win the fight along with Kicking Bear. Sitting Bull was right with us. His part in the fight was all good. My mother and Sitting Bull's wife were sisters; she is still living.

"The names of the Chiefs in the fight were: Crazy Horse, Sitting Bull, Lame Deer, Spotted Eagle and Two Moon. Two Moon led the Cheyennes. Gall and some other Chiefs were there but the ones I told you were the leaders. The story that white men told about Custer's heart being cut out is not true." [2]

Flying Hawk was there and he saw and knew. He was last of the survivors of that historic episode, and it is fortunate that coming generations could have a truthful and reliable account from him before he too had passed to the Spirit World Beyond.

Late that afternoon, the Indians set fires to the grass in the valley. Prairie fires are short lived. In less than a few hours, when the clouds of smoke lifted the soldiers could see in the distance the departure of the entire Indian village. Not only were the Sioux and their allies well armed but they were well horsed as well to so effectively disperse. This long, slow procession of ponies and travois headed mainly toward the west, and before darkness set in, not an Indian was in sight. It was the 26th, and Colonel Gibbon was coming south along the Little Big Horn, right on time, and yet, too late.

It was the next day, the 27th, that Colonel Gibbon's men discovered Custer and his command. All the bodies, including Custer's, were buried on the battlefield where they fell. Markers were set to indicate where they were buried. A year later, Company One of Custer's old Seventh Cavalry returned to the battlefield. Custer's body was exhumed and sent to the post cemetery at West Point, the United States Military Academy. The bodies of every officer except one and two civilians were exhumed and sent to the homes of their relatives for reburial. The remaining bodies of the fallen soldiers, those who 'had fallen into camp' of Chief Sitting Bull's vision were exhumed and reburied in one large grave on the top of what is now known as Custer Hill, where they remain to this day.

After this momentous battle, the various bands made off in different directions. Most of them went right back to their fall schedules, gathering lodge poles here, hunting there, and occasionally brushing with the military. Scattered as they were, the army could not bring about effective strikes, but they were a bother to the Indians. Some, on encountering the army, quietly gave up and went back to their reservations, while others kept dodging the soldiers and remained free for another year or two. Sitting Bull sought refuge in Canada for a period of years. Many of his followers became permanent Canadian Sioux. Crazy Horse, after dodging around in the north country and finding his people starving due to the absence of game and buffalo, was finally compelled to return in just over a year. The last great resistance was over, and life on the reservation was about to begin.

Leadership, Size, Tactics and Endurance: Why the Army most often failed in their many battles with the Sioux.

1. *Sioux Leadership.* - Sioux leaders were most often in the thick of combat and wisely used the terrain and even the weather to their advantage. Crazy Horse and Red Cloud earned over 80 coups each. Along with Sitting Bull these leaders were fearless in battle. They were selected as leaders not by politics but by their proven abilities and success in combat encounters.

2. *Conservation of combatants.* - Sioux chiefs generally would retreat and pick a better time when they started to lose in an encounter. The Army had a tendency to throw more men into a losing effort.

3. *The Sioux/Cheyenne Warrior.* - Totally fearless and combat confident. They installed fear and panic in most of the troopers even when numerical odds were not in their (the warrior's) favor. The backgrounds of both adversaries were also in stark contrast. The Sioux/Cheyenne warrior had much more combat experience mainly through fighting other tribes as well as the Army.

"(They) were the best cavalry on earth. In charging toward us they exposed little of their person, hanging on with one arm around the neck and one leg over the horse, firing and lancing from underneath the horses' necks so that there was no part of the Indians at which we could aim." Captain Anson Mills.[1]

4. *Size.* - The average Sioux warrior was often six inches taller than the average cavalry soldier, who was generally selected from the 5 foot 5, to 5 foot 6 range. The Army preferred and selected lighter, uniform sized men for their horses. Most immigrants were much smaller than the Northeastern American tribes where the Sioux originated. In the 1700s to 1900s, primarily because of diet and protein deficiency, European immigrants were considerably smaller, compared to the abundantly fed eastern tribes down through the centuries. The Iroquois, Hurons, Cherokee, as well, were large people. Knight's armor in modern European museums proves the size difference. A modern American woman of today, would not be able to fit into said armor.

5. *Trained and Conditioned Mounts.* - Horses were kept in prime physical condition on an open range primarily by Indian youth, eager to exercise the warrior's battle horses daily for them. Warriors recognized that a slow, unconditioned horse could easily result in death or capture. Army horses were too often kept in garrison or stockades and hence winded much sooner than Sioux/Cheyenne mounts. When the Cavalry would lose their mobility on winded mounts the Sioux warriors were at a tremendous advantage. Endurance was an important factor which the battle chiefs planned upon and played to.

6. *Horsemanship.* - Regarded as the finest light cavalry even by their adversaries. Having both hands free by guiding their mounts with their knees in close combat, was a major reason.

7. *The Horse.* - Gunfire was commonly, almost daily experienced by domestic Plains Horses heavily experienced in buffalo hunting. Children played upon the horses in mock combat games. In actual combat, Sioux horses rarely bolted or threw

their riders whereas many Army horses reared or bucked their riders upon their first encounters. These horses were often captured and retrained as effective war and buffalo hunting horses. Army horses were the major source for Chief Red Cloud's battles. At the Little Big Horn, the entire Sioux/Cheyenne encampment was significantly mounted to be able to disperse effectively in a matter of a few hours.

8. *Captured Weapons.* - Initially the Bow was no match against the muzzle loader yet through decoy tactics Army weapons, ammunition and horses were repeatedly captured. At the Little Big Horn the Sioux and Cheyenne were well armed with modern weapons which, years later, modern metal detectors would prove.

9. ***The Winchester.*** - Rangers at the Little Big Horn battlefield readily admit that the Sioux had the Winchester repeating rifle. The Army troops had no repeating rifles. 200 or more such rifles are estimated to have been in the hands of the Sioux. 200 or more such weapons against 600 single shot cavalry who had to hold onto their bit and rein equipped horses was a tremendous advantage for the Sioux warrior who had both hands free while he was mounted.

10. ***Religious and Spiritual Beliefs.*** - Their Spirituality provided a determined and courageous attitude for the plains warrior. Their Benevolent Creator was not considered fearful, punishing and wrathful. Their belief in a Spirit World was closely tied to family devotion, honor, duty and sacrifice for the tribe, if so needed. Being less fearful of death was a warrior's combat asset. Fighting for freedom and upon their own land was highly inspirational as well.

Curley, the Crow Scout, brings news of the Custer fight to the Steamer Far West
Drawing by Charles M. Russell

Black Elk and the Missionaries

The Spirit World should be a very relieving place, if unalterable Truth is its ultimate atmosphere!

Do Indians have religious prophets? I would consider the Oglala named Black Elk as more of a visionary than as a prophet upon which the white man, both the Christian and the Islamic seem to place a greater reliance. Indians I have known, mostly Sioux, shy away from all-knowing prophecy because they truthfully admit that when dealing with Mystery there are simply too many unknowns. I say that, not looking for argument. It is simply the way and how we have observed upon our own life journeys. It is all that we can offer; what we have experienced and are too respectful, even now, to try and embellish and change its direction.

Exponential Math

From my experience with the white man's proclamations, most seem to be more in error than they are right on. We constantly hear the doomsday predictions which never happen. I personally shy away from so-called prophecy other than what is scientifically obvious such as real facts on over-population and the disasters it can bring. An evidentiary disclosure such as what happened to the folks who over populated Easter Island is an example. They had no choice but to sail away into the vast ocean to save their own lives and thin down the population behind them. Some found other islands and a goodly many, no doubt, perished at sea. When too many billions populate this planet in a short time to come, it will be a much greater calamity. There will be no unpopulated islands to sail off to. Exponential math has its truth. It is the way God has ordained it and there is nothing much we can do about it except beseech to Creator, of course. Whether or not Creator will respond to our own folly, we do not know for sure. Will Creator have Mother Nature continue to respond according to what we observe happening now? If the Extremists clamor with emphatic, "NOs," then what proof do they have? If the waving of their Bibles

Medicine Bundles Burning

(Multiply and subdue the Earth!) goes on for another century or two with no results, and the human race is in deadly throes from planetary heating and an unlivable swelling of the world population by then, what will be their answer then?

Thor Heyerdahl impregnated my mind years ago with his description of Motane Island, a ghost island that once held abundant life, but man had literally killed it and he too had to flee for his survival. Its environmental message is too important to not reappear in this work from an earlier writing.

A Once Lush Island in the South Pacific

Motane was once a thriving island. Before World War II, Thor Heyerdahl wrote of his observations in the book *Fatu-Hiva, Back to Nature.* [1]

The island (Motane) was where modern man had beaten nature. He had entered this South Sea paradise intent on improving conditions for himself and his uncivilized local host. Through bringing plants and domestic animals, he had also upset the whole balance of a life lived in accord with local conditions.

"Failing in his effort to help the islanders in order to benefit from them, white man withdrew from the island as soon as he confronted his own shadow, and the encroaching jungle followed at his heels, often right down to the island shore, until everything it had lost was re-conquered."

Captain Cook estimated a local Polynesian population of one hundred thousand when he ran into the island group in 1773. After him came European settlers, whalers, and missionaries. A good century later, in 1883, the total census was 4,865. By 1920, the population was down to 3,000, mainly due to European germs and living conditions. On Motane, the death rate was so high that not a single survivor had remained to tell the story of what had long since become a ghost island.

The Europeans brought a different living system and they brought disease. "On Motane, local history ended. Perhaps the last surviving Polynesian died on the family's pandanus mat on just this paepae where we were sitting. Perhaps the last desperate family embarked in their canoe to escape to Hivaoa, whose mountain crests could be seen in clear weather. Or perhaps the last survivor was a child left alone between the trees and the animals. We shall never know."

With no humans, the domestic animals ran wild and the sheep were the survivors. With flesh-eating man gone, the sheep of Motane multiplied. Hordes of wild sheep consumed all within reach, and when famine hit them, they devoured the roots of the grass and the bark of the trees turning Motane into a desert. "Motane's biological clockwork had not only stopped, but was set in backward motion, until the hands showed a visitor pretty much what our planet looked like before life emerged from the sea. If the Moana's crew managed to catch the last of the scraggy sheep, then the miniature world we saw from our hilltop would more or less match Planet

Earth, in the period when life was confined to the ocean and the air: the remote era when eroding rock had liberated the first salts and minerals ashore, which, dissolved in water, had combined with sunlight to fill first the ocean and then the air with creatures swimming and flying around the lifeless coasts. But if all the world were reduced like Motane, how many million years would we have to sit alone on our hilltop paepae waiting for algae to be washed ashore and develop into grass and trees once more, or for fish to jump ashore and acquire lungs and legs and fur a second time? The tiny fish we had seen jumping in the surf area on the cliffs of Fatu-Hiva had certainly jumped like that for hundreds of thousands of years, and not one of them was as yet ready to take the first leap on the long road toward kangaroo or monkey. Better to take care of the world we had. It would take a long time to get a new one."

Thor Heyerdahl wrote this passage back before WWII.

Planetary Heating

Planetary heating is now getting some startling proclamations from leading scientists based on real, measured and observed factual data which is convincing to me and yet the white man's religious leaders seem unmoved and many oppose the scientists. According to Bill Moyers in a startling speech to the Center for Health and the Global Environment, Harvard Medical School, they (religious leaders) smugly declare that biblical prophecy is being fulfilled and many are out rightly pleased with the downward environmental spiral of the planet despite the fatal outcome for two-legged which can result. [2] I do wish I had their confidence...if they are right! They could possibly be! For not long ago, the Indians indeed thought that the Benevolent Creator had blessed the wahshichu immensely. No doubt that is why so many tribes readily embraced the white man's religion. They had a more powerful God obviously, as we were constantly beaten back; as simple as that. The buffalo have all but vanished and look at how productive the lands are now! Yes, the white man can offer many convincing counter arguments. It would be a lie, would it not, to not allow his view; his accomplishments? The Oklahoma tribes had little problem changing their spiritual view.

Something inside, however, tells me to support Mr. Moyers, especially when I compare what modern science is observing and warning; this something cannot be denied. I guess that I have become too schooled in the concept of Direct Observation. There is simply too much evidence that planetary heating, thinning ozone, depleted resources, over-population and water scarcity are real. Other environmental topics or subjects also exist beyond these five such as the newly discovered methane emissions from melting permafrost. These catastrophes become more warranted as each succeeding scientific study reveals.

Native Worldview

There is a big difference between Native worldview and White Man's worldview when one compares the influences of each others' religion. If we wish to understand the Red People, the one that kept his Nature-influenced values, is there some man-made rule which states we should not at least attempt to understand their spiritual worldview? I have combined the information offered from old Black Elk with that of his son, Ben Black Elk, the interpreter of every word of the book, *Black Elk Speaks*. Ben was a personal friend and influenced me beginning when I was a child. Even when I was a Marine pilot I would stop and see him when he worked at Mt. Rushmore after landing a military machine at the Ellsworth Air Force base near Rapid City, South Dakota. As military pilots we had to perform cross-country flights as part of our training. I would often choose my hometown which had the convenient military field nearby. At the University of South Dakota I helped bring Ben to the campus wherein he offered several lectures. My close friend by then, beautiful Connie Bowen saw to it that Ben was always comfortably housed. Ben Black Elk was most appreciative. Ben was the interpreter between his father, Nick Black Elk and the writer, John Neihardt who authored the book *Black Elk Speaks* back in the thirties before I was born when this great revelation was written. The book has gone on to many millions of readers and has been printed in numerous languages.

Dances With Wolves

I have often been asked my opinion of the movie, *Dances With Wolves*. I think it presented our culture, our worldview in a far more truthful light than other Hollywood portrayals. The Sioux in that movie came across as deeply respectful of Nature and the Wamaskaskan (the animals). No one cut the heads off the deer, elk and the buffalo, and hung them up in their teepees as the white man does. (The older bulls or bucks should be allowed to live for healthier reproduction because they have proven their immunity to the chronic wasting disease.) Such an odd, arrogant custom the wahshichu has.

The Vision

We have already learned of the powerful vision the elder Black Elk experienced. I will add a brief expansion of that happening without any major elaboration of the Six Powers.

In a time when the tribe enjoyed the freedom of the Great Plains, a powerful vision took place. This event occurred several years before the famous Custer battle, no doubt in the very camp of Oglalas under Chief Crazy Horse's command. A boy named Black Elk was a young boy when he had such an open, understandable vision as it pertained to all of Creator's Nature which surrounds us. It began with the Wamaskaskan, the animal creations, finned, flying and four-legged, all in a myriad of gracious display. Yes, whatever was responsible for such a powerful vision did include the Wamaskaskan. His vision took him into a Rainbow Covered Lodge of the Six Powers of the World.

Two spirit men carried this young boy upward to the Spirit World. On a cloudy plain, thunder beings leaped and flashed. A bay horse appeared and spoke: "Behold me!" The boy walked on toward a cloud that changed into a tipi with a rainbow for an open door. Within, he saw six old men sitting in a row. He was invited to go through the rainbow covered lodge door and told not be fearful.

He went in and stood before the six old men and discovered that they were not old men but were the Six Powers of the World. Of the powers, the West Power, Wiyopeyata, (pronounced with a guttural –we yoke-pee ahh tah) spoke first. When the West Power spoke of understanding, the rainbow leaped with flames of many colors over Black Elk. The West Power gave him a wooden cup filled with water and spoke. "Take this, it is the power to make live." The West Power gave him a bow and spoke. "Take this, it is the power to destroy." The West Power then left and changed to a black horse but the horse was gaunt and sick. This is the way the Vision is best described and for deeply interested readers regarding the spiritual, I suggest any of my previous non-fiction books and of course *Black Elk Speaks* by John Neihardt or *The Sacred Pipe* by J. Epes Brown. Each Power spoke in the above manner.

The Six Powers concept is a helpful tool, an almost essential ingredient to generate an understanding of Nature's Code. Millions of readers are familiar with the concept. The book, *Black Elk Speaks* has sold millions of copies and these in turn have been passed on to numerous other readers. It is printed in numerous languages as well.

John Neihardt

Black Elk intended that the world should know of his vision. Several writers had earlier attempted to secure Black Elk's story but he was not satisfied with them. When John Neihardt came to his cabin, he told Neihardt that he was the one he was waiting for. It was in the fall. Black Elk said that it was too late that year to relate his vision. "You come back when the grass is so high," the holy man held out his hand to indicate the height of spring grass, "and I will tell you my story."

Ben Black Elk interpreted between Neihardt and the holy man, Black Elk. Ben was well satisfied with the finished writing, *Black Elk Speaks*. His satisfaction should dispel the false accusations which have been heaped on John Neihardt as self composing. Here we have the interpreter being very satisfied. Wouldn't one who had ordinary common sense and a bit of intelligence easily discern that a son is generally, usually going to know which are his father's words and which are those of someone else? Especially when he interpreted a long conversation both ways - in English and Lakota! Ben always spoke glowingly of the finished work as, "My Father's book!" It was published in 1932, but at that time there existed so much prejudice and ignorance that it went into remainder and copies were sold for 45 cents apiece. It wasn't until thirty years later that the importance of such a profound vision would be rediscovered, thanks to the interest of Carl Jung and Dick Cavett. The book has now sold well over a million copies and has been printed in many languages, including Japanese.

With Our Own Kind

The reservation missionaries made a strong attempt to dislodge Black Elk's vision and were almost successful. Why? All that I can surmise on their behalf is that it intruded on their belief system as this writing will be judged. It was also quite convincing if one would rely on direct observance of what all surrounded us. Many Sioux know little about it, or they believe the detracting dogma perpetuated against it. That is their loss; my opinion. I harbor little remorse for those who deny direct observation. It is the choice they made while on their Earth journey; a foolish choice; my opinion. Hopefully, there exists a Spirit World in which we can be with our own kind. That categorization, also hopefully, will not be a separation by race or worldly accomplishment, but one of how well we utilized our mind while here upon this journey. How much did we place into this greatest of gifts which Benevolent Creator has designed specifically just for us? Courage, bravery, generosity and sharing - the four cardinal virtues of the Sioux may also have their importance toward our final destination. I deeply hope that when one enters the Spirit World, one will be able to go or be placed with one's own kind. 'According to your truths!' This could be the real 'Heaven or Hell' most of us wonder or ponder about, if we are at all truthful. We will seriously elaborate upon this theme in a latter chapter.

There are many from all walks who are taking a serious look at this vision. Joseph Campbell's remark that this vision is the best example of spiritual imagery is very appropriate. There are many people who have discovered the visible Six Powers of this earth and who are now relating these daily entities in balance, acknowledgement and kinship to their everyday lifestyle. Black Elk lived at a time when Chief Crazy Horse, Chief Red Cloud and Chief Sitting Bull were alive and in power. As I said earlier, I believe that these three leaders we have studied were spiritually respectful men who believed that it was the Six Powers (Shakpeh Ouyea) who regulated the known world to the Sioux under the laws, actions and powers of the Creator, Wakan Tanka, as those leaders understood it.

Canton Insane Asylum

The Canton Indian Insane Asylum was created in 1902 while Black Elk was in his middle age; a time when the United States' official Indian policy was assimilation. The Federal Canton Indian Insane Asylum was built out of brick at Canton, South Dakota, in the eastern part, south of Sioux Falls, the largest South Dakota town. I even have a picture of it sent to me by a Canton township person. It demonstrates how brutal and primitive the mindset of the government officials was, as well as the church people who lobbied for it. Leonard Bruguier says whatever the intent behind the asylum, it was a convenient tool for reservation agents. Bruguier is a member of the Yankton Sioux and was Director of the Institute of American Indian studies at the University of South Dakota.

Many Indians who went into Canton simply disappeared. A large graveyard is now part of the Canton golf course. Some 200 bodies, former patients, are buried between the 4th and 5th fairways.

Bruguier: So in order for the agent to feel more comfortable being surrounded by yes-people, it would be very easy for him to say 'This person's insane,' and have him shipped to Canton to be administered by a whole different set of rules. Basically you'd just be able to get rid of them.' It is alleged that medicine men were also incarcerated with no symptoms whatsoever of 'insanity.' This too was a method to wipe out the old religion. [3.]

Is it any wonder why I am an ardent proponent of the concept of Separation of Church and State? How dangerous life was made for an innocent group of people. Yet, recently a congressional candidate in Minnesota won a house seat with the opposite view. Throughout the nation, this view has elected house and senate seats. I hope that the Sioux

Federal Indian Insane Asylum - Canton, SD

(Lakota/Dakota) never copy the structure of an organized priesthood or ministry. Presently, a medicine man or medicine woman is not a part of any form of organized hierarchy. I commend those Protestant church organizations that have direct control of their clergy through their own immediate membership which includes selection or expulsion of ministers, major church expenditures and property ownership.

Black Elk's 'Conversion'

After the Custer battle Black Elk settled on the Red Cloud Agency. He was a part of the short-lived Ghost Dance and had been in Europe with Buffalo Bill Cody's 'Wild West' shows. Returning to the reservation he took up his call once he found that he had strong healing power. His reputation grew and he had many Tetons coming to him for various afflictions.

In 1902, Black Elk had an experience with a Jesuit missionary, Father Aloysius Bosch, who came upon Black Elk innocently doing a healing ceremony and was promptly set upon by the angry priest from Holy Rosary Mission. The yet young visionary and practicing medicine man had his altar dismantled and sacred objects (peace pipe) thrown on the ground. The burly priest yelled at the Indians in attendance and told them to go back to their camps. This account is partially recorded by Raymond DeMallie, author of *The Sixth Grandfather*, and the negative portions (from an Indian's point of view) have been excluded or told not according to Neihardt's notes. Hilda Neihardt told me personally she was quite set out against DeMallie whom she had given permission to see her father's notes and primarily by this omission to offer the full story. She was extremely disappointed that he omitted key materials in the so-called 'conversion' controversy that modern academics are constantly bringing up regarding Black Elk.

What was omitted was that Aloysius Bosch returned to the mission, and under a clear blue sky, lightning hit the priest's horse and he was thrown from it and died. Another account holds that the lightning killed the horse and broke the priest's leg. Either way, the interfering priest was badly set upon. The Indians naturally believed that the priest should not have been so disrespectful to the Native Way and went on happily with their healing ceremonies. Within a few years of relative peace and freedom, along came Father Lindebner and did the same thing. Black Elk was grasped by the neck and yelled at, "Satan Get Out!" Black Elk was a slight man and not a typical Sioux warrior whom a priest would have a hard time in so subduing. He was also in the throes of despair at the time from the loss of his wife with children to raise. After havng been thrown physically into a wagon by the overreacting Lindebner, S.J. and hauled to the Holy Rosary Mission to be exorcized by one Father Joseph Zimmerman, S.J.; Black Elk was forcefully converted. He was issued a pass for his compliance and now could travel freely upon the reservation. In time, as long as he did the bidding of the missionaries, he could travel to other reservations as well, which he did.

Canton Asylum was in full operation at the time and the Sioux 'Grape Vine' certainly knew of it. Numerous books clamor regarding this superioristic 'conversion', egotistically championed by the likes of Raymond DeMallie, Clyde Holler, and the Jesuit writers, Steltenkamp and Steinmetz. Oddly these men offer little focus on the profoundness of the Vision despite the reference to it from Joseph Campbell to Bill Moyers; **"the best example of Spiritual Imagery!"** Also, none of these academics mention in their writings, the foreboding asylum which waited for medicine people who would not toe the missionary line. More than one holy man was 'converted' to avoid this horrid place and more than one medicine man who would not comply was forever doomed behind the restrictive bars at Canton.

Deloria

Vine Deloria, well-known Yankton Sioux writer, and now deceased, never mentions it (Canton) in his extolling of the 'Big Four', Episcopal breed missionaries, one of whom was his Grandfather. His Great-Grandfather had to kill four Sioux; the white man's God told him so, regarding conversion and the book is thus dedicated. I have to be honest however, and admit that his first and last of these killings, the guilty victims definitely deserved their fate. The breed priests, Lambert, Deloria, Ross and

Walker, who renounced the old Way, are dubbed proudly as the 'Big Four'. Their pictures are in his book, *Singing for a Spirit*, and are dressed in their missionary finery wearing those 'Mickey Mouse' hats that we also saw the Diocesan Catholic priests wear. That is what we Indian youth used to call them. By 1900, '12,000 (Indians) were converted', he proudly states. Evidently the 12,000 disappeared, for the Wakpala mission became a ghost church. Chief Eagle Feather and I used its abandoned basement over a quarter century ago to hold a *Yuwipi* Spirit ceremony heavily attended by spiritually hungry Hunkpapa. DeMallie disrespectfully refers to the *Yuwipi* as a 'conjuring' ceremony. What the reader will discover in later chapters regarding this ceremony is definitely not 'conjuring.' If my Great Spirit told me to go out and kill four Indians to join some new religion, I doubt if I could do it although I have to respect the great-grand father, Saswe, as I said, for taking out the two who deserved their fate.

Vine, Sr.

The following is an interesting note. I was reading a book of Vine's father's the well-known missionary in South Dakota. At the very end, I was totally surprised in finding my name. Vine Sr., stated that he wanted his ashes flown over a particular Dakota area by none other than me, the Sioux pilot, Ed McGaa. Afterwards, he passed away. Maybe, my strong return to my people's old ways as well as my championing of the Return disparaged the fulfillment of Vine, Senior's specific request, by relatives, as I was never contacted. At the time of his writing, however, Vine, Senior, was well aware of my Sun Dance return and public championing of the Old Way. Deep down inside, despite being a converted churchman, he obviously respected my stand to issue such a personally important request.

I can't help but think of the old traditionals however, bleakly attempting to hold onto the old Sioux Way at that time or the ones doomed at Canton Asylum. Reservation missionaries, mostly white ones, had a strong influence on the government agents. Yes, it is interesting how some so-called scholars can omit some hard-core evidence that does not support their egotistical, religious superiority.

Wah ste aloh

I must remind the reader: My spirituality is my choice for myself, but I do not hold it out as superior for your needs or your mindset. I know that sounds highly unusual in this proselytizing, I-know-everything world. My tribe is still intact. Possibly, that is the reason it works for me. Most readers are not specifically from a tribe. Nature will take care of everything, eventually, one way or another, is my reassurance. Simply carry on, care for your offspring, appreciate and be good citizens. If you increase your knowledge base as you are presently attempting to do, then that is well and good, (wah ste aloh) my opinion. Leave it at that. Mystery is mystery and we should definitely not be fighting or arguing over it. Wah- steay- ah- loh!; spoken firmly, it is a very pretty word, and we use it often to compliment.

Prior to Canton being investigated and soon afterwards shut down, Black Elk boldly told of his powerful vision, Standing Bear standing beside him to verify; every word passing through his interpreter son, Ben, while Enid Neihardt, John Neihardt's daughter served as stenographer. John Neihardt listened to every word and often broke into the old man's running conversation to ask a question to verify a particular point. The old man would frequently lapse off into a deep nap, revive, and continue on. The missionaries were greatly disturbed when they discovered they had been omitted from the telling and demanded from Neihardt a copy of his manuscript.

Conversion Squabbles

When asked, by Neihardt, "On what grounds do you make such a demand?" The Jesuits replied that they indeed had a right to such information since Black Elk was now, 'one of theirs'. They also believed that they could then 'edit' on behalf of Black Elk. John Neihardt not being of any particular white man's faith, simply scoffed and refused to deliver. The Jesuits were highly incensed and not used to being rebuffed on what was 'their Sioux reservation,' but little could they do about it. Such was the accustomed pomposity of the reservation missionaries over the Sioux. Later, the writers previously mentioned, came along to seriously distract from this simple yet deep discourse given beside a log cabin in far out Manderson, South Dakota. Author, Julian Rice should also be added to the list of 'conversion squabblers'. All have neglected to explore what I presume to be the major issue of Black Elk; his Vision! The academic writers however, have tied themselves in knots as to what degree Black Elk agreed or did not agree to be converted! I will guarantee an interesting evening, should some University include me in an open meeting or discourse with these writers. 4. See; Review of Clyde Holler's Sun Dance Books and related commentary on other writers by Dr. Dale Stover.

I had the fortunate opportunity to view Susan Zucotti, *Under His Very Windows*, the renowned Jewish scholar debate some Academics regarding Pius XII when 4,000 Jews were rounded up within his view with gunfire outside the Vatican and he lifted nary a finger in protest. They were sent to their deaths at Auschwitz. I think the University Academics owe the same favor to the experienced traditional-supporting Indian writers. Notice, I use the term experienced and will also add - connected; such as; personally knowing tribal medicine people. Dr. Bryde would be an excellent partner. I do have that Juris Doctorate so should qualify academic-wise.

Shouldn't a religion stand for God's ultimate objective; that we sincerely cultivate and practice Truth? I mean, real, real sincerely as if the Creator was right before you and you were about to divulge what you genuinely observed with no alteration, no ulterior motive such as control or just to please someone? Wouldn't a man, about to tell a powerful happening held up inside of him for decades and along with much supporting evidence and a personal friend right there to help verify, and your very own son, to serve as an interpreter: wouldn't this be sufficient enough evidence to pass on to a narrator or a recorder who has the immediate opportunity to question or have repeated what he did not at first comprehend or understand fully? Why would religious outsiders be needed to further the truth of the relating? Why would they want to "edit" this work? Is that how organized religious history has been explained or verified down through time? Actually, yes! Is this what they call the 'sanitation process' or 'political correctness' in order that the control of the people comes first? This thought process is what the Indians faced when they had to deal with the treaties to a high degree, is my opinion. The white world and the Indian world indeed were very separate when it came to basic human understanding and carrying out the full meaning of the word: Truth! The Spirit World should be a very relieving place, if unalterable Truth is its ultimate atmosphere!

As I have said repeatedly in many of my works; I firmly believe that Mother Nature is about to deliver some very ultimate Truths. Why? Because human has allowed himself to be misguided and misdirected by the un-truths which are incompatible with Mother Nature's environment. It is right there in Black Elk's vision: The Blue Man of corruption, deception and greed. The 109th Congress is one of the foulest examples. The world is falling apart all around the Blue Man in the Vision and the Earth Spirit has politely called out to truthful human for help. Now, She is beginning to act forcefully! It can't get more specific. It is as simple as that. Time will certainly tell. Planetary Survival: what will your record be? Once you enter the Spirit World.

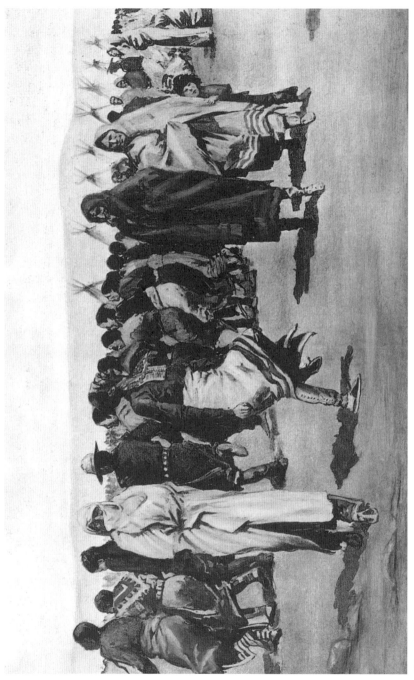

Ghost Dance

Ghost Dance

Beware two-legged - when he makes up prophecy.
Thunder Owl, Mdewakanton Sioux.

It had been fourteen years since the defeat of Custer. After that battle, the various Sioux bands returned to their reservations and tried to settle down, but these were restless and unhappy years. Most of the people knew that further fighting was useless because of the superior number of the soldiers; yet, the desire to wander and follow the buffalo was like a burning thirst in them, even though they knew that there were no more buffalo to follow. Of all the reservation years, these were the hardest, because these were the people who were fresh from the plains and who had grown up in the old way. The next generations to follow, although they would find it hard, would not find it nearly as hard as these who first came off the plains to live on the reservations. Up and coming young warriors who were seventeen and eighteen years old at the time of Custer were now in their early thirties and just reaching their prime as fighters, but they could not fight. The very things they had lived for and had been trained for were removed from them, and they lived in constant frustration.

In their despair and frustration, they were willing to turn to and to believe in anything that would offer them the slightest hope of returning to their old way of life. As we saw in an earlier chapter, the Sioux were a naturally and deeply religious people. In their despair, they prayed and prayed and sought visions from God for guidance and deliverance. They were willing to listen to anyone who claimed to have information from God for a way out of the agony of their frustration. It was at this point that a Paiute Indian by the name of Wovoka entered the scene. No one can understand Wounded Knee without understanding what Wovoka offered for deliverance and how eagerly all the tribes on the plains seized his advice. What Wovoka had to offer was the Ghost Dance, and it was primarily this ghost dance that became the force that shaped Wounded Knee. Many people think that Wounded Knee was simply this: a bunch of soldiers went out to meet some Indians. They surrounded them and tried to take their guns away. When a shot rang out, the soldiers shot most of the Indians down. This is not the complete story of Wounded Knee at all. One has to understand the causes leading up to Wounded Knee (starting a year prior to the massacre) and the causes that brought about the fight that very morning. Mistakes were made on all sides, as we shall see, and one has to understand all these factors in order to have a true picture of Wounded Knee.

The influence of Wovoka began in 1889, just two years before Wounded Knee and many miles from it. Wovoka, as we said, was a Paiute Indian, and he lived in Nevada. His father, Tavibo, had claimed for twenty years to have had visions from God in which he was told that there was a great earthquake coming by which all the non-Indians would be swallowed up, leaving only the believing Indians, who would then be able to go back to their old way of life. It was another of the continual 'Doomsday' predictions. Very few, even among the Paiutes, believed in Wovoka's father.

After the death of his father, Wovoka lived with a non-Indian family who were very religious people regarding the white man's beliefs, and he read the Bible every day. Wovoka himself was very religious and listened eagerly to the stories of the Old Testament. He was especially moved by the deeds and prophecies of the prophets of the Old Testament. The family with whom he lived was named Wilson, and Wovoka even took their name and went sometimes by the name of Jack Wilson.

On January 1, 1889, there occurred an eclipse of the sun which terrified all the Paiutes because, like the Incas of old, they were sun worshippers and they regarded the eclipse as an attack on their God. After the eclipse, Wovoka told the people that God wanted the Indian people to do a certain dance. He told them that on the day the sun died (the eclipse) that he, Wovoka, was taken up into the other world of heaven where he saw God and all the Indian people who had died in the past. Here they were happy, had plenty of game, and enjoyed all their old time sports and joys. God told him that he must go back and tell the Indian people the following:

    a. They must not quarrel with one another, nor quarrel with the non-Indians, but live in peace with everyone;

    b. They must work and not lie or steal;

    c. They must be good and love one another;

    d. They must do away with any thought of going to war again, neither with other Indian tribes nor with the non-Indians;

    e. They must do a sacred dance which he, Wovoka, would teach them;

    f. If they did all these things, they would be united with all their dead friends and relatives in heaven when they died.

This sacred dance would be the Ghost Dance. Since the Indians believed that Wovoka had brought this information from God, they began to regard him as a Messiah, as Jesus was declared by the white man as a "Messiah"—an Anointed One of God. Wovoka himself fell into this and even referred to himself as the Messiah. For this reason, the reaction this had on the other tribes was called the Messiah Craze.

It must be noted clearly that what Wovoka taught the Indian people had nothing of war in it at all. In fact, his teachings were explicitly against war and forbade it. The main hope that Wovoka held out to the people, if they followed his teachings, was that they would be reunited in heaven with all their dead relatives and friends when they died. We shall see that the Sioux added something to the original teachings that was going to cause them much anguish, trouble and needless deaths which would include a famous and respected chief.

The Ghost Shirt

Wovoka had his vision in 1889. News of the vision and Wovoka's teachings spread through the tribes of the plains like a prairie fire. In just a few months, tribes from the Indian territories of Oklahoma, and practically all of the Western tribes sent delegations to Wovoka to get his teachings first hand. The Sioux first heard of Wovoka's teachings through the Cheyennes. The Sioux, as we saw, were naturally religious and over-eager to adapt new religious ideas to their own religion. This natural religious bond, plus their own frustration at losing their way of life, made them seize upon Wovoka's ideas as a starving man would seize offered food.

When the Pine Ridge Sioux learned about Wovoka late in the summer of 1889, they immediately held a great council at Pine Ridge and selected a delegation to go to Wovoka and learn his teachings first hand. The delegation consisted of Yellow Breast, Flat Iron, Good Thunder, and Broken Arm of the Pine Ridge Reservation as well as Kicking Bear from the Cheyenne Agency Reservation. They traveled for five days by train in order to reach Wovoka at Walker Lake, Nevada. On returning, another great council was held to hear their report.

It was from this meeting that a dangerous addition to Wovoka's original teachings was made. It was most likely the Sioux who added the idea of the ghost shirt. Most likely it was Short Bull and Kicking Bear who came up with this idea. The Sioux were told by Kicking Bear and Short Bull that, if they wore this certain shirt called the ghost shirt, it would stop bullets and they would be safe from any attacks by the non-Indians and non-Indian soldiers. By now, there were 30 to 35 tribes containing over 60,000 Indians practicing the Ghost Dance, and the Sioux were the only ones to add the idea of the ghost shirt. This dangerous idea that bullets couldn't hurt them was going to make some of the Sioux eager to fight and it was going to be a provoking factor in causing the outbreak to follow.

After the report of the delegation that had gone to see Wovoka, many of the Pine Ridge Sioux took up the Ghost Dance with enthusiasm. All over the reservation, dances would go on for hours and even days. Some groups were small and other groups were large, but to the non-Indian people on and near the reservation, Indians dancing meant only one thing: a war dance. Few non-Indian people knew that the Indians had all kinds of dances such as religious dances, social dances, and many others, and that to the Indians a war dance was only one of many dances. But, as we said, the non-Indians didn't know this, and when they saw dancing Indians, to them it meant that trouble was coming. They did not know that the Ghost Dance was a religious "prayer dance" and that in dancing the Ghost Dance, the Sioux were actually praying for peace and deliverance, not war.

Indian Agent

At this time, there was a brand new agent on the reservation, Daniel Royer, who had only been in office for a few weeks and who was not at all familiar with Indians. Dancing Indians, to him, meant trouble and as he looked out over the Pine Ridge Reservation, he was terrified at all the dancing that was going on. In a panic, he did a very foolish thing: he sent for soldiers. He sent the following telegram to his superiors, "Indians are dancing in the snow and are wild and crazy. ... We need protection, and we need it now. The leaders should be arrested and confined in some military post until the matter is quieted, and this should be done at once."[1] Thus it was that the two fears fed each other: fear of dancing Indians caused the soldiers to come in and prepare for trouble; fear of the soldiers caused the Indians, to prepare for trouble.

1. Modern Indians. Ghost Dance Chapter

General Brooke

There were already a few soldiers regularly stationed in Pine Ridge, but on November 20, 1890, General John R. Brooke arrived with a huge number of troops consisting of five companies of infantry and three troops of cavalry equipped with one Hotchkiss and one Gatling gun. The stage was set on the Pine Ridge Reservation. Almost three weeks later, something was to happen that would put the events in motion toward the Wounded Knee tragedy. The event, which took place about 250 miles to the northwest of Pine Ridge and which put the northern forces in motion toward Wounded Knee, was the death of Sitting Bull which occurred on December 15, 1890. The death of Sitting Bull frightened a peaceful old chief named Big Foot, and he and his Minicoujou people left their Cheyenne Reservation to camp on the south fork of the Cheyenne River.

The army regarded this leaving as a hostile act and sent orders to Col. Sumner to bring Big Foot back to the Cheyenne Reservation. Col. Sumner had been watching Big Foot for months and knew he was perfectly peaceful but, following orders, he sent an interpreter out to Big Foot's camp to tell him to come back. During the night, however, some of the young warriors talked to Big Foot and told him that, if he went back, the same thing might happen to him that happened to Sitting Bull. They persuaded him to slip away and head for Pine Ridge. Big Foot also had another reason for going to Pine Ridge. His Minicoujou people had been practicing the Ghost Dance, and the fact that some of the Indians who had been killed with Sitting Bull were wearing ghost shirts at that time shook his faith in the Ghost Dance. He wanted to go to Pine Ridge to talk to Chief Red Cloud about the Ghost Dance and the ghost shirts and to get his advice. The moment he slipped away, he was declared hostile, and the soldiers on the Pine Ridge end were alerted to his coming. Red Cloud, at this time, was beginning to be quite dubious as to the merits of the 'bullet-proof' claim and the frenzied attention it was drawing.

When General Brooke in Pine Ridge received this news of the probable arrival of Big Foot and his band at Pine Ridge he sent out Major Whiteside with a force of soldiers to find Big Foot before he could reach Pine Ridge. The authorities on the Pine Ridge end, thinking that Big Foot was hostile, didn't want any hostile group coming and stirring up the Pine Ridge Sioux. As it was, the Pine Ridge Sioux were stirred up enough by the Ghost Dance movement, and the army feared that any hostile group coming in might be the spark that would set off the powder keg. It was the plan of the army, therefore, to find Big Foot, take his guns away, and hustle him back to his home base before his group could get together with any of the Pine Ridge groups.

Major Whiteside

Heading out from Pine Ridge in a northeasterly direction, Major Whiteside sent scouts out ahead to find Big Foot's band, promising twenty-five dollars to the first scout who found them. The scouts did not find Big Foot's band; on the contrary, Whiteside's scouts were watering their horses in a stream north of Porcupine when they suddenly found themselves surrounded by Minicoujou scouts. The Minicoujous took the scouts to Big Foot who had become very ill from pneumonia during the trip and who was traveling in a wagon. From these scouts, Big Foot learned that Major Whiteside was camped near Wounded Knee Creek and he told the scouts to go back and tell Whiteside that he was coming in to see him and that he wanted no trouble.

When the scouts returned and told this to Whiteside, he took his 225 men and 10 officers and rode up to meet Big Foot's band that was now slowly moving toward Wounded Knee Creek. At a big hill called Porcupine Butte, he met the band slowly coming toward him with the warriors in the lead. Taking no chances, Whiteside fanned his men out in battle formation in front of the band and ran his two cannons out in front of the line. The Minicoujous kept coming, and the warriors spread out in a skirmish line. Some of the warriors got off their horses and tied up the tails of their ponies in preparation for a fight. Others of the Minicoujou warriors raced back and forth, waving their rifles and giving their war cries. It was a tense moment, and fighting could have broken out at any moment if anyone on either side had made a false move. Behind the Minicoujou warriors came Big Foot's wagon with a white flag attached to it.

Whiteside's orders were to disarm the band and to bring them in as soon as possible. He had originally planned to do that as soon as he saw the band. Now, however, with the warriors riding up and down ready to go into action at the slightest provocation, his scouts pointed out to him that this was impossible right now. He just could not send word to those heated up warriors to put down those guns, get off their horses, give them up, and come walking along behind him. Whiteside rode up to Big Foot's wagon and told the chief that he wanted him and his band to go with him to Wounded Knee Creek and to camp there for the night. Big Foot said that that was exactly what he had planned to do anyway, and so the Minicoujous surrounded by the soldiers made their way slowly to Wounded Knee Creek where they camped for the night. The soldiers surrounded the Indian camp so closely that no Indian could slip out and escape. The army set up a special, large tent with a stove in it for the ailing Big Foot, and Whiteside sent a doctor to treat him.

Forsyth

The next morning Col. James W. Forsyth arrived with more soldiers and took command of the military operation to disarm the Minicoujous. Altogether, he had about 500 soldiers, and the Minicoujous, men, women, and children, numbered about 350 to 400, with about 100 to 150 of them warriors. Since they so greatly outnumbered the Minicoujous, Forsyth did not think they would try any fighting, but he was taking no chances. On the hill overlooking Wounded Knee Valley, four Hotchkiss guns had been mounted. These were small, cannon-like guns which could rapidly shoot shells that weighed two pounds and ten ounces and which exploded on hitting. They could shoot effectively for a distance close to a mile. Most of the Indians knew that any kind of resistance was impossible, but they hadn't reckoned on some very die-hard ghost shirt wearers who had their shirts on under their blankets and who still believed that the shirts would stop the bullets.

On the morning of December 29, 1890, after both sides had eaten breakfast, Colonel Forsyth sent Major Whiteside into the Indian camp to get down to the business of disarming the Minicoujous. The Eyapaha or camp crier, named Wounded Hand, was sent throughout the Indian camp to announce that all the men were to assemble in front of Big Foot's tent for a council. When the men had come together, it was explained to them that they must go get their guns and put them into a pile by Big Foot's tent. The soldiers remembered clearly all the gleaming rifles that they had seen the day before when they first met the Minicoujou warriors drawn up in battle formation in front of the rest of their band. Also, the testimony of many of the Indians after the massacre indicates that, though many carried very old guns that weren't much good, there were also many who had Winchester repeating rifles and carbines.

Most rifles, especially the older models, came from the Army, in the first place. More than one skirmish or contest had been won by the Sioux who mostly out horsed the soldiers on their sturdier and better conditioned mounts. Soldiers on spent, winded mounts, soon lost their weapons. Sioux horses were not kept in confining stockades. They were used to being ridden and often. Even the children played their part in keeping the Sioux mounts superbly conditioned.

Note: The Winchester: In 1858, a Winchester Arms Company rifle mechanic, named Henry devised a new rifle with a 15 cartridge magazine. The gun was operated by moving the trigger lever down and back to its original position. This extracted the spent cartridge, carried a fresh shell from the spring-activated tubular magazine into the chamber, and cocked the hammer ready for firing.

The rifle sold well, and in 1866 the Winchester Repeating Arms Company was established at New Haven, Connecticut. Soon afterwards an improved version of the 'Henry' rifle was produced. It was however the 1873 model that was the most successful Winchester. Over the next 40 years the company sold 720,610 of these rifles. That would be about 144 of these rifles per Teton warrior; and there were those idiots who expected the Sioux to keep on fighting and hence condemned Chief Red Cloud for realizing that further resistance after the Treaty of 1868 signing would eventually see the Sioux forces overwhelmed.

When the warriors were told to get their rifles and pile them up, they began talking among themselves as to what they should do. They finally decided to send two men in to talk to Big Foot and ask him what they should do about giving up their guns. Big Foot, after thinking a minute, instructed them to give up only their bad guns. These guns were used for hunting. Without them the people would have a hard time subsisting for there was still much game, mainly deer and antelope upon the plains. In the creeks and river breaks, mule deer and white tail were yet numerous. One of Forsyth's interpreters who had gone along with the two men understood what Big Foot had said and he advised them to give up the good guns too. "You can buy guns," the interpreter said, "but if you lose a man, you cannot replace him." Big Foot answered, "No, we will keep the good guns."

The two men went back and told the others what the chief had said. Instead of sending all the men at once back to their camp, Forsyth sent them back to get their guns in groups of twenty. The first twenty to come back brought back two broken and very old rifles and laid them down. In regard to the surrendered guns, an observer later said, "They were long used, no doubt, as toys are by children, but they formed no part of the splendid Winchesters owned by the warriors." As each group of twenty came back, similar old rifles were put on the pile, and the soldiers could see that they were getting nowhere.

Forsyth had Big Foot carried out to tell the warriors to give up their good guns. This was a huge mistake on the part of Forsyth. Big Foot said that they had no more guns, as they had been seized by the soldiers when they were back at the Cheyenne River Agency. Forsyth then asked Big Foot where all those guns were that the soldiers saw the day before when they first met the Minicoujous by Porcupine Butte. Big Foot just repeated that the guns that his warriors surrendered were all the guns that they had.

Finally, Forsyth saw that the only thing he could do was to search the camp, as well as the men and women in it, most of who were covered with blankets under which it would be quite easy to conceal a rifle. It wasn't long before the good guns began to show up. Warriors who had not wanted to take any chances on losing their guns had left them with their women to hide. The women tried every trick they could think of. Some sat on the ground with their wide skirts spread out over the guns. One elderly grandmother was lying on the ground apparently quite sick as she indicated by her moaning. Under her was found a Winchester repeater. Some guns were found inside wall pockets of the tipis, while others were found packed in the wagons for the trip to Pine Ridge. To avoid any accusations of indelicacies involving the Indian women, enlisted men were not permitted to go inside the tipis; only officers were allowed to do this.

Yellow Bird

It was during this tipi to tipi search, which took considerable time, when the first mistake was made on the Indian side. The one responsible for this mistake was the old medicine man, Yellow Bird. He was a firm believer in the Ghost Dance and the bullet-stopping power of the ghost shirt. As both men and women grew restless during the search for guns, Yellow Bird began dancing around the warriors, singing and occasionally picking up a handful of dust and throwing it into the air in the direction of the soldiers. He kept yelling at the warriors, apparently urging them to do something. Yellow Bird kept this up during the long search for weapons, and the warriors grew increasingly more restless. Finally, one of the army interpreters told Col. Forsyth what Yellow Bird was trying to do and what he was saying to the warriors. "Don't be afraid," he kept telling them. "Let your hearts be strong to meet what is before you. We all know that there are lots of soldiers around us and they have lots of bullets, but I have received assurance That Their Bullets Cannot Penetrate Us. The prairie is large and the bullets will not go toward you. The bullets will not penetrate you." 2. Forsyth gave orders to an interpreter to tell Yellow Bird to sit down and keep quiet, and, after Yellow Bird had completed his latest circle around the warriors, he sat down and lapsed into silence. 2. Modern Indians- Ghost Dance chapter.

In the meantime, the tipi to tipi search was coming to an end. The search had turned up 38 rifles, but most of them were old and not much good. Only a few of the rifles that had been found were Winchester repeaters. The rest of the rifles that the soldiers had clearly seen the day before on first meeting Big Foot's band remained to be found. Since the whole camp and all the women had been searched, there was only one place left where those repeating rifles could be, and that was under the blankets of the warriors themselves. Through an interpreter, Forsyth told the warriors that he did not want to conduct a personal search, but wanted each warrior to come forth like a man, remove his blanket, and put any concealed gun on the ground. About twenty of the older men said, "Hau," got up, and moved toward the Colonel. The younger warriors made no move to comply and Yellow Bird jumped up and began yelling at them again, whirling around and throwing dust into the air. After the older men had passed between the soldiers, removing their blankets and revealing no weapons, Major Whiteside and Lt. Varnum started passing the young men between them. From the very first three who went past, they found two rifles and a quantity of ammunition. At this, Yellow Bird became more excited, and Philip Wells, one of the interpreters, got Big Foot's brother-in-law to try to calm him down, but with no success.

Black Coyote

At this moment, one of the Minicoujous named Black Coyote, seeing that his rifle was going to be discovered, 'took it out from under his blanket and began to wave it around over his head.' Turning Hawk, one of the survivors, explained later that Black Coyote was a "crazy man, a young man of very bad influence and, in fact, a "nobody." 3. Joseph Horn Cloud and Dewey Beard also explained later that he was also deaf. Black Coyote kept yelling that the rifle belonged to him, that he had paid much money for it, and that he wasn't going to give it up unless he was paid for it. Two soldiers approached and tried to take it away from him. In this struggle, the gun went off in the air. At this moment, Yellow Bird leaped to his feet, let out a fearful yell, and threw a handful of dirt into the air. Immediately, the camp was in an uproar as the soldiers instinctively returned fire. Bullets of the soldiers that missed Indians hit other soldiers, and bullets fired by Indians at the soldiers hit other Indians. Wild confusion followed with smoke and dust making it hard to see who was who. Big Foot was killed in one of the first volleys. In the beginning, the soldiers who had been surrounding the Indians were afraid to fire because many of their own men were still mixed up with the Minicoujous. Captain Gapron, one of the officers commanding the Hotchkiss guns, noticed that one of the gunners was so nervous that he was afraid the man would fire out of sheer excitement. He ordered the friction primer removed from the gun so that it couldn't be fired at the troops. As the groups separated, the surrounding soldiers opened fire, and the Hotchkiss guns on the hill did enormous damage. In the smoke, dust and confusion, old men, women, and children were killed and wounded. Since many of the Indian men and women were wrapped in blankets, it was difficult to tell the men from the women in the confusion of the fight. When a warrior went down, the one nearest to him, man or woman, would seize his rifle and begin to fire back. The soldiers, seeing only the flash of the rifle and a blanket covered figure through the dust and smoke, fired back, and a number of women were killed in this manner. Dewey Beard, an Indian survivor, remembered later only the glint of brass buttons through the murk of the confused fighting. 3. Modern Indians, G D Ch.

Smoke and Dust

The fight with the Minicoujous and the soldiers all mixed up together in the smoke and dust lasted about five minutes and, to this day, it is impossible to tell who killed whom. During this time, soldiers very likely killed as many soldiers as Indians killed Indians. After this first five minutes, the Indians broke for cover, joined by their women and children, and the soldiers, who had been in the camp, headed for their original positions outside the camp. Later on, an officer said that he admired the way in which the Indians handled their Winchesters. These apparently were the good guns that Big Foot told his people to save.

The cannons silenced the fire from the camp shortly after both sides ran for cover. Only a few Indians, who had taken refuge in the tipis and fighting from there, had remained. Yellow Bird was one of these, and he had sought shelter in one of the Sibley tents that had belonged to the scouts. From here, by slitting a hole in the canvas wall, he shot several soldiers before someone noticed where the fire was coming from. Cavalrymen riddled the tent with bullets and a Hotchkiss gun fired two shells directly into it. Later, Yellow Bird's charred body was found within the remains of the tent. The main and final action now moved down to the dry creek where most of the warriors had followed the women and children for shelter. A Hotchkiss gun was moved down from the hill to zero in on the gulch because "bullets were coming like hail from the Indians' Winchesters," as Corporal Paul Weinert was to recall later. "The wheels of my Hotchkiss gun were bored full of holes and our clothing was marked in several places. Once a cartridge (weighing two pounds) was knocked out of my hand just as I was about to put it in the gun, and it's a wonder it didn't explode. I kept going farther, and pretty soon everything was quiet at the other end of the line."

With the main fighting over, one by one, wounded people started coming out of the dry creek and, helped by the soldiers, made their way to the hospital area set up north of the cavalry camp. Phillip Wells was one of those who went down to the village to see how many wounded could be helped. About a dozen people were badly wounded, but still alive. One of the wounded survivors named Frog was being helped from the village area when he saw a burned Indian body lying within what had once been an army tent. Looking around for someone who could speak Indian, he saw Phillip Wells, one of the interpreters. He called Wells over and asked, "Who is the man lying burned there?" Wells told him that it was Yellow Bird. Later, Wells related that Frog raised himself up a little higher, raised his closed fist, pointing it in the direction of the dead Indian, shot out his fingers (which among the Indians is a deadly insult meaning I could kill you and not be satisfied doing it. I am sorry that I could not do no more to you), and then used words trembling which I could not catch. But he said this, which I did hear, speaking as though to the dead man: "If I could be taken to you, I would stab you," and then turning to me he said, "He is our murderer; only for inciting our young men, we would have all been alive and happy."

The disarming of the Indians was the main mistake. Later, an Army General, General Miles would have sense enough not to attempt the same as Forsyth in a related situation. They had always had their arms for hunting and to give up your hunting rifle, especially a coveted Winchester was a difficult thing to do especially for a hungry people who needed to supplement other rations from what game still remained. To give up your source for food procurement especially to one who constantly lied to you and whom you could not trust, yes, would be a difficult thing to do. Had Major Whiteside been in command, from his actions the day before; refusing to demand the Minicoujous guns, quite possibly he may have used wiser protocol on the fateful morning compared to Forsyth's mistake.

The fighting had lasted a little over an hour and when it was over, 146 Minicoujous were counted dead and were later buried. The dead Included 84 men and boys, 44 women, and 18 children. These were not the total Indian dead and wounded, because many others were carried off by surviving Indian relatives and friends. It was, therefore, impossible to make a count of these. Fifty-one wounded Indians were taken to the Pine Ridge hospital and, of these, at least seven died later, mainly because, out of fear, they would not let the army doctors treat them. Thus, the total known Minicoujou dead numbered 153. Very few of Big Foot's people escaped death or at least injury. Among the non-Indians, there were twenty-five dead and thirty-nine wounded.

In asking the question, "What caused Wounded Knee?" one would like to be able to point his finger at one single thing and say "This caused it, or that caused it." In the case of Wounded Knee, this is impossible, because there were a number of things causing it, and each one of these things could not have caused it alone. Each one of the factors involved, leading up to the final tragedy, depended on one or several other factors.

All the Factors

Therefore, one cannot point to any one thing and say that it was the cause. To explain Wounded Knee fully, one has to point to all the factors involved and to note their connections.

Wounded Knee was brought about by:

a. Wovoka.

b. Kicking Bear's and Short Bull's invention of the Ghost Shirt protection.

c. Forsyth's attempt to disarm the Sioux of their weapons and hunting rifles. Why did the Army have to have the Indians hunting rifles? No soldier had been killed, at least in any significant numbers since the Custer battle, 14 long years earlier, wherein most every one will or should agree that Custer deserved his fate. Because Indians are doing a superstitious dance is the reason to disarm them? Even an Army General wisely would not carry through with this request under similar circumstances less than a month later when 4,000 angry Sioux decided to finally come back into the settlement of Pine Ridge from their holdout in the Badlands.

d. Yellow Bird's obsessed, blind faith in Wovoka, Kicking Bird and Short Bull and the 'bullet-proof' power of the ghost shirts and hence stirring up the young braves.

e. Federal Indian Policy of not honoring their Treaties. This Policy of Greed culminated in the frustration of the people for the preceding 14 years which, in turn, goaded them to strike out at almost any provocation, plus Yellow Bird's inciting the warriors, plus the presence of the soldiers.

f. Federal Indian Agents 'Jumping at the Gun': Their over-reaction to the Indian's Ghost Dance participation

g. All these factors working tgether and influencing one another caused Wounded Knee, and one does not have a true picture of the tragedy unless he sees all these connections.

Chief Flying Hawk

Chief Flying Hawk had this to say about the Great Chief of the Sioux (Red Cloud) in his contest with the Federal armies; he called him the Red Man's George Washington.

After the Custer fight and when the Indians were starving, and then Wounded Knee, Red Cloud made a speech about it. [3]

Chief Red Cloud's Speech

"I will tell you the reason for the trouble. When we first made treaties with the Government, our old life and our old customs were about to end; the game on which we lived was disappearing; the whites were closing around us, and nothing remained for us but to adopt their ways. The Government promised us all the means necessary to make our living out of the land, and to in-struct us how to do it, and with abundant food to support us until we could take care of ourselves. We looked forward with hope to the time we could be as independent as the whites, and have a voice in the Government.

"The army officers could have helped better than anyone else but we were not left to them. An Indian Department was made with a large number of agents and other officials drawing large salaries - then came the beginning of trouble; these men took care of themselves but not of us. It was very hard to deal with the Government through them - they could make more for themselves by keeping us back than by helping us forward.

"We did not get the means for working our lands; the few things they gave us did little good.

"Our rations began to be reduced; they said we were lazy.

"That is false. How does any man of sense suppose that so great a number of people could get work at once unless they were at once supplied with the means to work and instructors enough to teach them?

"Our ponies were taken away from us under the promise that they would be replaced by oxen and large horses; it was long before we saw any, and then we got very few. We tried with the means we had, but on one pretext or another, we were shifted from one place to another, or were told that such a transfer was coming. Great efforts were made to break up our customs, but nothing was done to introduce us to customs of the whites. Everything was done to break the power of the real Chiefs.

"Those old men really wished their people to improve, but little men, so-called Chiefs, were made to act as disturbers and agitators. Spotted Tail wanted the ways of the whites, but an assassin was found to remove him. This was charged to the Indians because an Indian did it, but who set on the Indian? I was abused and slandered, to weaken my influence for good. This was done by men paid by the Government to teach us the ways of the whites. I have visited many other tribes and found that the same things were done among them; all was done to discourage us and nothing to encourage us. I saw men paid by the Government to help us, all very busy making money for themselves, but doing nothing for us.

"Now, do you suppose we saw all this? Of course we did, but what could we do? We were prisoners, not in the hands of the army but in the hands of robbers. Where was the army? Set to watch us but having no voice to set things right. They could not speak for us. Those who held us pretended to be very anxious about our welfare and said our condition was a great mystery. We tried to speak and clear up that mystery but were laughed at as children.

"Other treaties were made but it was all the same. Rations were again reduced and we were starving--sufficient food not given us, and no means, to get it from the land. Rations were still further reduced; a family got for two weeks what was not enough for one week. What did we eat when that was gone? The people were desperate from starvation - they had no hope. They did not think of fighting; what good would it do; they might die like men but what would the women and children do?

"Some say they saw 'the Son of God. I did not see Him. If He had come He would do great things, as He had done before. We doubted it for we saw neither Him nor His works. Then General Crook came. His words sounded well but how could we know that a new treaty would be kept better than the old one?

"For that reason we did not care to sign. He promised that his promise would be kept - he at least had never lied to us.

"His words gave the people hope; they signed. They hoped. He died. Their hope died with him. Despair came again. Our rations were again reduced. The white men seized our lands; we sold them through General Crook but our pay was as distant as ever.

"The men who counted [census] told all around that we were feasting and wasting food. Where did he see it? How could we waste what we did not have? We felt we were mocked in our misery; we had no newspaper and no one to speak for us. Our rations were again reduced.

"You who eat three times a day and see your children well and happy around you cannot understand what a starving Indian feels! We were faint with hunger and maddened by despair. We held our dying children and felt their little bodies tremble as their soul went out and left only a dead weight in our hands. They were not very heavy but we were faint and the dead weighed us down. There was no hope on earth. God seemed to have forgotten.

"Someone had been talking of the Son of God and said He had come. The people did not know; they did not care; they snatched at hope; they screamed like crazy people to Him for mercy; they caught at the promise they heard He had made.

"The white men were frightened and called for soldiers. We begged for life and the white men thought we wanted theirs; we heard the soldiers were coming. We did not fear. We hoped we could tell them our suffering and could get help. The white men told us the soldiers meant to kill us; we did not believe it but some were frightened and ran away to the Bad Lands. The soldiers came. They said: 'Don't be afraid - we come to make peace, not war.' It was true; they brought us food. But the hunger--crazed who had taken fright at the soldiers' coming and went to the Bad Lands could not be induced to return to the horrors of reservation life. They were called hostiles and the Government sent the army to force them back to their reservation prison." [4]

Was the Ghost Dance a part of Sioux culture? Historically it happened. It can not be denied but it was short lived, very short lived. Chiefs Sitting Bull and Red Cloud did not take part in it and Chief Big Foot was rather skeptical once he received news of Sitting Bull's death.

The 'bullet-proof' ghost shirt was a conjuration of the two aforementioned Siouxs, Kicking Bear and Short Bull. It had no connection to the major Sioux ceremonies listed earlier in this work. I would consider it as a tragic, misleading historical episode which began through the invention of two men. It portrayed no spiritual credibility in comparison to what one experiences in the major Sioux ceremonies we will now study in the following chapter. I leave it with the quote found at the beginning of this chapter:

'Beware two-legged - when he makes up prophecy.' Thunder Owl, Mdewakanton.

Sun Dance

The Sun Dance in hot July or August for four days without food or water and the Vision Quest on Spirit Mountain or a Bad Lands butte are the two most grueling yet confidence building ceremonies a person can endure if you truly seek the Spiritual.

10

Church, Temple, Mosque or Sweat Lodge?

Beseechment to Creator

Beseechment or Ceremony should offer a deeper look into the Sioux mindset. Ceremony is merely human's attempt at some form of communication into a Spirit World, so to speak, or an attempt to express respect, appreciation and communication to one's concept of Higher Power. When Christians or Muslims go to their churches or mosques, a Sioux presumes that these folks are going to attempt to communicate to their Higher Power. Likewise they would hold the same precepts for the Jewish folks who attend their temples. Religion basically is the same all over the world but unfortunately most sects refuse to accept this obvious fact. Too bad, human's ego can so quickly make lethal, resources-consuming wars out of it.

For the sake of attempting a realistic approach toward understanding of a Nature-based culture, let us view what I consider as the major ceremonies held by tribal people among the Great Plains. Each ceremony is distinct. Each had its role when the tribe was yet free upon the plains. Modern traditionalists now depend upon these ceremonies to keep their Spirit Path intact. Remember this well. They had several thousand years to perfect their beseechment methods. Obviously they honed these communications fairly well judging from the results you are discovering and what you will further glean in the remaining chapters.

In my opinion, the most important 'ceremony' is your own inner thoughts which one advances daily upon one's journey while here upon the planet. If one never attempts a formal ceremony yet steadily contemplates toward one's Higher Power and includes the well-being of the planet and its inhabitants, as I hope most people do, one can 'get along' so to speak without ceremony. Most people including many plains Indians never attend tribal ceremony. Ceremony however, brings a vast enrichment into your life. I will never regret the many ceremonies I have been so privileged to experience.

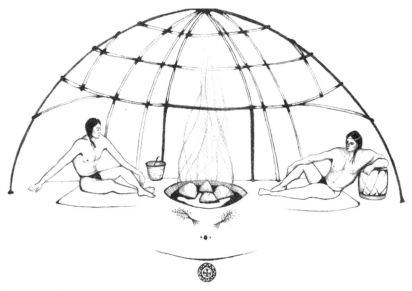

Sweat Lodge

The formal ceremonies:
 Sweat Lodge
Vision Quest
Pipe Ceremony
Yuwipi Spirit Calling
Sun Dance
Give Away Ceremony (Ceremony for a departed mate).

Ceremony

What is ceremony? It could be described as a gathering of people to beseech, respect, acknowledge, thank or recognize their concept of the Great Spirit or their Higher Power. Down through time, people of all tribes held ceremony. Ceremony was not performed only by Native Americans. Tribal peoples world-wide beseeched or gathered in groups to solicit communication to their Higher Power. Celtic people beseeched to the Higher Force through the Four Directions long before the age of Columbus.

Those Sioux who respect and are aware of Black Elk's vision recognize the Six Powers as integral to life for all living entities upon this planet. In ceremony, these entities are called upon or recognized. In all of the ceremonies that I observed Chief Fools Crow and Chief Eagle Feather conduct, these entities were always recognized, yet the main indication to me was that both renowned holy men were beseeching to the Great Spirit, Wakan Tanka.

Vision Quest, Sweat Lodge and Sun Dance

Specific ceremonies for the lone individual, the group beseeching together or a specific ceremony for a large gathering are as follows:

Vision Quest is the one ceremony designed for the lone individual.

A group ceremony would be Sweat Lodge, the Give-away ceremony or the mysterious Yuwipi ceremony (the Spirit Calling). The Oh do huh- the Give Away ceremony, generally is practiced a year after the death of a departed mate and may be designated as a group ceremony.

A larger ceremony in numbers of participants and on-lookers would be the tribal Sun Dance. All ceremonies beseech to Creator or to Creator's forces or as some say, the Spirit Helpers. The Four Directions or Six Powers are generally included in these beseechments as well.

The Sioux, the Lakota/Dakota people, were the last of the big tribes to come in from their natural freedom on the plains. Consequently, they retained more of their culture, more of their religious ways than those tribes that have spent several centuries under the rule of the dominant culture. Other tribes do not like to hear this or admit this fact but if ego can be shed, it allows us to understand why the Sioux have retained so much more of their culture in relation to most other tribes. The Navajo, Apache, Hopi and the Pueblo tribes have also retained their language, culture and religion. The geography of their lands allowed them a high degree of privacy and less intrusion from the dominant society. For centuries, however, the patriarchal and too often exploitive and brutal Spanish Church has exerted a strong influence among the Pueblo and the Navajo. The Pueblo suffered severely under the close scrutiny of the Spanish church for a period of time and even recently, many of their ceremonies were opened in conjunction with Catholic priests. I saw this with my own eyes on a trip to the Southwest. The Mormon Church has made deep inroads among the Navajo.

In Sioux history, and from the perspective of the famous visionary Black Elk, a holy woman appeared to one of the Sioux bands. Many believed this episode happened when the Sioux were entering the Great Plains and leaving what is presently Minnesota. It may have happened when they were close to the pipe stone quarries which are still worked in southwestern Minnesota. The woman was called the Buffalo Calf Woman and taught the people the use of the pipe in seven sacred ceremonies.

These ceremonies were:
1. The Sweat Lodge
2. The Vision Quest
3. The Sun Dance
4. The Making of Relatives
5. The Keeping of the Soul
6. The Womanhood Ceremony
7. The Throwing of the Ball

These ceremonies are explored in detail through Black Elk's words as told to Joseph Epes Brown who later wrote *The Sacred Pipe*. These seven ceremonies were actually banned by the Federal Government; among them were the Sun Dance and the Keeping of the Soul ceremony. Times change, however, and at present, two ceremonies, the Peace Pipe ceremony and the Spirit Calling ceremony, are practiced more frequently than two of the original ceremonies listed above. Not that they were superseded by the seven ceremonies of the Buffalo Calf Woman, as mentioned earlier. I have a supposition that it was the Yuwipi or the Spirit Calling ceremony that warned and led the tribe to make their initial exodus to avoid the early white man many centuries ago. Most Northern tribes had versions of this ceremony which called into the Spirit World beyond. Of course, white man's religious leaders vigorously brand any and all Indigenous spiritual methods of spiritual communication as mumbo jumbo and heretical. That is their problem, not ours. They do not and obviously will not have such capability; therefore they have to resort to untruth in their relentless attempts to discredit. It will be interesting to observe them once they enter the Spirit World.

Some ceremonies have changed very little and their essence or meaning remain the same. The Pipe ceremony is probably the most popular of the Sioux ceremonies in this day and the Sweat Lodge could well be the second most popular ceremony or a ceremony that more people, many of them non-Indians, have become familiar with. Often a pipe ceremony or a ceremony beseeching to the four directions will be within a major ceremony such as a Sweat Lodge, the Sun Dance or a Yuwipi (spirit calling) ceremony. I call the newer category, listed below in terms of popularity or participation, the Seven Mother Earth ceremonies. If practiced, they can convey a meaningful connection in establishing a spiritual relationship with Mother Earth and all of the rest of the Great Spirit's creation. I use my own personal terminology simply to emphasize a later time and the higher frequency of ceremonial practice or usage that these ceremonies have proven to exhibit. Tribal people are free to apply their own terminology.

These Mother Earth ceremonies are:
1. The Pipe Ceremony
2. The Sweat Lodge
3. The Vision Quest
4. The Sun Dance
5. The Making of Relatives
6. The Giveaway
7. The Yuwipi Spirit Calling.

Ceremonies have a wide range. The Vision Quest is for a lone individual and takes place in an isolated area. The lone vision quester usually beseeches up on a mountain, a hill or on a badland butte. The participant is attempting to commune with the Great Spirit and often receives communication through the lesser entities that are created by the Great Spirit. The vision quester seeks direction, guidance and spiritual advice for his or her earth journey. Maybe a bear or another animal will appear in their dreams while they are on the mountain and maybe the bear will have words. Maybe a real live bear will come by, or an eagle or another winged, or four-legged will appear close by or maybe the winged will hover right over the vision quester in a most unusual manner. I have had such an eagle experience while vision questing on Bear Butte Mountain. These acts would be considered symbolic and also convey acknowledgement from the natural world.

I have mentioned elsewhere in this writing but it is worth repeating: Did not the white man's Jesus Christ go out into Mother Earth and fast and pray for many days, isolated and alone and therefore could be considered as Vision Questing? Did not Moses do the same, much earlier in time? I respectfully supposition that Mohammed, who was also devout and deeply spiritual, did he not pray and beseech at times in a like manner to his Higher Power? I find it disturbing that the religious leaders of these faiths, except for a few Indian reservation Jesuit priests, never have the courage or deep respect to do likewise. Yet, they adamantly proclaim to the masses to follow their personal example. The ones I have observed are far more focused toward filling their purses than following the true footsteps of the religious leaders they so ardently proclaim to follow.

The Sun Dance is opposite from Vision Quest in that in this ceremony, in the not too distant past, the whole tribe would gather out in a spacious area to camp and be together. The tribe would offer their annual thanksgiving to the Creator for all that it has provided. This obviously was quite pleasing to Wakan Tanka, Great Spirit. The memorable Lone Cloud Sun Dance that I personally viewed is adequate proof to me. To be annually thankful in a four day display of thanksgiving seems a bit more appropriate than sitting down and having a large turkey meal and calling that event one's annual Thanksgiving. We are so divorced from true appreciation to Creator in this modern age. Does Creator miss those super sincere folks of the past who roamed this continent? One would think so. Maybe the heating of the planet and the consumed, lost resources caused primarily by foolish over-population will bring about such tragic consequences that the survivors will indeed learn dearly what they should have appreciated.

In modern times, it is a community or a certain medicine person's following that will gather to view a Sun Dance. Relatives of the Sun Dance pledgers will most certainly be there. I am making plans to attend my nephew's fifth year participation and also my grandnephew's fourth year pledge. At this event, as an 'old timer sun dancer' back when few participated, I was honored to be one of several who accepted the pledger's pipes during the final day when all would break their bonds to the Tree of Life at the Sun Dance circular arena's center. Over one hundred pipes were presented and accepted. So there we have two ceremonies that are considerably different, sharing a common belief in the Great Spirit that controls all things except for the two-legged who are allowed to make their own decisions. Other tribes had Vision Quest as well and they also had their own way of expressing an annual thanksgiving to their concept of the Great Spirit.

In between, there are the ceremonies where people come together in lesser numbers than they would at a Sun Dance. The Sweat Lodge and the Yuwipi spirit calling have a similarity and are ceremonies where a smaller group of people will pray, beseech or acknowledge together. The Give-away or Oduhuh ceremony is quite practical. It commemorates the passing of a loved one, usually one's mate. This commemoration usually takes place approximately one year after the mate has passed on. Details of this ceremony may be found in *Mother Earth Spirituality*. You white people should adopt this ceremony for your loved one, once you learn to understand how rewarding it can be for the one who must live on after their life-mate has gone Beyond. It will be a powerful medicine for you and you do not have to give up your church affiliation to perform it as long as you have an understanding and hopefully a sympathetic minister or priest. In fact, many non- Indians have used their church hall to honor their loved one in this manner. The Sweat Lodge also is in more detail in the Mother Earth writing as well. As I have said several times, we do not intend to own you. I realize that our Way is highly unusual but it has a deep respect for real truth and freedom. All faiths should have positive teachings. Why should a two-legged prevent one from learning the best each has to offer?

In a sweat lodge, a group gathers together in a small igloo-shaped lodge usually large enough for five, ten, or twenty people to sit in a circle and beseech or pray. The lodge is covered and hot stones are brought into the lodge so that the people will sweat and become very clean. Steam will be generated by pouring water over the heated stones from a ladle. A bucket of water is placed beside the one who will be conducting the lodge ceremony. The steam and one's sweat make an individual quite refreshed. Usually, there are four parts to the sweat lodge. The lodge that I have seen Chief Fools Crow and mostly Chief Eagle Feather conduct was in four parts. I am influenced strongly by Black Elk's vision; therefore I conduct a sweat lodge as following:

The first door or endurance is to the West Power and acknowledges greetings and welcome to the spirit world. The second endurance is to the North Power and acknowledges truth, cleanliness and meditation. The third endurance is to the East Power and acknowledges knowledge, wisdom, understanding and peace. The individual prayers are often said during this endurance. The fourth endurance is to the South Power and acknowledges healing, honoring yourself, family members, special friends and the commitment to protect Mother Earth.

The most important part for me is when the people each say an individual prayer to the Great Spirit. I think that a lodge should be held wherein people are allowed, without fear, to pray individually and from the heart with a minimum amount of distraction or discomfort. The darkness certainly precludes distraction. A more detailed account of this ceremony and other related ceremonial descriptions are found in *Mother Earth Spirituality*. John Fire offers his sharing of the sweat lodge ceremony in the chapter, Inipi—Grandfather's Breath, *Lame Deer, Seeker of Visions*. Mikkel Aaland, Sweat; is a very informative book. 1. J. Bruchac also has a Sweat Lodge book.[2]

The white man generally terms his formal beseechments to their Higher Power concepts as worship. To me, Indian ceremony is more of a calling out to the Spirit World than a worship service.

Before a ceremony is to begin, the people participating usually gather together in a circle or stand facing the leader of the ceremony. If sage or sweet grass is available, this offering is lit and the smoke bathes the participants (smudging). Sage, especially, has a very definite, pleasing odor, more so when it is lit and the sage smoke permeates the area. The Catholic Church utilizes incense in some services I have attended, especially at funerals. Certain items such as a drum or a peace pipe, if present, are also smudged with the pleasant smelling grass or sage.

A welcome is extended to the spirits to enter the ceremony. Who are these spirits? It appears that they are simply former humans who were once here and understand what our ceremony is about. Except in a Yuwipi spirit calling, we do not address a specific spirit but assume that they are indeed attending our calling. Possibly, we ourselves will become observing spirits once we pass on to the spirit world.

The leader will then beseech to each cardinal direction, west, north, east and south. Most often, the people will also face each direction as it is called upon. I usually hold up my personal wotai stone to use as my portable altar when I beseech to each direction. I hold it outward to the direction I am calling upon and recognizing. Bear in mind that each direction is an entity created by the Ultimate Creator in order for us to live here upon this planet. If the life-bearing sun did not rise from the East direction we would have no life. If the life-giving rains refuse to come out of the West upon this hemisphere, then we would not have our life-sustaining crops. The cattle and grazing ones would have no grass. White man takes all of Nature around us for granted and refuses to acknowledge or realize what reality is in a spiritual way. Therefore he remains extremely ignorant as to unlocking Nature's door and can never access the Code to save the planet, by such an attitude.

I always turn to my right in a clockwise manner as I go from one direction to the other. In this northern hemisphere, water spirals in this manner when it drains through an orifice. Therefore, I want to reach into an encompassing harmony or at least recognize this. In New Zealand and Australia, indigenous people turn ceremonially from right to left to be in their harmony. A medicine wheel ceremony or a power of the hoop ceremony recognizes the meanings of each of the four directions and often is a recognition and connection with Father Sky and Mother Earth as well. Bear in mind, these entities are considered as extensions of the Great Spirit because they are created by the Great Spirit. Throughout this work, this theme will be often repeated in one form or another. At the conclusion of the beseechment to the Six Powers, the Great Spirit is often formally invoked. I usually make a statement thanking the Great Spirit for giving us the Six Powers which allows us our life.

When a peace pipe is used in connection with this ceremony, tobacco is placed in the pipe after some has been placed back to Mother Earth from where it came. We place only tobacco or a substitute for tobacco, such as kinnic kinnick (red willow bark), in the peace pipe. We do not place any form of hallucinogens in the tobacco. This is absolutely contrary to natural harmony and extremely disrespectful. The mind is inhibited when hallucinogenic products are so used. This result is, no doubt, very displeasing to the spirit world to which the beseechment is being directed. The pipe is then the portable altar and pointed to each direction as its (the direction's) power, teaching and meaning is recognized.

I **do not** recommend that non-Indians use the peace pipe in respect to Arvol Looking Horse's request that only Indian, tribal Native American pipe carriers so do. Chief Looking Horse is the Keeper of the Sacred Pipe. A long list of Lakota practicing medicine men who have signed a statement are in disagreement however, with this edict. For harmony and avoidance of needless argument, I recommend that the wotai stone can just as efficiently be utilized. I personally have been gifted a peace pipe by Chief Fools Crow himself and also made a pipe myself. Both have been given away even though I am as qualified a pipe carrier as any. I base this statement on the fact that my teachers were Chief Fools Crow and Chief

Eagle Feather in the six sun dances I have been a participant under their direction. I loathe religious or spiritual argument however and am quite comfortable with my wotai stone. The spiritual results of my ceremony are no different than when I used the pipe. That is what truly matters.

Before a sweat lodge, Chief Bill Eagle Feather would open with a pipe ceremony. When he was teaching me this lodge ceremony, he would often have a woman formally open the Sweat Lodge. One of his reasons was that we all come from a woman. Another reason was that the Buffalo Woman was a powerful figure in our history. He also recognized that Mother Earth is very powerful and that we are all made from Mother Earth. Bill was a practical holy man. It seemed that just about everything that he taught me or spoke to people about made a lot of common sense. He was a "no-frills" holy man and did not take long to make his point. He also had a strong sense of humor which he was not afraid to employ, even in ceremony. He definitely was not an angry man. He was a great teacher from my perspective. When Bill would conduct a sweat lodge, he would address each of the four directions at separate times within the Sweat Lodge ceremony. Everyone within the lodge would have their special time to pray out loud and individually. This procedure, he pointed out to me, was highly important.

Wotai Stone

You, yourself can beseech, acknowledge, respect or seek to the spirit world beyond. Most people now use a simple stone which they carry. If you want to pray but are uncomfortable with something this new, then go to your church and sit and pray or to the place in your home where you pray.

How do I use my stone? I hold it outward at arms' length or hold it up in an offering posture as though I am presenting. I face a direction and call upon what I contend is the power or the representation of that direction. "Oh, West Power, Oh Wiyopeyata," I call out. "I thank you for the life giving rains. I thank you for the fluid, the motion you allow me while I am on my journey across this planet." I have thanked and recognized a gift from God through one of its creations. "Oh spirit world that I associate with the west; Oh spirit world look on and be with us in our small ceremony tonight. We will beseech and acknowledge to the Great Spirit through that which it has created and you are welcome." I have extended a pleasant welcome and in this scenario I would be in an evening ceremony. If I was alone in my home, I would probably say, "I thank you, Great Spirit, for letting me enjoy this day." I might point out something in particular that I learned or experienced that day.

Six Powers and the Spirits

Because the West is where the sun goes down, darkness comes and there is much less distraction. In the daytime, most of us are busy making a living. Our focus then is in another area of life. The night is not something to be fearful of or "spooky" of. Why in the world should you be afraid of what Benevolent Creator has created... the dark (Earth's shadow)? Darkness and night are created by the Great Mystery. It allows one to concentrate more and be less distracted, especially in a group. In a dark sweat lodge, you are not distracted by what someone is wearing. You are able to concentrate on the prayer you will be speaking out loud. Don't you like to have someone's attention and focus when you make a special effort to go and visit them? Many of us believe that the spirit beings listening in want our attention without distraction.

By praying to or including spirits in a ceremony, am I praying to another entity and not God? Considering where these spirits are, I believe that they are much closer to the Great Mystery than I am. I also think that it is the "higher planed" ones, those who are becoming very highly evolved, who are able to have the "spiritual intellect" to observe our ceremony or beseechment. Their conduct while they were here as a human probably allows them to understand what we are doing because they were more observant, more focused, less distracted by those who were far from Creator's blessed and revealing nature teachings. Maybe they placed more information, which they gathered daily, on their 'Disks of Life' which I mentioned earlier. It wouldn't seem practical that the 'blank disks'; those that settled for soap operas or were beer guzzling, non-balanced couch potato Charlies will evolve to such a level or spiritual plane. Like the spirit guides that enter the foretelling ceremonies to help the holy men make accurate predictions, these on-looking spirits that we hopefully cultivate are familiar with what we are doing. Those with "blank disks" have no knowledge of what we are doing, therefore, they are not present and we are spared their ignorance.

To put it bluntly and I am sure that my fellow traditionalists will concur: I feel much more confident in beseeching through these 'Spirits' than I would thru a Falwell, Pat Robertson, Jesse Jacksons, priests, bishops, sky pilots, evangelists, mullahs, clerics and even popes.

I get in touch with my concept of the Higher Power mainly through my everyday thoughts. Maybe this could be called an informal basis. The Native American, no doubt, had this very same informal basis. They were such a spiritual people before their exposure to the dominant society. I believe that this informal reaction of thinking about and relating to Great Spirit was almost automatic. They believed that the Great Spirit was always around them and was constantly revealing itself through its creations which were so highly visible to these people. Consequently, most of them were very reverent and harmonic people. Go out into Nature. A butterfly suddenly floating before you or a tiny waterfall made by a fallen tree across a stream can make you think about God.

Do not leave out the animals, the finned, winged or four-footed in your beseechment. The Wamakaskan are already in their own communion with Wakan Tanka. I would say that they have some "direct connections." Even if you live in a city put out bird food or water. The winged will soon stop by and become your friends. Talk to them.

Did not the Wamaskaskan appear in the great vision of Black Elk? In a later Spirit Calling ceremony the animals will play a prominent role.

Prayers are usually personal but some songs are structured and for those who are familiar with Black Elk's vision, there is a clockwise structure within the beseechment. In a group ceremony such as Sweat Lodge or a Yuwipi ceremony or the tribal Sun Dance there exists a definite structure, however an "official" or a fearful atmosphere does not (seem to) emanate. Respect is very apparent but it is not cast in a demanding or fearsome tone.

Power of the Hoop

I often perform a semi-formal ceremony which I call a Power of the Hoop ceremony when I want to get in touch with the higher power, or whatever mysterious spirit forces there are around us, that seem to be concerned about our earth journey. I also use this means when I want to center toward or focus on a particular area or need. Often when I rest or sit in a place to contemplate, I draw a circle in the air with my hand and draw two intersecting lines in the circle. This act signifies the four directions and the circle of life. It also can be called the Power of the Hoop and can stand for the Six Powers of the World. I am simply emphasizing at that moment that the Six Powers are all around me and that I am an extension of these powers which were put here by the Creator. I believe that these Six Powers are extensions of the Great Spirit and so in a more remote sense, we two legged are extensions of the Great Spirit through these powers. Regardless, your life, how you conduct it, is your ultimate prayer.

I would like to point out that we are physically made up of three of these six powers; the Sun Power, which is within Father Sky, provides our energy, our electronic ability; the Earth Spirit, which gives the approximately 20% material for our bodies, and the West Power, which takes up approximately 80% of our bodies in the form of water and henceforth gives us motion and fluid for our physiology. Some of my information will be repetitive as are other aspects within this writing. It is intentional because I believe that it is that important and establishes a strong base for you to become established within the Natural Way. You do not learn a song, how to hunt, fly fish or become good at a sport if you do not follow some repetition.

The other three powers that I observe, sense and feel are within my spirit. They are not as physical as the first three (West Power, Mother Earth and Father Sky) that I have mentioned; they are more from the mental aspect or are a part of our decision making.

From a standpoint of personal prayer; the North Power helps us to recognize endurance, cleanliness, truthfulness, honesty, removal, independence, provision, preparation and politeness. Once learned and recognized, this power is within us. Native peoples often wintered over in the cold, north climes. Their survival depended upon their ability to endure and prepare for the long winter. Polite manners, quietness, respect for space and truthful conduct were virtues to live congenially within confining space limited by restricting snows and cold. The sweat lodge was used to keep clean during the winter. Little water was needed and snow was often used to make cleansing steam. When the snows melted in the springtime Mother Earth was washed clean. The virtue of cleanliness comes through very strong if I think and identify in this manner.

The East Power reminds me to always appreciate a new day. When the red dawn appears in the east, new experiences, new happenings will accumulate more knowledge upon my Disk of Life. I will strive to be cognizant of what is unfolding before me. After the sun has coursed across the sky, I will contemplate what I have learned. In time I will discourse with others and weigh their opinions where this new information might be relevant. When we share new knowledge, wisdom can come into being. Wisdom leads to understanding, and peace can follow. Understanding, wisdom and peace were strong words which Black Elk identified in his vision. Wisdom associated with spiritual contemplation becomes Grace. These were the gifts from the East Power. I believe the thoughts, memories and deeds related to these virtues carry over into the spirit world.

Growth, medicine, healing and bounty are from the South Power. We all have to make a living. We have to provide, especially if we have dependent children or relatives. If you wish to hone your ability to provide, then beseech to the South Power. Ability, determination, interest, skill, improvising and perseverance are traits that I associate with this direction because they are needed to provide food, shelter and clothing. Itokaga (South Power) was created by the Creator specifically for provision. It is an extension of the Creator. Why shouldn't we beseech in a specific manner to it? Medicine is made from the plants; their stems, roots and fruits. The South Power causes these plants to grow and all of our foods as well. Even the buffalo was a result of the gift of Itokaga, because it fattened and lived from the grasses that grew tall as a result of the summer sun causing all things to grow. If I was unemployed or was unhappy with my occupation or situation, I would beseech to the South Power. If I was physically sick, I would beseech to Itokaga. If I did a ceremony for a person who was physically sick, I would face that person to the South Power. For those who are very compassionate and seek to help and to heal; they will be helped greatly if they explore the medicines and herbs and also seek spirit helpers that have gone on with their knowledge of medicine and healing. Naturally, they should seek knowledge from those who are yet living. These kind and loving people will be very pleasant to be around in the spirit world, like butterflies and flowers.

So, these three powers, North, East and South, are of the mind when they are ascribed to humans. The characteristics, the traits and virtues of The North, East and South Power; we can implant these upon our Disks of Life. They will then become a part of us. The application of endurance, truthfulness, seeking of knowledge, ability to share wisdom and understanding, along with our own example of bravery or courage, all help us to harmonize and fit in with our surroundings.

Do not forget and I repeat; the West Power is our fluid, the life-giving rains. Fluid allows our bodies to have motion. The fifth power is the sun's energy which flows through us and of course, the sixth power, Mother Earth's elements and minerals make up our physical being. All of these entities are placed here by the Ultimate. Even the most ardent detractors cannot truthfully deny this fact.

Free Choice

The benevolent Creator has even given us free choice as to how we shall use what is symbolized and made obvious by these powers. If we want to avoid and ignore them, then we have that choice to do so. If we want to sit and detract, make fun of or be jealous and contribute nothing, we have that power also. It will be a long, cold time for these kind in the spirit world. Who will want to associate with them? What is upon their mind except empty, useless detraction? They have avoided the harmony that is so evident in Nature. I believe that jealous detractors are paid back severely in the Spirit World, especially those detractors who tell vile lies within their detraction. They will be in a foreign place when they enter the Spirit World. I believe strongly that the spiritual realm is so close to the Great Spirit that disharmony is absolutely not condoned, tolerated or allowed. Yet, their distractive habits and character will be with them as will be their former addictions. They will truly be miserable and have to look back with many regrets. Good, harmonic spirits will avoid them because they will have nothing in common to share. This is a much more practical supposition of the Beyond than what the white man has conjured for us and which I suspect the major purpose was to control.

Spiritual Imagery

Joseph Campbell said it right. The description of the Six Powers is a strong part of my spiritual imagery of this Great Spirit while I walk my Earth Journey. It certainly helps me identify with and feel related to what I pray to. If it works for me, then what is it hurting? I have no intention of forcing others to believe this way yet there will be many over zealous ones who will take offense that an indigenous back- grounded person has decided to put his spiritual suppositions, thoughts and experiences down in response to innocent questions that have often been asked by Dominant Society members.

I do not want anyone to haul children off to boarding schools and separate them from their parents and certainly want no one placed in gas chambers if they do not believe in the Six Powers as a form of spiritual imagery to help recognize the Creator's creation. It is all Mystery. Even the zealous religious detractors do not have the ultimate answer which they proclaim. They cannot be truthful and say, "I do not know for sure. You might be right or maybe there exists some truth in what you are expressing."

In the case of a nomadic tribe, there was no specific place to worship although certain geographical areas were deemed as or regarded as significant holy places. Often a tribe, a band or a religious group would return on an annual basis to conduct ceremony in a particular area. Bear Butte in the Black Hills has been a vision quest area for many Sioux. In these modern times other tribal members, especially those from the surrounding plains tribes, come to this promontory at the eastern edge of the Black Hills to vision quest and hold sweat lodges.

Worship

I am probably a bit unusual. I do not place much emphasize on worship. In fact, I am not too fond of the word, worship. If I do worship, then naturally I worship the Great Spirit.

Does this Almighty Creator that has created unfathomable space and time have any need for my mere worship? I respect and am thankful to this vast entity but when I visualize the concept of worship, I view an ant or a tiny insignificant bug crawling by and saying to me, "Praise you, Eagle Man. Praise you, Eagle Man."

What is that statement going to actually do for me or what significance does it amount to?

I occasionally sit through a church service and hear the people exhibiting their worship. Once in a while I am asked to speak in churches. Obviously, these are the more liberal churches whose numbers are growing. To be polite, I will attend their services when I am asked. In my opinion, it is good if churchgoers are receiving sincere enjoyment or a wholesome, spiritually-enhancing feeling from their worship. Occasionally, there will be a good service and I have heard some extremely good messages from ministers or priests. Some of these words, some of this knowledge, I believe was meant for me to hear or be exposed to. I do not rule out these services entirely. I am not better than these people nor do I consider myself beneath them. I just come from a different area of religious or spiritual exposure and of course, I have my own thoughts on the subject.

I have to be true to myself and do not want to lie regarding many questions that often arise. In the old days I would have surely been burned at the stake if I would have made the statement that I am not exceptionally supportive of the word "worship."

Bad Taste

I have a past that has left a bad taste regarding church services. My sister and I had to go to church every Sunday under the fear of going to hell if we missed mass. A mortal sin and you would burn in hell if you died before going to confession. The white man was so smart that he could even categorize sin in different degrees. It was no question, we were not wanted in the redneck neighborhood church where the congregation looked down at us, so we would go across town to a big cathedral and sit in the back. We would get there late and leave early: Two dark little Indian kids sneaking in back. I don't think many people knew we were even there yet God knew and we were free of this mortal sin and could relax for another week. In church, people would worship God yet they could be very prejudiced during the week. My sister and I did not have much of a social life while we were growing up. While we were small, kids did not seem to care if we were Indians. Yes, kids had a good degree of the Code then. We had a lot of fun playing, but once puberty came about my friends changed. My poor sister even dropped out of school because she did not have much of a social life. She was shunned by her grade school friends who did not want to risk their chances at popularity once they reached higher grades. Thankfully, I had sports and some new friends who just wanted to play ball. I also danced Indian. That was fun. I stayed in school.

Once I sneaked off with a white friend from sports who was good to me, so I went to his church. They seemed to worship more than ever. There was a lot of praising of God in songs and in their words. They seemed to be a happier group of people. Their songs were easy to sing and I enjoyed trying to sing with them from a hymn book. There was a girl there too and she was good to me. We had cookies and Kool-Aid afterwards so I went back the next week. Where I went to my church there was very little socializing, at least not on a weekly basis like this Protestant church. But then the priest found out about it and scared me into staying away from that church. When you have a young, forming mind, you can easily be manipulated. Those fears can become entrenched, but thankfully we are allowed our maturity if we choose to take it and can cast inhibiting fears aside.

At Christian funerals, often there are more worship phrases of Jesus than talk of the deceased, and what the deceased did and stood for. I went to a relative's funeral recently and the minister said very little about the deceased. It was disappointing because I wanted to hear more about the person we were having a funeral for. The same thing happened at my sister's funeral. This time I spoke up when this deacon-type asked if anyone wanted to come forward and say some words. He made a big mistake. I said quite a few words that they did not want to hear (the authorities). I said I would not talk about their Jesus and that my sister strongly followed the Indian's Natural Way by the many sun dances she attended. Most of the audience appreciated it when I told about the many positive qualities my sister exhibited down through her Earth journey.

There are exceptions, however. At my brother's funeral, the priest told us that we could conduct the ceremony since this was the desire of my brother before he died. His two sons wanted the service to be held that way also. The Catholic priest, a Jesuit, was very understanding so we went ahead and had an Indian service with substantial mention of my brother's military background and artwork. The many Indians in attendance voiced their approval of the ceremony. We all thanked the priest who said some words also. There was a considerable amount of harmony at that service.

Language

Naturally, indigenous people prayed or beseeched in their own language. After the dominant society placed the various tribes on the reservations, and the majority was converted to Christianity, the people learned to pray in English. The Sioux language was forbidden at both the missionary school and the federal government boarding school. Despite this harsh but effective procedure to eradicate culture, language and religion, the native language managed to persist and survive. Many Sioux still speak their language fluently as do the Navajo and other southwestern tribes.

Many other Native Americans are not fluent in their tribal language, however, and these people make up the majority of native-descended people. When they pray and beseech, they do so in the English language. I recently watched a full-blooded appearing California Indian lead a sweat lodge ceremony in Hawaii. He used the Sioux phrase, Mitakuye Oyasin— For all our relations, throughout his ceremony but it was the only native language that I heard during the course of the ceremony. I think that this phrase was all the native language he knew. The music within the lodge was chanting instead of songs.

I am not fluent in Lakota although I do understand and make use of many of the subjective names and phrases. I also can sing songs in my language. I have discovered that the Sioux language is exceptionally beautiful for singing. It is so much easier to sing a song or compose a spiritual song with it in contrast to attempting to sing spiritually in the English language. Wakan Tanka, Wakan Tanka, is much prettier and has a deeper and fuller resonance when sung in Sioux rather than singing one of the English translations, such as Great Spirit, Great Spirit. It seems that the Lakota/Dakota language was honed to a very spiritual degree down through time because of the people's closeness to ceremony. Singing and beseechment must have been a major ingredient within the development and evolvement of the language. Their values and lifestyle were a part of this development as well. To learn Sioux songs however, requires participation with Sioux people although many tape and CD recordings are being made to instruct.

Lakota Beseechment and Song

Consequently, if the Natural Way should become more and more a part of this land, I believe that Sioux language could become the spiritual language of the future, at least, in song and beseechment phrases. Sioux Songs are being sung in all parts of the world. As time goes by and people continue to communicate and travel, the richness of Sioux language in ceremony, especially the singing of beseechment songs, will continue to spread because the songs add so much to a ceremony. On a trip to Australia, I was pleasantly surprised to discover people who sang Sioux songs rather fluently. There are many tapes out now of Sioux dance songs and even some beseechment songs. Cinte Gleska (Spotted Tail) College at Mission, South Dakota offers a set of good tapes on Lakota (Sioux) language. I should not become too optimistic however as Dominant Society's organized religion will constantly thwart any advancement of natural based Spirituality. According to them, we are starting to become a threat to their religious edicts.

Aside from individual tribal languages which are coming back, in North America we all do speak and understand a common language. The English language does provide for our communication among all tribes and of course with the dominant society.

Does this religion have an initiation procedure or ceremony? I am not aware of an initiation ceremony into Native American spirituality, at least from the Sioux perspective. An initiation ceremony was not one of the seven ceremonies referred to by Black Elk.

Ownership

There is an avoidance of ownership in spiritual values. One cannot own the Four Winds, the eagles, the streams and certainly not the Spirit World. Conversely, one should not be owned. Our spirit is the most free entity that we have. I do not intend for anyone to own mine. In old tribal warrior societies there were initiations but these were more in line with acceptance according to your reputation rather than an initiation. One had to prove oneself worthy to be a part of a particular society. These societies represented social structures more so than existing for religious interest. The Silent Eaters were older warriors who had paid their dues upon the field of combat and generosity from the hunt. They would meet to discuss the welfare of the tribe. The Dog Soldiers were a society, considerably younger and still building upon and establishing their reputations. They served as the front line of defense. This society lived among themselves and were placed strategically in the camp where they could defend and react suddenly to attack. In peacetime they were the hunters and the scouts. At a certain age, young men would enter the realm of the Dog Soldiers. They would be required to perform certain tests of skill or prowess, often learned from an older teacher.

An initiation ceremony such as baptism, first communion or confirmation was not within the scope of Sioux religious ceremony, to my knowledge. These would be considered 'ownership' ceremonies which Siouxs would avoid.

Sun Dance

Except for a very few, most will never experience this ceremony as it is a tribal thanksgiving and most are not of a tribe, but it is important knowledge to know about as it helps one to further understand the spiritual depth of the old traditionals. And even a closed ceremony gives us insight into the development of intuition when we hear or read the stories of those ceremonies.

There are many, many summer sun dances now held on the reservations in the Dakotas and especially on the Rosebud and Pine Ridge Reservations. When I was younger, there was but one Sioux Tribal Sun Dance held at Pine Ridge Reservation. This ceremony was banned by the government in the early 1880s. Sporadically it was done in secret out in lonely areas of the reservations by brave and stubborn holy people. It did not return in public form until the 1950s after the old prophet Black Elk died. Chief Eagle Feather, the true Sun Dance Warrior, said he was going to bring back the Sun Dance, "Out in the open," and Chief Fools Crow said, "I will pierce him." How a young half-breed boy that was only a mere pow wow dancer the night before that famous event, could be at that first modern era, public sun dance is indeed more than coincidence, but I was there and sitting beside my step-grandmother. It was a pitiful crowd but it was out in the open, defiant and the beginning of the Great Return. Oddly, missionaries and government authorities paid us little attention. They were so used to winning that a couple of old holy men were considered harmless. The small crowd proved that.

Frank Fools Crow was the Sun Dance Chief for the six sun dances that I took part in the later sixties and early seventies. My first Sun Dance I was not pierced since I had just returned from war. The next four Sun Dances held at Pine Ridge, I was pierced and my last Sun Dance was way up at Green Grass on the Hunkpapa reservation where the sacred pipe resides and at that Sun Dance all of we dancers did not pierce. Chief Fools Crow and Chief Eagle Feather both officiated at that ceremony.

In my time, tribal Indians only took part in the piercing ceremony and I believe that all of the participants were Sioux, either Oglala, Sichangu, Hunkpapa, or Minnicoujou. Maybe a few of the other Sioux were also represented among the pledgers as one in my limited capacity did not go about asking for credentials. My mother warned me that I might not be allowed to dance as I was not a full-blood and only half-Indian. A friend, Sonny Larive, also a half-breed or 'mixed-blood' had danced the year before so I didn't quite believe my mother, who would have been relieved had I been rejected as the missionaries were pressuring her to somehow forbid me to dance. They were fearful that we younger ones and me as a combat warrior would set an example for the young to return to the old way. They were right! At my last piercing Sun Dance, the arena was vibrant with many young Sun Dance pledgers. Fools Crow had to have help from other holy men to pierce all of us. The once pitiful crowd almost two decades before had grown to a huge throng that swelled to the periphery of the arena.

Now it is a different world in regard to Sun Dance. No longer is there one Sun Dance on one reservation as in my time. It grew as it would have to. No longer could one Sun Dance manage the thousands of pledgers now coming from many reservations and off- reservation as well. Throughout Sioux country it spread. I believe there are over fifty summer sun dances a year in the Dakotas alone. Some are small, 'family' sun dances. Others have over a hundred male pledgers and twenty to thirty supporting women dancers.

You can go to some Sioux reservations and see Sun Dances ranging from wide open (meaning non-Indians can participate as pledgers) to closed Sun Dances that require you to show a tribal enrollment card before you are admitted to watch or participate. Some of these Sun Dances are so strict that your non-tribal spouse, if you have one, cannot be admitted with you even if you are an enrolled tribal member. One of the most beautiful and respectful Sun Dances I have seen in years was such a closed Sun Dance conducted by an honorable Oglala holy person, Rick Two Dogs, on the Pine Ridge Reservation. Those of Indian descent, 1/4th, 1/8th and 1/16th and enrolled tribal members are finding themselves most welcome at many of the so called "closed" Sun Dances. My Nephew, (1/4th) and his son (1/8th) just finished their fifth and fourth Sun Dance on the Pine Ridge Reservation in which there were over 100 participants (dancers/pledgers). They pledged to dance at least four sun dances.

However, I have heard too many negative reports regarding the wide-open Sun Dances which have been held. The most important negative point I have observed personally is the attitude of many young white men who have participated in some of these open ceremonies. Too many have become instant holy men and have gone on to discover some tribe in their lineage and which they now believe vehemently they are a member of. Worse, too many have quit learning and searching for they now know everything that needs to be known in the realm of the spiritual. How one Sun Dance can bring all of this about is indeed baffling.

Proclamation

As mentioned above, the Keeper of the Sacred Pipe, Chief Arvol Looking Horse has issued a Proclamation regarding the usage of the Sacred Pipe and the restriction of non-Indians in certain ceremony.

Quite surprising to me, many traditional holy men have taken a dissenting stand, however, that our religion (spirituality) should not become exclusionary and have maintained that young non-Indians also need the medicine of the Sun Dance, especially those who have taken their pledges to dance at least four years. No different than for some of my own relatives, non-Indians too want the strong medicine of the tribal ceremony to combat former problems with drugs and alcohol. This is not the sole reason why they participate but for many of the young it is an important factor. The more open medicine men voiced some strong rebuttals to the proclamation advocating consideration for these pledgers to fulfill their pledges and for the ceremony not to be exclusionary and went ahead with their summer Sun Dance as planned. There are indeed many strong traditionals who conduct sun dances who feel this way. It is a difficult situation. A I have mentioned, I did observe that many of the 'card carrying' (registered and enrolled) Indians were down to _ and 1/8th Native blood and their children were even less at a 'closed' Sun Dance I viewed of over 100 dancers. At 1/8th and even 1/4th, the Native lineage is hardly discernable. The Native American is the most intermarried to other races of all the minorities in the United States and hence the blood line becomes thinner much more rapidly. Those who advocate totally closed ceremony must be reminded of this fact as time most certainly moves on.

Chief Fools Crow's Sun Dance

My description of the Sun Dance is based on what I viewed under Chief Eagle Feather's and Chief Fools Crow's direction. The Sun Dance is a time when the people thank the Great Spirit, publicly and out in the open as a tribe. It is also a time, that certain men can and will fulfill their Sun Dance vows, usually for a favor or a request that was made in time of need. A desperate hunter might take a vow to be pierced in the forthcoming Sun Dance if he would see a winter deer to bring back to hungry people. I personally took a vow to pierce in the Sun Dance if I would come back from the war in Vietnam. No one forced me to take this vow and the pain that I endured was of my own choosing much like a woman who gives birth to a baby. She chooses her own pain so that the people might live. A Sioux woman can also dance in the sun dance, but she does not pierce because she has given her pain when she bears children. Such is the depth and recognition of woman in Sioux ceremony. Many of our service men take a vow to dance in the Sun Dance if they come home safely from Iraq.

Around the Sun Dance tree, placed earlier in the center of the tribal arena, the sun dancer would dance. Singers are gathered around a large drum to sing old tribal songs. For me, these songs are hauntingly beautiful. Four days the dancers would fast and pray around the tree and sleep in a small tent at night not far from the arena.

On the fourth day, a bed of sage would be placed beneath this "tree of life" and the dancer would be taken to this spot and be pierced in the chest by the Sun Dance Chief, the intercessor for the ceremony. A pair of small slits would be made in the man's skin and a wooden peg would be skewered through; in and under the skin. The end of a rope would be brought down from the tree, and it would be attached to the wooden peg by a buckskin thong. The other end of the long rope would be attached toward the top of the tree. The dancer would rise after he was attached and would slowly dance backward, away from the tree's base to the end of his rope. Other dancers would be pierced and after all were pierced the piercing song would be sung and the dancers would dance inward toward the base of the tree to beseech strongly to the Great Spirit who we believed to be looking on. After the dancers touched the tree, they would go back, away from the center to the end of their ropes. Four times, this beseechment would take place. The on- looking tribe would be in very serious prayer, with very little distraction. The tribe praying together in a concerted effort was considered to be far more powerful and beneficial than the drama of the Sun Dancers. This was the main focus of the Sun Dance — the tribe praying as a unit, praying together — an annual tribal Thanksgiving to Creator, Wakan Tanka.

The drama of the piercing assures an unbroken, non-distracted spiritual focus. After the fourth beseechment, the dancers would be free to lean back and break themselves free by putting their weight upon their tether to the tree of life placed into Mother Earth. The rope is their spiritual umbilical. When the peg would break through, their sun dance vow would be fulfilled. The tribal Thanksgiving would be over.

Such is a description of the Sun Dance as the way we experienced it and which is a personal and a freely self-chosen sacrifice. No one is required to Sun Dance and the majority of tribal members do not actually become pledgers or Sun Dancers. Some variations of the piercing have now entered the later sun dances in contrast to our time.

Enhancement, Honing, Spiritual Intuition

I look back now at Chief Fools Crow and Eagle Feather. They were truly bull Orcas for humanity. Their Intuition (Mysterious Power), like the great stately beast of the sea which has no enemies, their mysterious power could occasion wonders which no human could match. I firmly believe their participation in the Vision Quest, Sweat Lodge and Sun Dance highly enhanced their gift of Spirit Calling. I could care less about what foolish detractors will claim against them but can only warn such ignorant that they will have to face all they detract upon in this Spirit World beyond if it is based on the real truth we see constantly emanating from Creator's creations. That is a pretty heavy thought and they should think very seriously about what it means. Both holy men were advocates of the powers and confidence one could also derive from the 'Wotai' stone. Like the 'Lone Cloud Sun Dance', both were awesome encouragement that I had found a better path for myself. Ceremony can strongly hone many gifts. Bear in mind that we are dealing with Mystery. Some may not arrive at what I would like to explain. I realize I have limitations but hope by presenting what I have observed, many will understand more fully. By now, the reader should realize how some men and women, who respect Nature, do have a grasp of the Code.

As we participate more in spiritual ceremonies, we learn or at least appreciate how Nature truly does educate us. Tremendous confidence is gained when you experience such an event as the Lone Cloud Sun Dance which seemed to be encouraging to us. The next step is to develop a bit beyond preparing for our earthly journey and giving thanks. Can we talk to Creator's Helpers as well?

11

Participation

> *"Cowardice asks the question - is it safe? Expediency asks the question - is it politic? Vanity asks the question - is it popular? But conscience asks the question - is it right? And there comes a time when one must take a position that is neither safe, nor politic, nor popular; but one must take it because it is right."*
>
> Dr. Martin Luther King, Jr.

Ceremonies for Accessing the Code

If one is in a large city with minimal access to nature, I will have to admit that participating in Nature-based ceremony may be a bit difficult. The white man has come along with concrete and pavement and covered Mother Nature up! What purpose will it serve for such a confined person to explore further down Nature's trail? I cannot offer a truthful answer, wherein I believe I would attempt to satisfy such an individual. If one is able-bodied, however, Nature should become available if one will simply take the initiative. Just raising plants in one's dwelling will allow you within Nature's purview. The Japanese are pressed for space yet have miniature rock gardens which keeps them closely connected. I do not promote keeping pets confined within the walls of apartments or condominiums, but many people find certain of the smaller breeds of dogs that seem to enjoy their city habitats. One can always champion the cause for more city parks and especially the dog runs and parks offering freedom for dog lovers. I am so fortunate that my pet gets to hunt freely in the wide spaces of Dakota and Iowa. One does not have to be a fisherman or hunter however. Thousands, actually millions of city folk travel to the many parks America can offer.

Ceremonies can help the individual to grow in their life's quest. I believe ceremony is our tool to hone one's intuitive abilities. They enable you to be surer of your perspectives toward truth. Many ceremonies are universal. I hope the universal ceremonies can be rescued from some erroneous designed form of ownership in order that all creeds and tribes may rightfully enjoy the blessing of our common ceremonies. It is my belief, however, that some, a very few, ceremonies are tribal, and maybe not meant for everyone.

No one owns Vision Quest

Vision Quest is a ceremony that was practiced by many tribes down through time and not just the Native Americans. Vision Questing or spending an isolated time out in Nature is not owned by any Indian tribe. The Christians claim their Jesus did fast and pray out in the wilderness. Moses, I understand, went out alone to a mountain to commune with his concept of the Higher Power. I did the same on Bear Butte Mountain to fulfill my instructions from Chief Fools Crow through Chief Eagle Feather. "Go up on the mountain and fast and pray before the next sun dance." These were my instructions.

I had a rather startling quest. A rattlesnake actually snapped a portion of my peace pipe off, on a dark stormy night, just below the bowl where the pipe maker had carved an ax blade. The top portion of the pipe was a bowl for peace and the ax was for war, since I had been a combat warrior. The ax portion was snapped flush.

When I told my experience to Fools Crow he raised nary an eyebrow and calmly sent me to Chief Eagle Feather in a nearby reservation with the simple words, *"Wah ste aloh!"* (It is good!) I was a bit perplexed but assumed he considered me as more of Chief Eagle Feather's student and politely did not want to interfere.

Chief Eagle Feather was slightly more informative once I described my vision. "You had a good vision quest, Nephew. Now you get your things ready for the Sun Dance." I concluded that you should not expect a holy person to give you a detailed explanation of your quest (if there is any). Your own observations are what are most important.

A Jesuit Priest Quests for a Vision

Father William Stolzman became the chairperson of the Medicine Men and Pastors' Meeting held at the Rosebud Reservation from 1973 to 1979. The meetings sought an exchange of information, spiritual discussion between the spiritual leaders and lay persons of the Sioux Tribe, and the pastors, priests, and laypeople of the white man's faith. It was well attended for a reservation function which met bi-monthly, nine months out of the year. With Lakota relatives present, often there were as many as forty people present per meeting. My main mentor, Chief Eagle Feather, was a regular participant. Unlike most priests, Father Stolzman became a very open-minded priest through contact with the traditionals. He discovered Natural ceremony, and described his own personal observations in his book *The Pipe and Christ*. Father Stolzman described the dark rain clouds that threatened his solitary vigil on the mountaintop as he faced the Four Directions and prayed.

"As I faced the West, the wind became more and more ferocious. The black flag in the West was long, and it whipped me and lashed me painfully. How hard and

testing is the West! The wind became so strong that I seemed to lean 45 degrees into the wind to keep my balance. Finally when I could no longer stand, I descended into the pit and sat facing the West. The wind roared, the flags slapped, and the lightning flashed from the West overhead. Suddenly, 'Yehhhhhhhhhhh...,' the most blood-curdling eagle scream I have ever heard! It was a thousand times louder than any eagle cry I had ever heard before. The wind immediately stopped! The sudden silence was shaking. There was only the snapping and crackling of the lightning in the West... and the lingering memory of that frightening eagle's scream. I sat and shuddered. It was the Wakiyan, the Thunder Bird, controller of storms.

"The lightning then moved to the South. Something was wrong. This was contrary to the way it should be. It should have turned toward the North! Only later did I understand that this was a sign of the companion of the West, the contrary one, Heyoka, the Clown. With the wind quiet, I returned outside to pray. As the lightning moved to the South, the wind began to come from that direction. With it came a fine mist. As it touched my face, I could not help but think of tears. I did not want the mist to come into the square, so I prayed, and even the mist stopped. (This was amazing, for at the medicine man's house a mile away, the people were anxiously praying for me. They were having a downpour, and it hailed several times. In fact, the entire region suffered the worst hail storm in years that night.) On the hill, however, there were only wind, lightning, and thunder.

"I began to hear voices coming out of the floor at the southern edge of the pit. There were thousands of voices resembling the drone of a crowd. I bent over and cupped my ear in order to pick up some words to discover if they were speaking to me in Lakota or English. After a few minutes the voices stopped. These were the voices of the dead who journey south to the place called Tate Makoce, what White men call the 'Happy Hunting Ground.'

"I remained for quite a while in the pit, praying and feeling very close to the earth, to which the bodies of the souls had returned. Then I decided to go outside. As I got up to leave, the earth gave a great heave one direction and then the other. I was bounced back and forth from side to side in the pit -- gently. It seemed as if Grandmother Earth was showing her presence and love by rocking me back and forth in the 'arms' of the pit as a little child is rocked in the arms of its grandmother." [1]

The rest of Father Stolzman's story though full of how Nature communicated with him during his Vision Quest, is most informative of how the experience changed his life:

"My prayers had been answered. In fact, every time I have gone to the spirits on the hill my prayers have been answered. Yet they are always answered in ways I have never expected. I have studied some psychology, and I know that a person can sometimes unknowingly program himself to see what he wants to see or symbolically hallucinate events for the past. Every time I go to the spirits I find their response to be a total surprise. I guess if there were no surprises, they would be giving me nothing new, and there would be no need for their coming. When I try to set up expectations for them, they refuse to come at all." [2]

Father Stolzman's books are evidence of a new openness I never saw in the many missionary priests I knew as a child. His participation in ceremony helped to develop his intuition by attuning his senses to Nature and learning to take meaning from winds, eagle cries, lightning, and spending a calm night out in the open on a hilltop surrounded on all sides with thunderstorms and hail. All of these entities are created and obedient to Creator alone.

Before we leave Father Stolzman, I would like to recommend his book, *The Pipe and Christ*, for those readers who are not ready or able to completely embrace the Natural Way. His book is very informative regarding ceremony, culture, values, and beliefs on both sides of the coin. Many of you are just too laden with too much fear, from what I have seen. Some of you are not that fearful but choose to simply blend both Christianity and the Nature realm. Might be a smart move; you are covered on both bases. My mother seemed to manage that approach. (My father preferred the Natural Way.)

Participation in Vision Quest, Sweat Lodge and Sun Dance recently affected my nephew. He was always a respected person from my point of view but I saw a profound integration of newfound confidence and pride when I conversed with him after he finished his Vision Quest and Sun Dance under the tutelage of a Sioux medicine man. I also have another nephew who hasn't touched alcohol for years because of his many Sun Dances and related ceremonies. A grandnephew had the same blessed reaction.

All these young men are much better prepared for life. The ordinary quarrels and pettiness of daily living have no meaning to them; they have higher goals. This transformation has definitely honed their intuitive abilities. My nephews were not sitting and listening in some academic Indian Studies classroom. They were out upon Mother Earth in all three ceremonies, Sweat Lodge, Vision Quest and Sun Dance. Physically they were immersed in a totally different medium than what Dominant Society experiences. I stood in the arena during the breaking time, holding my nephew's pipe. The drum beat was mesmerizing, powerful, haunting. The dancers, mostly young men, went in to touch the tree four times, as I had done decades before. Under that vast western sky, many memories returned, of the old sun dances past.

On his fourth year, the fulfillment of his four year pledge, I was called upon to be one of the pipe acceptors near the ending of the ceremony. The sun dancers bring forth their pipes to the acceptors. My mind went back to decades before when three acceptors, accepted our pipes and only eight of us were pledgers. One was a woman. I remember her name. Mary Louise Defender. Now my Nephew is making ready for his fifth sun dance, even though his initial pledge is fulfilled. It is an arduous, tough sun dance near Kyle, where Chief Fools Crow lived. We call it the Marine Corps/Airborne of all the sun dances. It is very demanding of the one hundred and more pledgers but so deeply powerful. I am so fortunate to view such beautiful 4 day ceremony and the pride and confidence I reap, when I see the strong young sun dancers and the medicine people. Yes, I am deeply proud that I stood up for the Way, way back then, when so very few showed their colors. Our Way will definitely live, is the message I receive.

Sacred Places

At this point, if you are not tribally enrolled, I suggest strongly that you do not vision quest at Bear Butte Mountain in the Black Hills. Be polite. Stay away from places the Indian people deem sacred. They are going back to their once-banned religion now and Bear Butte gets very crowded in the spring and summer. I used to Vision Quest on Bear Butte and was the only person up there at night but now there is a tremendous upsurge in Native people returning to the old ways. There are plenty of other distant peaks and mountains and Badlands buttes, and all very isolated too. All over America, even in the east, mountain and hill tops remain vacant - go there. Remember, this is a ceremony just between you and your concept of God (Creator). It is owned by no one or any tribe. It is a universal ceremony, but I believe the native people be given some allowance since the Christian-dominated government (and missionary influenced) wrongfully banned us from ceremonial participation. There is much to catch up on especially for the young.

I do not want to trouble the reader with any mechanics of a Vision Quest. Some want to ask: What do I bring? How long should I stay? What will I see? Can I take a drink of water? What is really important; is for you to simply get up and go do it! At the rate this world's population is increasing, I would not wait too long. How long and where you go is your decision unless you are fortunate (or maybe unfortunate) to have a teacher in these matters.

In summary, I believe Vision Quest is the most important ceremony you will ever do. It is simply the isolation of yourself out in Mother Nature for a brief period of time. I believe it develops and promotes one's intuitive abilities as long as you remain a 'hollow bone' which Chief Fools Crow spoke of and revealed in Thomas Mail's book, *Fools Crow*. All the powerful holy men I knew honed their spiritual intuitive gifts with this ceremony. It is the first ceremony a Sun Dance leader will insist you perform prior to your first Sun Dance.

We have observed a non-Indian's response to Native ceremony in which he directly participated. I was worried for Father Stolzman, however. I imagined that his authorities would know about his well-meaning books in which he had simply told the truth regarding his observations and experiences and yet they would set upon him and force him to recant. Why? Simply because he says good things (Truth) about Indigenous beliefs and practices in which he directly took part. They could consider his direct involvement as detracting from Church Dogma and rules.

He laughed when I expressed my worries. He said, "Don't worry about me. I am too old to bother with and besides I am building a new church right now."

So let us go to another non-Indian who has had a powerful experience with a Medicine person.

How The Spirits Healed Bird Flu
By Celinda Reynolds Kaelin
© October 2006

This account is the truth of what only I experienced during these sacred ceremonies. Others also had powerful interactions with the Spirits, but I can only write what I know to be truth, not of others. I am deeply indebted to Eagle Man, Ed McGaa, for opening the door to these Lakota ways which feed my spirit and made these ceremonies possible.

Grandfather Mike issued his invitation on the last day of Sundance, when I explained how ill I was. "Bring me 402 tobacco ties and I can heal you." With this oblique reference to his Spirit Guides, I knew he was offering a Yuwipi. Grandfather Mike was my Sundance Chief. When I returned home, I prayed with my C'anupa (Sacred Pipe), but failed to receive either confirmation or warning, so I just let the matter go.

Several months later, in October, I have a dream about Grandfather Mike. He and I are sitting on the ground in total darkness – no fire, no lights, no C'anupa – and we do a ceremony together. As he rises to go, he looks at me one last time, "You'll be all right now." And then he is gone, and the dream ends. When I awake, I know that this is the Yuwipi and the confirmation from Spirit that I had been seeking. I call Grandfather Mike and recount my dream.

"Yeah. I also came to you in my dream last night. You were near this big mountain [Pikes Peak] and then there was a white building with a bell tower [the old schoolhouse near our ranch] and there was a beautiful tree that was bent like it was dancing [a Ute Prayer Tree near the ranch]. Usually the Spirits protect me, and don't let anyone near me that way. Yes, it is time for the Yuwipi. Come next week. Bring me 402 tobacco ties, and four tobacco flags with the colors of the four directions. Also, you need to bring your Pipe and a gift for the healing."

"What can I bring you that you need?" I want to be certain that my gift will be appropriate.

"Well, I need some guns."

I am mute for several minutes, and this silence speaks volumes about my aversion to guns.

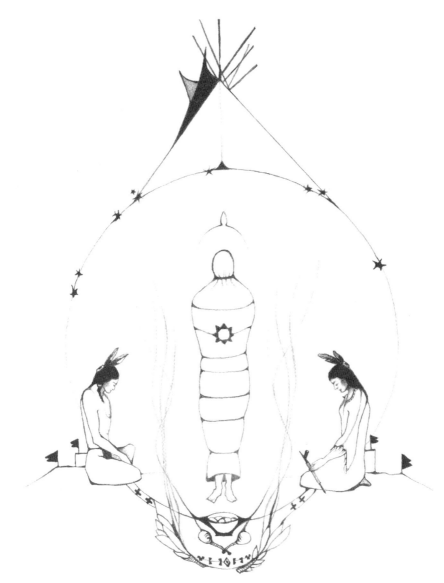

Yuwipi

"We need guns to hunt for food. While we were at Sundance, someone broke into my trailer and stole all my guns. Hunting season is coming, and without guns we won't have food for the winter."

I'm sure that he can hear my sigh of relief. "Okay, I'll bring you some guns."

"This healing will take two ceremonies, so we will do the House Ceremony for two nights."

With this, we end our conversation on the preparations, and I begin one of the most incredible experiences of my life.

Fortunately, I live in the high mountains of Colorado and have several friends who are avid hunters. They help me acquire the coveted hunting rifles in just a few days' time. Making the tobacco ties, however, requires three days of hard work. I first pour the tobacco into a wooden bowl, then hold it to the four directions and ask each of the Grandfathers to fill the ceremony with light and love. I know that like a sponge, the tobacco will hold these prayers and our ceremony will be protected from any negative energies who will be sure to avoid the light and love. I then place a tiny pinch of this tobacco into each of the 402 two-inch squares of red cotton cloth, tying each one at the top, then binding them together into one long rope with cotton twine.

My friend, Elizabeth, invited us to hold the ceremony at her house near Porcupine. We arrive late in the day and I immediately set about preparing the meat and vegetable soup for feast after the ceremony. An hour later, we arrive at Grandfather Mike's home a few miles away. Pungent smoke from the Sweat Lodge fire fills the air as we walk to his humble trailer. I had filled my C'anupa at Elizabeth's, asking Creator to surround Grandfather Mike with love and support his work for the ceremony.

"Ah, good, you brought your Pipe."

I am always delighted by Mike's deep bass voice, and find it curious that such resonance emanates from his tall, gaunt body. He sits on the edge of the couch and begins to smoke my Pipe. I am amazed at his concentration, or *waableza* as Black Elk called it, in spite of the blare of the television, children jumping on the second couch, a teenager talking on the phone, and Lolita cooking the evening meal while visiting with her daughter. In the midst of this chaos and cacophony, my Pipe veils Mike in wreaths of silvery smoke, his every puff sending small circles like sacred hoops. The C'anupa's bowl is empty of every tiny flake of tobacco in a matter of minutes. This seems a miracle in itself, as my Pipe is notorious for requiring a good set of lungs and at least 30 minutes of smoking time. Electricity runs up and down my spine as he smokes, indicating the presence of Wakan Tanka's spirit, or *wocangi*, the whole time.

Mike returns my C'anupa to me, and adds.

"Ah, good. You understand these ceremonies, and it makes it easy to work with you."

"Shall I bring your gifts for the ceremony now?" I quietly ask. Mike nods his assent.

My husband Harold and I hurry to our car and gather the coveted rifles and shells. What a gift is given us in seeing the joy of Mike and his sons as they enthusiastically examine each of the rifles. It's like Christmas in October, and we are Santa Claus.

When the excitement dies down, we all proceed to the Inipi, or Sweat Lodge, where we will cleanse ourselves before the Yuwipi. Mike's Lodge is quite large, and its dome shaped structure can easily accommodate about 35 people. Many people join us in the darkness, but I can't see how many or who they are. Mike holds an Inipi every night and everyone in the community is welcome. As we settle ourselves in the darkness around the Stone Cradle, the Fire Keeper brings in 75 large gray stones that have been heated until they glow red hot.

"Boy, this is going to be a Warrior Sweat!" I catch myself worrying, and work hard to discipline my thinking into prayer and not on the searing heat that I know will come with the first ladle of water.

"We will only do three doors, and the fourth door will be the Yuwipi," Mike instructs as the singing begins and he pours the water.

Almost immediately, small blue lights emanate from the stones and dance around in the darkness. Mike is praying in Lakota, and there are many voices speaking in hushed tones. I don't realize until later that these are the Spirits talking to Mike.

After prayers to each of the Sacred Directions, the door to the lodge is opened and we all gulp in the crisp night air, preparing ourselves for the next round, or "door." At the end of the third door, we file out into the chilly darkness and dry our wet clothes with a towel. We then climb into our cars for the drive to Elizabeth's house. She and her family have been busy moving all of the furniture out of her modest living room and covering the windows with black plastic and blankets.

My prayer ties and flags have been purified in the Inipi, and they are now placed to create a man-sized rectangle in the middle of the room for Mike's altar. A large coffee can is placed at each corner and the flags (attached to a red and blue staff) for the four directions are held in place in the can with dirt. An assistant unrolls half of the prayer ties to enclose the rectangle. An extra coffee can is placed in the center on the west end, and Mike attaches an eagle head and other sacred items to the staff. Wakinya Sna Mani, Mike's son, smoothes gopher dust at the base of this staff and traces symbols in it with his finger. He then places three rattles on the west side, then ties eagle bone whistles to the remaining staffs.

"My son Mike (*Wakinya Sna Mani*, Sound of Distant Thunder) will do the Yuwipi tonight as he is learning the ceremony. This is only his second time, so watch, and you're going to see something interesting."

Now Grandfather Mike and his assistants completely cover Wakinya with a star quilt until he resembles a mummy. Methodically, they secure it with a rawhide thong around the neck, chest, waist and feet after first binding his fingers behind his back. I marvel that Wakinya can even breathe at this point. When they lay him face down in the center of the hoshika or altar, I am sure that it must be virtually impossible to breathe.

"Creator, have pity. Surround Wakinya with white light and love and help him with this ceremony." I quietly send a prayer to Wakan Tanka to help my little brother.

Harold and I are instructed to sit just outside the altar on the west side. About thirty other guests have filed into the room, and we all sit cross-legged on the floor around the perimeter of the altar. It is a tight space, only about eighteen by twenty feet, so we are only inches from the prayer ties outlining the altar. The singers, four young men, occupy the northeast corner. As soon as Wakinya is face down on the floor, the single light bulb in the middle of the room is unscrewed, and the singing begins.

Almost immediately, flashes of blue light emanate from the center of the altar and begin to dance through the air. Rattles fly around the room, their rhythmic clatter sounding over my head and in front of me. As the crescendo of sacred songs increases, the eagle bone whistles also take flight and their piercing sound sends chills up and down my spine. The Lakota say that the eagle bone whistle is the voice of the Creator, and the wocangi that I'm feeling lends credence to this teaching.

"Wow! Look at those lights! This is incredible!" I catch myself with these thoughts, and struggle to discipline mind back to prayer.

Soon, I hear Wakinya's muffled voice speaking to a someone low to the floor and close to his face. His head is only about eighteen inches from where I sit.

"Celinda, the Spirits want you to stand up and tell them what you want."

As Wakinya instructs, I struggle to my feet in the darkness and gulp a deep breath.

"Tunkashila, Grandfather, at Sundance I was very sick. When I went to Grandfather Mike, he told me that the Spirits would heal me with this Yuwipi. So, please Tunkashila, have pity on me and heal my lungs and my liver and the tumor that I have. Tunkashila, I also ask that you bless my brother Wakinya Sna Mani and all my Lakota brothers and sisters here so we may do the work of healing the Sacred Hoop." I end my request with the traditional Lakota blessing, " Mitakuye Oyasin! (We are all related.)"

As I finish speaking, the rattles become agitated, and now they are touching me all over my upper body, especially my chest and my abdomen. After a few minutes of this concerted activity, Wakinya addresses me again in his muffled voice.

"The Spirits thank you for your prayers. They say that they will heal you. In return, they would like you to come when the grass begins to grow and give a Wopila Ceremony."

When I agree to this, the singing begins again, and Wakinya continues a dialog with several other strange voices while the rattles work on me.

"Hau Kola, Wopila Tanka!" I silently thank the Spirits as they work.

Then the strange voices and the blue lights travel around the room, talking to each of the participants. They are speaking Lakota, and each person quietly responds to them as they are addressed. I silently promise myself to learn the Lakota language. Suddenly, a cell phone rings over near the singers, and its vibrant light goes sailing in a crazy zig zag pattern up to the ceiling and around the singers before someone manages to grab it and toss it through the curtain and into the kitchen.

A final song is sung, and when the lights are turned back on, Wakinya is sitting on the star blanket and the leather thongs are in a neat ball at his feet.

Grandfather Mike hands me his two-foot long ceremonial Pipe, and instructs me to light it and pass it around the circle. I take several deep breaths, and trying hard to draw the flame into the bowel. I struggle for a few minutes, quietly praying to the C'anupa for its help before I get a feeble wisp of blue smoke. After four quick puffs, I pass the C'anupa to my husband Harold who is seated at my left, and then the Pipe travels around the room.

"I can see that your lungs are not working good. The Spirits have shown me the herbs I am to heal you with. Tomorrow morning we will begin." With these words, Grandfather Mike reassures me that the healing will start right away.

We linger with Elizabeth over coffee the next day, and return to Mike's by mid-morning as he requested.

"Here, drink this. It's the medicine for your lungs. I was up at five this morning and went out and gathered these herbs. We'll go this afternoon and get the other two."

I pass the mixture under my nose and inhale its earthy aroma. I savor the pungent brew as I slowly sip from the steaming cup.

"You feel okay? Sometimes this can make people sick."

"No. It's wonderful and I love the taste."

"Okay, you finish that. I have to go to town and attend to business."

We sit outside Mike's trailer, basking in the bright autumn sunlight and watching Mike's grandchildren as they play. Suddenly, a familiar sick feeling comes over me as I recognize the energy of the pneumonia that made me so ill for many years. I understand that this is the medicine at work, purging my body of this old energy. I crawl into the back seat of our car and doze fitfully as my lungs heal. Harold busies himself with the young men who are preparing for tonight's Inipi.

It is late afternoon when Mike returns from town, and I am still feeling wretched. Mike pulls up a chair and we chat for a while in the late afternoon light.

"The Spirits have told me that this Bird Flu will be very bad, maybe kill 60 million people. They want us to bring Elders from the four corners of the world and do a ceremony. If we do this, they can heal the Bird Flu and maybe only a few thousand people will die."

"Mike, thank you for telling me this. It has been heavy on my heart. Just recently, the news reported that over 8,000 birds fell from the sky at Lake Qinghai in China and that the virus will soon spread to humans. Thank goodness we can do something to help. I will talk to Woody at the World Council of Elders, and we will make the arrangements for a Bird Flu Yuwipi."

My mind is still on this wonderful opportunity to heal this pandemic when Mike continues.

"Do you see this scar on my finger? It's from a snake bite. I was gathering this Wakinyan medicine one time and a rattlesnake was wrapped around its roots. They do that to protect these sacred plants. The Spirits taught me all about healing with herbs, and I know over 60 different plants for healing. There are only certain times of the year when the Wakinyan medicine can be gathered. I will be back in a while."

With this, Grandfather Mike heads off up the hill behind his house to gather this most sacred medicine for my healing. I had thought that it would take him hours, but he returns in about half an hour and explains how I am to use the remaining herbs.

"Mitakuye Oyasin!" I breathe this brief Lakota prayer as I crawl into the Inipi, honoring this sacred space as the womb of Mother Earth. I still feel awful, and pray hard as the water is poured on the mound of red-glowing stones in the center.

"Unci Maka, Mother Earth, have pity on me. Please take the spirit of this sickness from my body and harmonize it so that I can be strong for the ceremony tonight." A flood of wocangi flows from my hands into the earth, and I instantly feel better.

Afterwards, we all file into Elizabeth's small living room for the second night of House Ceremony. Tonight, Grandfather Mike will be the Yuwipi man.

"Yeah, you're going to see a lot of Spirits tonight. They're going to pound on the door as they enter so that you'll know they're here."

In a matter of minutes, Mike has his altar laid out and his assistants are binding his fingers behind his back.

"Tighter. Tighter. Do it so that it looks like it's cutting off the blood." Mike instructs the young men as they lace his fingers together with a leather thong.

Soon he is wrapped in a star quilt and lying face down in his altar. Someone unscrews the light bulb, but doesn't remove it as they did the night before.

Again, the blue lights flash and move around the room as soon as the singing starts. Within a few minutes, the rattles and the eagle bone whistles follow course.

As rattles fly over me, small bits of material fall onto my head and shoulders, and I think that the Spirits must be sprinkling us with rice much as we do for a wedding. Suddenly, there is a heavy banging on the door. The pounding is repeated again and again as the room fills with strange voices while Spirits flood into our small space. Some of their voices are like hoarse whispers, some are a high nasal pitch, and others are deep and nasal pitched. I can't figure out how the Spirits open the door, as people are packed into the room and at least three are seated right in front of it. There is no room for anyone to stand up, much less move around.

"Wow! This is amazing! How fantastic!" Again, I have to catch myself and channel my mind back to prayers instead of wonderment.

As I stand with my palms open and outward, the Spirits began to doctor me. Small, warm hands are placed on my chest starting on the left side. I count up to ten different hands on my lungs, but am distracted as the rattles trace over my kidneys and liver ever so gently. Someone's head is pushing against my hands, and when I allow it to pass upward between my palms, I feel thick silky hair with a part in the middle."Tunkashila, Wopila Tanka!" I thank the Spirits as they work.

Slowly I become aware that I can no longer hear Grandfather Mike's labored breathing from within the blanket. Just then, the woman next to me whispers in my ear.

"They have taken Grandfather Mike! Pray hard!"

I catch my breath in order to listen again for Mike's breathing. His head was only inches from me, but now I can hear nothing.

"Tunkashila, have pity on us. What will we do without a Spiritual Interpreter like Grandfather Mike? How will we live? Who will help us to talk to the Spirit World? Have pity on us! *Wakan Tanka, oshi mala, ye oyate, wani wicinca!* Creator, have pity on us so that our people may live!"

Black Elk taught that this is the most powerful prayer we can send, and I breath it over and over as tears stream down my face for the return of this powerful and beautiful Medicine Man.

The singers send their hearts into their voice, the rattles soar around the room, and blue lights flicker everywhere. It seems like hours of prayer before I hear Mike take a deep breath.

"Wopila Tanka! Thank you, Creator." I have never felt so thankful in my life. The Spirits have returned Mike to us.

In his muffled voice, Mike explains that the "Spirits took me flying over the badlands."

I can hear the Spirits voices as they now pass around the room speaking to each of the people there. At one point, an owl calls and I can feel the air from its wings as it flaps across the altar and over to the woman in the southeast corner.

Now the tiny hands are gently and firmly pressing me against the wall. They place something large and warm on my left shoulder, and then they are gone. I don't dare to move or touch the object on my shoulder.

When the lights came back on, Mike is sitting cross legged on his neatly folded quilt and the leather thongs are rolled in a tight ball in front of him.

I take a deep breath and finally dare to look down and to my left. There is a perfect ball made from my prayer ties connected to a tail woven from the yellow, white and black prayer flags. This ball and tail are draped over my shoulder. I am still afraid to touch it.

My attention is now drawn to Harold, who is intently examining something between his fingers. We look around as the murmuring in the room grows louder. Almost at the same time, we realize that the Spirits have taken our lonely light bulb, completely crushed it, and sprinkled it over our heads like confetti.

I am still shaking from my experience of actually feeling the Spirits hands and head, and the close call we had when they took Mike. It is difficult to steady my hand when Mike hands the Pipe to me to light. With one easy breath I draw the flame into the bowl! Silver hoops waft toward the ceiling as I take four puffs and then pass the Pipe to Harold.

* * * *

Giant, wet snowflakes swirl around the GMC pickup as Tom, Woody, Ove and I begin our journey from Colorado to the Pine Ridge Reservation for the Bird Flu Yuwipi. It is early March, but I am not concerned about getting caught in a blizzard. When I prayed with the C'anupa to fill our journey with light and love, the *wocangi* was strong, so we will be all right.

The week before, our Pipe Circle had come together to do just this for the healing of the Bird Flu. When we were all gathered together, I held a wooden bowl of tobacco to the Four Sacred Directions and asked each of the Grandfathers/Grandmothers to come into this sacred herb, filling it with White Light and Love for the healing of this Bird Flu spirit. We then played Sundance songs as each person from the circle took a small square of red cotton cloth and placed a pinch of blessed tobacco into it, praying the whole time. When all of the 402 prayer ties were made, we then placed them at the center of our circle as we prayed with the C'anupa. Each member of the circle took four puffs of smoke and blew them onto the prayer ties. In this way, our entire Pipe Circle, the White Horse Circle, was lending their intentions and presence to the healing Yuwipi that was to come.

Each of these beautiful people from the circle also contributed what they could to help bring Ove from Sweden. He is the leader of the Four Sacred Warriors from the four nations of earth's people, and is to represent the White Race. We had hoped to bring one of the Mayan priests to represent the Red Race, but at the last moment our funding didn't come through. Now, we can only raise enough money to bring Ove. Through the Pipe, however, Grandmother says that this will be enough. Woody, from Hawaii, will represent the Yellow Race, and our Lakota brothers and sisters will represent the Red Race. The Black Race will be taken care of somehow. All races from the Four Directions will be represented – Black, White, Red, and Yellow – just as the Spirits had requested. This donation of money from our circle for the ceremony is a huge gift. Each of these beautiful people is quite humble, and most work at least two jobs to make ends meet. Most cannot even attend the ceremony with Grandfather Mike, and yet they trust Spirit implicitly and make this sacrifice on behalf of all humanity. They also do this in anonymity – no one will probably ever know how much they have given for the sake of all humans, and the winged ones, on earth.

"Ove, do you have a tradition of the Little People in your country?" I feel a compelling curiosity about these Spirits who will be working with us.

"Yes, we have the Little People and they often come to us in our ceremonies."

I know that Ove follows the traditions of his Scandinavian and Nordic people. He continues.

"Our little people are gray, and very few people see them."

My mind races through all of the accounts that I have heard of these strange beings. And I share this information with Ove.

"Clifford, the Ute Medicine man that I work with in the World Council of Elders says that they see them as green. He says that they came to him and taught him all of his healing ways. Frances Densmore, who documented many of the Native American songs and ceremonies at the turn of the century, recorded many of the Ute Medicine Men saying that their learned their healing from little green men. One of the elders of the Lakota told me that they see them as blue, and a friend of mine from Iceland said that they see them as purple.

"As I studied Lakota (Sioux) culture, I found numerous teachings about these Spirit Guides and Guardians, the *Manitoukala*. The Lakota say that our soul lives forever, and that we are in this physical body in order to learn and to grow spiritually. Their word for reincarnation is kini, meaning to 'return to life.' When a person has finished all of their work in the physical body, they can return as spirit guides or guardians of the earth, and these are who the little people are. Grandfather Mike says that we cannot see them, or we may die or go crazy. At the last Yuwipi with Mike, I felt their little hands and touched one's head and hair. Have you ever seen them?"

Ove is quiet for a moment, then responds.

"Maybe you think about them too much. Maybe you just need to let them do their work."

"Yes, you're right." But like a dog with a bone, I can't let it go.

"Ove, did you ever hear about the new research on geckos? Scientists have been intrigued as to how the gecko can cling to any surface, even glass, upside down. They thought originally that they had some sort of gluey substance on their feet, or that they perhaps created a type of suction with their feet, but found neither of these hypotheses to be true. Just recently, they discovered the geckos secret. It is something called Van der Waals force. Geckos have billions of spatulae, that resemble broccoli, on these microscopic hairs on their feet. These spatulae allow them to literally become a part of any surface on a subatomic level. Their feet actually become a part of whatever surface they are walking on! Maybe this is how the little people live within the earth and yet can come out and manifest as physical beings. I had a dream where one of these spirits took me flying within the earth, and then used the root systems of trees as highways to the surface. It will be so exciting to meet them again in ceremony!"

Ove is silent as I finish this last. He has already warned me not to overanalyze, but my mind seems to need a logical explanation. Finally, I honor his silence with my own and retreat into a meditation on the scenery passing by.

Black clouds curtain the horizon all around us as a spring blizzard dances from the mountains to the plains. Nonetheless, we are enveloped in a circle of sunshine throughout the six hour drive to Porcupine as the Spirits work for our safe journey. We arrive at Elizabeth's late in the afternoon. Tom and I will stay here while Woody and Ove return to Pine Ridge and their hostess Grandmother Marie. My brother Tom has come for this Yuwipi to represent the women and children of the world. We are to do Inipi Ceremony tonight (Wednesday), and also on Thursday and Friday before the Yuwipi.

It is not necessary to present a Pipe to Mike for this ceremony, as the Spirits are the ones who requested the Yuwipi. It is now Friday, March 10, 2006, and we enjoy a leisurely visit with Mike before we all go into the Sweat Lodge. As soon as the door is closed and the singing begins, blue lights emanate from the Grandfathers, the red-hot stones in the Stone Cradle at the center of the Lodge. These lights travel around the circle, flashing in front of each person as the Spirits address them. Sometimes we can all hear the dialog, and other times we cannot.

Spirit addresses my brother Tom, telling him to "listen to the White Woman as she speaks the truth." I am surprised and humbled to hear the Spirits speak of me this way, and silently thank them for the honor. Now, Grandfather Mike begins to laugh.

"They are calling him 'Jesus' (referring to Ove). They like his beard. Other Medicine Men on the reservation claim to bring Crazy Horse or Sitting Bull into their ceremonies. But I brought in Jesus! Yeah, I am the only one who can say he brought Jesus!"

And we all laugh at this joke from the Spirit World. I can't see Ove in the darkness, but I can hear his laughter as well. It is not often on the reservation that you see men with hair on their face and, obviously, the Spirits are enjoying this novelty. It helps that Ove's thick brown hair hangs loose clear to his shoulders, adding to the resemblance.

"Tunkashila, thank you so much for this ceremony. Tunkashila, thank you for offering this healing for the people of the earth. Tunkashila, I thank the Wakinya for giving us a safe journey." It is my turn to talk to the Grandfathers, and blue lights flash and the drum booms at this acknowledgement of the help from the Thunders.

"Tunkashila, I ask for special blessings for Grandfather Mike and for the Lakota people for they have given us these sacred ceremonies. Tunkashila, I ask that you have pity on my brothers and sisters of our Pipe Circle. They are all humble people, and many work two jobs, yet they have been very generous and made this ceremony possible. Tunkashila, have pity and bless them. Tunkashila, have pity and bless my half-side, Harold, for without him I could not do this work. Wopila Tanka! Mitakuye Oyasin."

When I finish, I cover my face again with my towel to protect it from the scalding steam as Mike pours yet another bucket of water on the Grandfathers. I breathe deeply of the vapors, the breath of Mother Earth, as I silently send my prayers.

"Unci Maka, have pity on me and cleanse my body of all negative energy so that I may prepare for this sacred ceremony. Help me to be like a hollow straw so that Creator's love may flow through me for the healing of the hoop."

Blue lights flicker around the stones and strange, whispering voices hold intercourse with Grandfather Mike.

"The Spirits say that this is a big day for the White Woman. The Spirits thank her for her prayers and say that some of them will be returning with her to her home."

I catch my breath at this last from Mike. Did I hear correctly? Why will they come home with me? Aren't they going to heal the Bird Flu here tonight? Instead of voicing these concerns, I am overawed and simply whisper, "Wopila Tanka!"

It is a short drive to Elizabeth's after the Inipi, and we all file silently into her small living room. Clarence and Clyde have been busy covering the windows with blankets and black plastic. All of the furniture has been set out on the porch, and we seat ourselves around the perimeter of the room, on our blankets with our backs to the wall. Mike instructs me to sit in the sponsor's seat, on the west end of the altar and just behind the center, red and blue staff. Tom sits to my left, and Ove to his left. Woody sits in the northeast corner with the singers. Grandfather has told us through the C'anupa that everyone in the circle represents the Black Race, as we all are descended from those few survivors who came out of Africa 70,000 years ago. Our circle of the Four Races (Black, White, Red, Yellow) of people is complete.

Yuwipi, the Lakota word for "Tie Up," is the historic term for this ceremony and is certainly appropriate. Grandfather Mike, however, prefers to use the term "House Ceremony." I wonder if this is due to the American Indian Religious Crimes Act of 1884, when all American Indian ceremonies were deemed a federal crime, punishable by imprisonment.

Mike's assistants once again lace his fingers behind his back, wrap him in a star quilt with ties around the neck, shoulders, waist, and feet and then place him face down in the altar. The single light bulb is carefully removed, and the drumming and singing begin. Almost immediately, blue lights flash and rattles fly around the room as the Spirits enter.

"Celinda, the Spirits want you to stand up and tell them why you are here."

"Tunkashila, last fall when I came for my healing with Grandfather Mike, he told me that you said we needed to bring Elders from the four corners of the earth and do this ceremony to heal the Bird Flu. You said that if we didn't do this ceremony, then as many as 60 million people might die from it. Tunkashila, you said that if we did this ceremony, then maybe only a few thousand would die. Tunkashila, we have done as you asked. We ask that you have pity on us. Tunkashila, we ask that you give special blessings to Grandfather Mike and to the Lakota people for keeping these sacred ceremonies alive. Tunkashila, we ask that you have pity and heal this Bird Flu, so that our people may live. Mitakuye Oyasin."

When I finish, Mike converses for a few moments in Lakota with a strange whispering voice near his head.

"The Spirits thank you for your prayers. They say that they will 'blow the flu the other way' so that it won't come on the reservation. The Lakota people are already struggling, and they don't have the medical services that others have. The Spirits will take special care of them."

There is a prolonged silence, and my heart sinks.

"Please, Tunkashila, have pity on all the people of the world. Please extend your protection to all people. Thank you so much for protecting the Lakota, but please have pity. Wakan Tanka, oshi mala, ye oyate, wacin wicinca!"

After what seems an eternity, the strange whispering voice speaks to Mike again. Then Mike's muffled voice continues.

"The Spirits say that the world is a big place."

Again a long silence.

"They say that they will bury the Bird Flu in the earth and cover it with dirt."

The Spirits again converse with Mike.

"This ceremony is your Wopila for this healing."

Relief floods through my heart, and tears stream down my face as the Spirits now go around the room, speaking to each and giving healings. A final song is sung, and when the lights are turned back on, Mike is sitting on his neatly folded star quilt and the leather thongs are in a tight ball in front of him. He is strangely silent during the ensuing feast, and gravely accepts our modest thank you gifts for the ceremony. How can we ever give enough for the work that he does as our Spiritual Interpreter? Will the world ever know the work that he does for all humanity, and how much he suffers in order to do this work?

* * * *

"Fairly preposterous, isn't it? I can hear the reaction of many who read this.

"Is it really?" I answer back.

"But...but..." they sputter. "First you start with this explorer, Captain Carver or whatever his name. This medicine man way back when. Then your experience at Fools Crows cabin. Granted, you did come back from the war... those predictions again...it can make a man wonder."

I remain silent.

"But...Eagle Man, what in the world would these Spirits ...why would they get involved with something as ahhh...big as this bird flu thing? It's a bit much." A gasp of exasperation. "After all the research you and that Dr. Bryde did on your tribe and those amazing leaders...now that was interesting...never knew that much was happening ...let alone some folks managed to preserve most of it ...it seems." Pause. "What in the world possessed you to come along with this preposterous 'Bird Flu' ceremony?"

Experts Puzzle over Bird Flu

By MARIA CHENG, AP Medical Writer **Sun Dec 10, 9:12 PM ET**

LONDON - Earlier this year, bird flu panic was in full swing: The French feared for their foie gras, the Swiss locked their chickens indoors, and Americans enlisted prison inmates in Alaska to help spot infected wild birds.

The H5N1 virus — previously confined to Southeast Asia — was striking birds in places as diverse as Germany, Egypt, and Nigeria, and a flu pandemic seemed inevitable.

Then the virus went quiet. Except for a steady stream of human cases in Indonesia, the current flu epicenter, the past year's worries about a catastrophic global outbreak largely disappeared.

What happened?

Part of the explanation may be seasonal.

Bird flu tends to be most active in the colder months, as the virus survives longer at low temperatures.

"Many of us are holding our breath to see what happens in the winter," said Dr. Malik Peiris, a microbiology professor at Hong Kong University. "H5N1 spread very rapidly last year," Peiris said. "So the question is, was that a one-off incident?"

Some experts suspect poultry vaccination has, paradoxically, complicated detection. Vaccination reduces the amount of virus circulating, but low levels of the virus may still be causing outbreaks — without the obvious signs of dying birds.

"It's now harder to spot what's happening with the flu in animals and humans," said Dr. Angus Nicoll, influenza director at the European Centres for Disease Control and Prevention.

While the pandemic has not materialized, experts say it's too early to relax.

"We have a visible risk in front of us," said Dr. Keiji Fukuda, coordinator of the **World Health Organization**'s global influenza program. But although the virus could mutate into a pandemic strain, Fukuda points out that it might go the other direction instead, becoming less dangerous for humans.

H5N1 has primarily stalked Asia. This year, however, it crossed the continental divide, infecting people in Turkey, **Iraq**, Egypt, Djibouti, and Azerbaijan.

But despite the deaths of 154 people, and hundreds of millions of birds worldwide dying or being slaughtered, the virus still has not learned how to infect humans easily.

Flu viruses constantly evolve, so the mere appearance of mutations is not enough to raise alarm. The key is to identify which mutations are the most worrisome.

"We don't really know how many changes this virus has got to make to adapt to humans, if it can at all," said Dr. Richard Webby, a bird flu expert at St. Jude Children's Research Hospital in Tennessee.

The most obvious sign that a pandemic may be under way will almost certainly come from the field: a sudden spike in cases suggesting human-to-human transmission. The last pandemic struck in 1968 — when bird flu combined with a human strain and went on to kill 1 million people worldwide.

In May, on Sumatra island in Indonesia, a cluster of eight cases was identified, six of whom died. The World Health Organization immediately dispatched a team to investigate.

The U.N. agency was concerned enough by the reports to put pharmaceuticals company Roche Holding AG on standby in case its global antiviral stockpile, promised to WHO for any operation to quash an emerging pandemic, needed to be rushed to Indonesia.

Luckily, the Sumatra cluster was confined to a single family. Though human-to-human transmission occurred — as it has in a handful of other cases — the virus did not adapt enough to become easily infectious.

This highlighted many of the problems that continue to plague public health officials, namely, patchy surveillance systems and limited virus information.

Even in China, where H5N1 has circulated the longest, surveillance is not ideal.

"Monitoring the 14 billion birds in China, especially when most of them are in back yards, is an enormous challenge," said Dr. Henk Bekedam,

WHO's top official in China. Of the 21 human cases China has logged so far, 20 were in areas without reported H5N1 outbreaks in birds.

"We need to start looking harder for where the virus is hiding," Bekedam said.

To better understand the virus' activity, it would help to have more virus samples from every H5N1-affected country. But public health authorities are at the mercy of governments and academics. Scientists may hoard viruses while waiting for academic papers to be published first. And developing countries may be wary of sharing virus samples if the vaccines that might be developed from them might ultimately be unaffordable.

That leaves public health officials with an incomplete viral picture.

"It shouldn't just be WHO as a lonely voice in the desert, calling for more viruses (to be shared)," said Dr. Jeff Gilbert, a bird flu expert with the Food and Agriculture Organization in Vietnam. All countries, need to understand that sharing will help them better prepare for a flu pandemic, he said.

Though scientists are bracing themselves for increased bird flu activity in the winter, there are no predictions about where it might appear next. The WHO's Fukuda said it would not be a surprise to see it appear in new countries.

* * * *

My reply to the 'Bird Flu' inquisitor. "Sir," as I said in the beginning, "Creator is all truth!" I drew a circle in the air with my finger and crossed its center horizontally with an imaginary line from East to West. I began at the top and again to make an imaginary line downward to the circle's bottom. The Power of the Hoop or the medicine wheel as depicted on the book's cover.

I offered a strong warrior's look. "Celinda is a truthful person. She has undergone the Sun Dance and the Vision Quest." A long pause. "That takes supreme courage and it makes you more truthful than when you started." I thought for a while. Should I tell him that those two ceremonies are a short cut to the Code - or at least they could be? I decided against the thought. He had too much to adapt to as it was.

"Therefore, I am hoping these Spirits we come in contact with…in ceremony, are of the same Truth." I continued. "Their predictions are what lead me to believe that they are genuinely sincere." I added, "The whole ceremony is sincere! The fact that their predictions always hold true (I have said that a few times.) seems to cement the thought that truly they are governed from where all Truth reigns. The White Man does not have this power of communication and therefore has to castigate what happens before mostly Indigenous folks and those white (Caucasian based) two-legged, whom sincere medicine people are now starting to open up to. Celinda Reynolds Kaelin simply wrote of what she experienced no different than Father Stolzman, and I believe her as I do the good Father."

I left the dubious inquisitor at that: Enough explaining. I really do not care whether or not other folks arrive to the same conclusion as mine. In the next chapter we will view a very powerful Spirit Calling by Chief Eagle Feather and after that ceremony we will dissect it to derive more clues as to the Spirit World beyond. Maybe we will also discuss or explore clues from the 'Bird Flu' ceremony.

These ceremonies enter into us or bring forth an entity who is not of this particular world - so to speak. Bluntly speaking - the Spirit entering ceremony and the divulging of needed information which human cannot extract on their own - they need help and therefore call for it. That the Spirit Helper carries our message to some very supreme force for desired results, demonstrates unquestionably, its (the Spirit's) mobility. After the following passage we will go on to the next chapter and one last Spirit Ceremony and then we can discuss this issue or quest more fully. It all connects to the Code, so have a bit of patience.

A Warrior's Beseechment

On my way to a national religion and ecology conference, I stopped to visit the Viet-nam Memorial in Washington, D.C., and found myself involved with ceremony.

Healing at the Wall

I was wearing a worn Marine Corps flight jacket and carrying a sea bag. A POW/Missing in Action booth appeared in the distance between me and the memorial. I noticed that several men, obvi-ously Vietnam veterans by their dress, were donating their time to the management of the booth. One wore an old army field jacket and the other's open shirt revealed a T-shirt that read "Vietnam Vet-eran and Proud of It." They spotted my jacket with its squadron and Phantom patches and greeted me warmly as I drew closer. I was no longer a stranger among the hundreds of other strangers who had been floating by on that spring day. After taking a sharp focus on my jacket's 100-missions patch, one of them asked where I had been stationed in Vietnam.

"Chu Lai," I replied as I relieved myself of my baggage. I asked if I could leave my sea bag in the booth.

By this time they had read my name and rank on my flight jacket and replied,

"Certainly, Captain. We'll watch your gear. Take your time. We'll be here when you come back." I was concerned for my belongings that were to be used at the religion and ecology conference. My drum and my pipe were in the bag and also my eagle bone whistle. I took out my eagle bone whistle and my buck-skin pipe bag that contained my peace pipe. I placed these items in the travel case I had hanging from my shoulder. The men looked at the fringed pipe bag but did not comment. I thanked them for watching my sea bag and walked toward the wall, where my past waited.

A great deal of anguish and lament can be found at the Vietnam Memorial. Fortunately, I am one of those who returned to a tribe that honored its own. My tribal chairman, Enos Poor Bear, even had me carry into battle the American flag that had flown over our Sun Dance. It was folded and placed under my ejection seat when I flew a mission. My squadron commander had it sent back to the reservation. Fools Crow, who was Sun Dance chief, had it flown again at the Sun Dance, and a recognition ceremony for those who served in Vietnam took place.

Memories flood back. Despite the tolling of time, combat memories and the ones you were with, living and dead, never seem to fade.

The skies of flak and missiles come back and so do the black, lightning-streaked, rainy nights orbiting over the South China Sea. Waiting to streak inbound to strike and be struck at. For me, the prolonged waiting at the very edge of fire-strewn skies was more disturbing than the actuality of combat itself. I can see the plane captains as we started our engines, the frenzied bomb crews rushing to reload us when a Marine battalion was being attacked by a dauntless and efficient enemy fighting for a cause they believed was worth fighting for.

I remember a touching scene when I was in law school and flying helicopters part-time for the Marine Corps Reserves. I took a Reserve helicopter back to the Hunkpapa people and helped honor their dead. Since this was during the time that draft-exempt college students were demonstrating, my non-Lydian copilot was amazed by the moving ceremony that took place far out on the Standing Rock Reservation. We circled to land and were met formally by a marching contingent of Sioux warriors who were members of the American Legion and the VFW. We changed quickly out of our sweaty flight suits into our dress uniforms in the belly of the helicopter. A recruiting staff sergeant in dress blues was also with us. We were told to march at the head of the contingent into the gymnasium. The assembled crowd cheered when we entered the building. Warriors spoke and women tremoloed. I had to speak to the packed gymnasium. I told the excited crowd that it was an honor to return to a land of tribal people who appreciated the sacrifice of their warriors. I told them how they had salved my spirit with their honoring medicine and how this medicine was deeply appreciated by all the living who returned. My nervous copilot, surrounded by a cheering, tremoloing crowd of Indians, had to speak also. I advised him, when he asked, to tell them that he appreciated a people who know how to honor both their dead and the living who return from a war.

After the speeches, we went outside. Close to the gymnasium were several rows of young cottonwood poles that had been planted in the ground. At the top of each pole a pulley was attached and a cotton rope hung down. Young Indian men and women waited with an American flag for each pole. Many Sioux warriors from this Hunkpapa and Minnecoujou Sioux reservation had been killed. A drum rolled and we stood at attention, holding our salute for a long time before the flagpoles. A flag for each departed warrior was raised on its own sapling staff, and the Sioux anthem and our national anthem were played. A singer chorused an ancient fight song while the Sioux women tremoloed. In the background, draped from two taller poles, the American flag and a tribal flag waved. It was an extremely moving scene cast upon the computer of life.

I left the Vietnam statue at the end of the wall and returned to the MIA table. It was a welcome relief from having just been to the wall. Sud-denly, in the midst of our conversation, the former corpsman asked, "Captain, you have a peace pipe, don't you?" When I nod-ded, he bluntly requested, "Captain, we come here all the time, Could you do a ceremony for us or some kind of honoring?" He turned toward the wall. "Could you take a bunch of us down to the wall and do something like I saw them do on the reservations?" He turned back to look me straight in the eye. "Name the time, Captain, while you're going to be here. We'll be waiting."

I didn't hesitate or fumble for the conference schedule in my shoulder bag. I was talking to combat warriors. *These men were never honored.* I spoke sharply. "I'll be back at ten o'clock. I'll be back at ten o'clock, the day after tomorrow morning," I hoisted my seabag to set off for the nearest intersection to hail a cab. After taking a few steps, I turned and told them to bring four solid-colored pieces of cloth - red, yellow, black, and white.

I can still see the light in their eyes. It is almost as vivid as my image of Bill Eagle Feather standing before the Sun Dance tree, tug-ging and pulling backward with his arms lifted to the skies. That was, and always will be, my most vivid, living memory. 'We will finally be honored,' was spoken out through their eyes.

My sea bag is a disguise, however. This container can do what fancy suitcases cannot. It can hold a thick round drum or hide a valuable buckskin, a beaded war shirt, heavy beaded belts, a bone hair pipe choker - gifted items that money cannot buy. No one yet has attempted to walk away with this rugged canvas that also con-tains an eagle bone whistle and a personally carved peace pipe that took me many hours to make. (I do not subscribe to the myth that you have to be given a pipe and cannot make your own.) The posi-tive ceremonial activity I have been experiencing with this pipe reinforces my belief.

In my travels I have yet to lose my sea bag that looks to the world as if it contains nothing worth taking and also diminishes my appearance - if I were to worry about impressions.

Ten o'clock came two days later. Four of us from the conference stepped from the cab. Two women and a black veteran, who had insisted on paying the cab fare, were with me as we walked to the ragtag group that waited.

The four colored cloths were placed on a table within the booth. I walked over to a stand of trees and plucked four branches for sticks. I tied a colored flag to each stick and passed them out to two warriors and to the two women. I took my pipe from its buck-skin container, assembled it, and hung the eagle bone whistle around my neck. I was wearing my buckskin war shirt under my flight jacket and could feel the warmth of the muggy day that was beginning.

In my pocket was my *wotai*. I squeezed it hard and told it to give me the strength and the distance of a mountain lion. My blood sis-ter, Jamie Sams, told me that a mountain lion is a lesson in the use of power in leadership.

Mountain lion stands on its convictions and leads you where your heart takes you. Others may choose to follow, and the lessons will multiply. You are never allowed to be human or vulnerable, if you call on the medicine of moun-tain lion. The pitfalls are many, but the rewards are great. You must always be aware of keeping peace. However, you can never make everyone happy unless you lie to yourself or others. Therefore the first responsibility to leadership is to tell the truth. Know it and live it, and your example will filter down to all within the pack.

I had to be the mountain lion that day and show no human emotion. For added assurance, I called on my spirit guide, Charg-ing Shield. His past consideration with me was a perfect reference for the moment. "You, oh stern, heartless-looking warrior, let me now be like you, without emotion. I will not cry. I will not draw forth tears. Although I was among these warriors and fought within the fire and steel of these modern battles, I shall be of that white man's steel, emotionless, while I do this ceremony. "

I thought of the eagle who allows only one chick to live in times of overpopulation, the buffalo herd that turns out the aged leader, the fox that casts out the deformed kit, and related harsh decisions made by the old two-leggeds who chose to walk into the blizzards or onto the ice floe rather than prolong their burden and loneliness. "I shall be you, Charging Shield (The Spirit image within my stone.). You who would never bend or cry." I called out to the four winds. I took on the scowl of one of the major powers within my stone. "Fall in," I yelled out harshly.

We assembled in a military manner. I was already beginning to sweat in my buckskin shirt. One warrior was heavy with tattoos and was comfortably attired in a black Harley-Davidson T-shirt and brown patent-leather vest. The vest bore his Vietnam ribbons and a motorcycle pin on one side, and on the opposite side a POW/MIA patch was sewn. I admired him for putting his ribbons on his vest. He reminded me of another warrior who had his com-bat ribbons attached to a leather plate on a Harley motorcycle that I saw in a parking lot. I felt good that whole day even though I never met that warrior.

"Fall in." I subconsciously repeated the command that was decades old in my memory. The group assembled in two squads. "Forward march", I called out like a drill sergeant.

The motley group obeyed commands from long ago and marched forward to halt at the beginning of the long black wall. We milled about for a few moments, and the other people on the walkway started to step back and stare at us. Such an odd sight we must have appeared. A ragtag band of veterans sprinkled with two women and led by a sweating Indian wearing a buckskin, beaded shirt underneath a pilot's jacket and carrying a peace pipe.

After a brief pause I led the group forward on the walkway. I was halted by a call. "Captain, here's a name." I turned and watched the burly, toughened man in the motorcycle shirt step for-ward to reach out to the wall. Looks are deceiving. He caressed the stone of the wall lovingly and began to cry. I feverishly called out to the spirit of the mountain lion and Charging Shield. I was the leader and would not cry at that moment. I would do all that later, but not at that particular moment. "Resolve!" an inner voice yelled at me. "Resolve! You shall show no emotion and not even be human at times. You are not allowed to be two-legged or vulnera-ble....You shall not be vulnerable." Somehow my eyes stayed dry and my voice did not crack.

It was a miracle that my voice did not choke at that moment. Such a strong, powerful man, unafraid to exhibit his feelings. Unafraid to reach unabashedly into his past with love and concern. When you watch such a strong man cry, you have great respect and admiration but it is very difficult not to release and cry with him. How fortunate it was that I had had my cry two days before. I stared at the Harley-Davidson eagle until the man looked at me and said, "Captain, here it is. This is my cousin. My real cousin. We played together when we were kids." The eagle, my natural namesake, fortified my resolve at this complex moment. He said the words so emphatically and innocently, as if they were still children playing. "He's here, isn't he? Captain, he's here?" he pleaded.

I said calmly, "Yes he is, he is here." My spirit shuddered at the powers that he so desperately wanted me to have. I called on my rock-hard spirit guide. "Charging Shield," I demanded in a warrior's voice. "Assure this spirit. Assure him that his cousin will be with him or I will cast you and my stone into the Potomac." I looked at the crying warrior squarely, unable to believe that I had to become a mountain lion. I took the stone from my pocket and walked toward him. I caressed it slowly across the name on the wall. Each letter I touched with meaning. I looked at him directly, fighting back the tears that wanted to well up when I saw the river flow from his eyes. "Mountain lion, Charging Shield, ... blizzards, ... fox," my words came out disjointedly as I fought to keep my lead-ership. The warrior began to sob when I took the stone from the wall and touched it across his shoulder blades. Such a strong war-rior he was. He reminded me of my vigorous and dynamic Viet-nam friend, Jim, from Ohio. "My friend," I said, "your cousin is now sitting upon you. Now let us proceed."

Within a few paces, another name was called out and the pro-cession stopped again. "Captain, we have another comrade who must be recognized." The corpsman came forward and cried out the name of a companion. I took my *wotai* stone and did the same as I had done for the Harley-Davidson warrior. The corpsman cried and this time it was easier for me not to cry. We went on, with each veteran in turn stopping the procession. Each time, I asked the spirit of the warrior to come into my *wotai* stone in order to do ceremony at the end of the wall. As we proceeded, the people on the walk-way stood back with reverence and respected the dignity of our meaning. It was all too powerful and real for anyone not to under-stand the depth of what we were doing. When we reached the end of the wall, we made our way through a group of high school stu-dents and marched toward the three figures cast in combat uni-forms and bearing the arms and equipment of the Vietnam warrior.

We stopped before the statues that seemed now to be alive. I placed each person who carried a colored cloth in the position of Black Elk's colors - red facing east, yellow facing south, black fac-ing west, and white facing north - and afterwards I gave a brief talk. Strangely, the high school students assembled and looked on with intense interest. Several black people, what looked like a Hmong couple, and whites from various walks of life gathered qui-etly. I offered my peace pipe to the four directions, down to Mother Earth, up to Father Sky, and lastly to Great Spirit. I cradled my pipe back into my arms and said:

"We are gathered here today as warriors, warriors who fought in a war that many of us did not fully understand. We fought in a time when politicians' sons were not in the front lines with us. Neither were the corporate heads nor their sons, or the chiefs and the sons of the chiefs of the many bands and groups that run this land. Some of us volunteered, some of us were drafted, but none of us came from the lead-ership of this country - political, religious, or economic lead-ership - and yet we were the only ones to go forth into battle. This long black wall is testimony to those who have gone on into the spirit world because of this battle far away in a foreign land. These surviving warriors who stand here are not of Native American ways and were not honored when we returned from this war, and that absence has been a severe handicap and hurt for us who have lived.

I stopped and took out my stone. "Within this stone," I began, "lies the spirits of those who have gone beyond and whose names are inscribed upon the wall. We have just taken them from the wall." I waved my *wotai* in a semicircle and called out in the direc-tion of the wall, "Oh, you warriors who have gone on, help us here in this land where you once were. Become spirit guides and descend upon the shoulders of your comrades to guide them in the wisdom and knowledge that you have gleaned from your new realm."

I brought my wotai down and waved it over the assembled war-riors, then walked among them touching the rainbow-rimmed agate to each man's shoulder. Returning to my position between the warriors and the statue, I continued: "Long ago, in the old days of leadership, and I believe a much more prudent leadership, the chiefs and their sons were the first in battle. This was a great detriment to foolish war. It is a lesson to be learned from the just people who are the ancestors of the land. When warriors went forth for the tribe and came back, or did not come back, they were honored - so that the people's way would live. Let all who are here today, let us honor these warriors who stand before us."

I placed my stone in my pocket and handed my peace pipe to one of the women before speaking to the figures in bronze. "We do not have time to lament, however. For the world has fallen into serious trouble from overheating, overpopulation, and pollution. In time, many millions of world citizens can be imperiled, and eventually, ultimately, this earth could become a black shell of life-lessness. Therefore, it is a new war that warriors must embark upon." At this point I turned back to face the assembled group and waved my hand at the wall. "The spirit warriors who surround this wall are no doubt aware of our planet's situation and no doubt would like to see those who are living channel their energies toward a new beginning. I call on you veterans to remain warriors, but to become new warriors, warriors for Mother Earth. I call on the spirits we have taken from the wall and placed upon the shoul-ders of these new warriors for Mother Earth to lead them toward a new environmental awareness. Take your past lament, your bereavement, and channel this energy toward fighting for Mother Earth, and let your spirit guide help you. *Ho.*"

The woman who carried the red flag spoke after she had sub-dued her tears. "Please forgive me. I was on the other side." She looked at the red flag of knowledge and almost cried again. "I was a demonstrator. I was a protester and now here I stand. I never knew what you have gone through and now I know and I am so ashamed." Her tears began anew and lasted for some time. The veterans stood silently and some shared their tears with her. I turned away and shared a few of my own.

"Please forgive me," she repeated emotionally. "Now I know and understand so much more."

The warriors nodded solemnly. The ceremony was over. The crowd stood stunned. It was as if time had stopped. We all became brief statues of dismay looking toward the White House, and then walked away. We would change this world with a duty of our own.

One last echo comes to me from that ceremony. "Captain, I sure do thank you," the black man spoke in a southern drawl. "I am released and got new direction. A bad, hurting weight has been taken from me." He gestured toward the statues where we had done our ceremony. "I thank you, Captain, and whatever tribe is out there that kept it all alive."

12

Death

"I know I have to keep breathing. Tomorrow the sun will rise.
Who knows what the tide will bring."

Castaway - starring Tom Hanks.
It offered some rewarding thoughts regarding life and death.

A guest entry by a dear friend, Medicine Story, Wamponaog tribal historian and author of *Return to Creation* (Revised). Medicine Story is a member of the Assonet band, Wampanoag Nation. See www.circleway.org, for information about all his books and recordings.

We are now together once more by Scargo Lake, listening to the murmur of wavelets conversing quietly with the shore. I return here to this scene of my childhood from time to time to remember and feel the space of my life growing from thoughts I sank once into the dark mystery below the surface in which the shadow of my soul peered back at me.

Where we sit now is in the old Nobscusset (Eastern coastal tribe) burying ground. It is a good place to conclude our thoughts and our journey together. The burying ground, which was next to my grandparent's house, has changed since I was a boy. Then it was completely unnoticed and neglected by the town. All overgrown with large thick bushes, tangled and wild. If you did not try to penetrate that thicket you would not see the old iron rail fence on stone posts that delineate the burying ground, or discover the small tablet that proclaimed it and informed that the chief, Mashantampaine, was lying there.

Since then the town has felt the consciousness that Native people began to arouse of our history, our existence and conditions today, and our determination to reclaim and honor the remains of our ancestors that have been desecrated by advancing civilization. So I guess they felt some local pride that they had preserved this place, and they came in and cleaned out the undergrowth and prettified and tamed it into a little park like their own graveyards. I have mixed feelings about that. I like it that they mean to do honor to our ancestors, that they will not put a mini-mall or a condominium here, and that people who come have a place to sit as we are, to rest and feel the peace of the trees and the lake, to give their minds peace and perhaps a thought of our old ones and the brief span of life that is given to each of us.

But of course to me personally it is not an improvement to impose human aesthetics and order upon a wilderness. There is order here now, open areas, walks, mown grass, planted flowers. Nice to think of the human care and attention it receives. But. Human ordering has brought the place under control, reduced it to fit into human understanding and utility. I guess I prefer my memory of it as an almost impenetrable thicket. There it contained the profound mystery of life, growth and death, untrammeled by human dread. There were places where only birds could enter, and other places barred even to the sun and wind. I might peer into this small area returned to the care of Creation and feel the unimaginable power seething within and sense something beyond my ken, something that reached out to still my breathing and stir eerily all the hairs of my body.

Well, this is a perfect place to explore our thoughts and feelings about death. Death, like birth, is an integral part of life, but until we are faced with it close at hand, as in the passing of a friend or loved one, or a near experience of it ourselves, we generally bar the subject form our minds.

Of course, there is no single Native culture in the Americas, but hundreds of quite different ones. There are generally held beliefs about the sacredness and the relatedness of all things, but the stories about what happens after this life are various. As with all human experience confronting the physical fact of death generates awe. The doorway of our tiny room of the known and familiar is for a moment thrown open to the vast and unfathomable mystery of existence.

Great stories abound. We love to titillate our senses with our ignorance and fear. Skeletons reconnect, bones find each other and stand and walk and sometimes re-grow flesh and hair. Some cultures are terrified of dead bodies, even burn their houses with them inside. Most merely respect them.

Our elders tell us everything has a spirit. Not only people, not only animals and plants, but stones and water and fire and wind – everything. Anyone who has witnessed the dying of a person notices that something palpably leaves the body at that point. The body is different then, somewhat smaller, less, it seems. What has left, the old ones called Manitou – Spirit.

The plains people put their dead on scaffolds, to be open to the sky and the journey of the spirit, to be cleaned by our relatives, the carrion birds and the wind and rain. A few cultures cremated. Most showed a concern, a respect and a tenderness for the remaining vessel of the departed.

Some built little shelters of wood or stone for the bodies, often with an outlet to the west or the southwest, the direction it was felt the soul would take on its journey. Many of our stories say Creator and our ancestors wait for us in that direction, and the band of filmy light that winds through the heavens was referred to as the Star Path that we will take on our last journey.

That respect and care for the bodies of the deceased is shown by dressing them in their finest regalia and placing beside them their most prized articles together with sacred tobacco, sweet grass and cedar. Often food was left as well, hoping the spirit of the meat or berries would follow the spirit of the person for sustenance on the trip. Many thought that the soul did not begin that journey for four days, being attached to earth and relatives. During that time, continued ceremonies might be held to show love, and urge the soul to depart.

In some of the old villages of my own people it seems people were buried beside their own houses. Probably it was felt that the deceased would want their bodies close to home where their families would look out for them. When the English moved in and displaced our people here, this town created this Indian burying ground to re-inter the bodies that were dug up. When I was a boy the town had forgotten about this place, and my grandfather engaged me to help him care for this place where ancient Nobscussets turned into earth and trees in the sacred cycle of life.

As population and towns grew, many old bones were being uncovered, and laws were passed to stop construction in such places until the indigenous descendants in the area could determine how to care for the sacred remains of their ancestors. Eventually laws were also created to return to Native people any bodies that were held by museums or other exhibits, so that they may be returned at last to the ancient earth of their homelands.

So now our people have begun receiving the remains of our ancestors, together with their sacred objects, from museums and archeological schools and societies. Some of them don't want to comply and must be pressed, but most of them are glad not to have the responsibility for these any more, and are glad to return them to us. And our people are very happy to have them back, to bring the bones of our old ones back to the earth they came from.

Since we never dug up our own dead once laid to rest, we have no ceremonies for re-interment. And it means we must deal with town officials and their burial rules. Some require caskets, and our people were not put in boxes, that they might more easily be assimilated into the soil and recycled to new life. Sometimes the remains have been treated with chemicals the earth may not want, and that is not a problem we have met before this industrial age. But survival of our people has always meant adapting and changing and creating new ceremonies to help us through the changes.

I can feel beauty and peace in the well-ordered cemeteries of civilization, but none of the hidden power of that fierce, elemental mystery. I think people do not want to have feelings they cannot comfortably deal with, but they also want to remember and honor the departed, and so focus on the beauty and order they can impose here.

I often remember sitting in a lovely cemetery with my best friend Fred when we were fifteen, watching the easy flow of the Shawsheen River and talking about life and art, philosophy and poetry, truth and beauty. But not about death. We kept our thoughts in the well-traveled realms of the known. It was only here, in the intense interior of this thicket, where all human art and science could not penetrate, that I felt the awe of all that lies beyond. The unfathomable presence, moving the cosmos concentrating itself in these few acres forbidden to our view.

Civilized man is uncomfortable with mystery. He demands to know, always questioning, as a child does. Well and good. There is an urge in our evolutionary instructions to pay attention, to watch and listen and learn. But we are uneasy when we do not understand. So too often we pretend we know. In that intellectual arrogance lie most of the problems we make for ourselves and our world. We make up stories to relieve our unease and our fear and then impose our fabrications on others. Humility comes hard for our species. Our ignorance means we cannot control, and that scares us, so we pretend we know and we try to control. With often dangerous consequences.

And the great mystery for us self-conscious beings is death. We build our religions and their stories to allay our terrors of a final dark. We cannot visit before the end of our journey on earth, so we send our spirits to accompany Orpheus, or Anubis, or Buddha, or Kali, or the Valkyries, or Virgil to guide us. Out Native cultures in North America have many tales of such journeys.

Often these stories are about young men distraught at the unexpected death of a beloved young bride. In one such story I am fond of, the young man is a great warrior and a chief, whose sorrow is so great he is unable to think about his people and sinks into despair. Finally he declares he will go to the Land of Souls and find her, as he cannot live without her. His elders try to dissuade him, but he is adamant and sets out on his journey towards the setting sun, guiding his way at night by following the Star Path in the sky, the trail of the Milky Way toward the southwest.

He continues in this manner for many months until at last he comes to a final hill beyond which there is only mist. Under this mist there is a great water, a still and silent sea, and on the shore one small lodge before which sits an old man. The chief tells the old man of his desire to go to the Land of Souls and is told he cannot go there because he still inhabits his earthly body. The young man weeps and pleads and touches the old man's heart so that he tells the youth he may make a brief visit, but he must leave his body behind. This the young chief is more than willing to do, so the old one strips the youth's body off his soul and hangs it like a robe in his lodge. Then he puts the soul into his canoe and paddles out into the mist.

Looking down into the water the chief's soul can see the bottom is strewn with the bones of other souls who have crossed over. Soon another canoe is spotted coming out of the mist, and the chief is overjoyed to see the soul of his beloved coming for him. Somehow she has heard of his arrival and his determination to see her. She brings him back with her to the Land of Souls, and they begin to walk together over sweet meadows and gentle hills where soft breezes carry the hum of insects, the trill of birds, and the scent of grass and wild flowers.

Happily they lie together then and no words or thoughts are needed to convey their love and joy in one another. Other souls pass silently by and can be seen to smile upon their bliss. Some he recognizes as relatives who have died, who only give a friendly nod and go on. After a long while the girl speaks.

"Grandfather Sun will leave us now and return to light another day on Earth. It is time for you to leave too."

"Then you must come with me."

"That I cannot do."

"Then I will stay here with you."

"That cannot be. You have been allowed this brief visit so that you can return and inform our people they have nothing to fear of death, and that all of us are waiting for you here where you also must one day come. I will always be with you in your heart through your life, and when you return to me we will be united never to part."

So she returned him to the old man who took him back and hung his body upon him again, and the chief made the long journey back to his people. He lived to a very old age and told all he met the story of his journey to the Land of Souls, a journey that all would one day make.

Other versions of this story contain conditions like those set for Orpheus and like him broken with tragic and cautionary results. But I like the sweet simplicity of this version, and certainly would like to believe the comfort of the chief's tale.

In most of the stories it is not the opposition of life with death that is central but the conflict between love and death. It is not the unknown we fear, it is losing the known, which has become so dear to us.

Death has much to teach us. I do not believe that people after they die would care at all (if they have any individual consciousness) what we do with their remains. It is only important to us the living, to confirm how we feel, not only about the departed one, but about death itself,

It is common for the closest relative to have a give-away and give the possessions of the deceased in the way he or she would have wished. The Sioux have a Give-away Ceremony called the O-du-huh. During the year after the deceased passes on, one's belongings are gathered and then given away. This way the deceased is re-remembered as friends or relatives accept their gift or memento and say words of their connection to the deceased. For many of us an old custom is followed of not mentioning the name of the departed for one year, after which another ceremony is held to remember what the person has left in our hearts.

The time of our loss is also a time of reminding us that our own demise is also on its way. We get to decide how we want to think about that. Do we want to believe it is too distant to consider now? Do we want to think about the meaning of our lives, what we have accomplished, where we are headed? Do we want to improve our relationships, get closer to loved ones, begin a new project? Maybe we will have a very high thought, in my mind, at least it is extremely important. Maybe we will ask our selves, "The Earth Mother is in serious trouble. What am I doing with my life, while I am yet here…to help her?"

Our ancestors were taught by Manito, or spirit, that when a dear relative died a special long lodge should be built. The body was placed near the center pole, and people stayed with it for four days singing and drumming. In honor and respect, but also, I believe, to encourage the soul to depart and go on its long journey. There are some people in Canada who still follow our traditional ways, but my own people, having been separated from land and each other for almost four hundred years, having lost our songs and ceremonies and language and having intermarried with the immigrants of many races and nations, are today in a process of using the ways of our mixed culture, the funeral practices of the Christian relatives infused with elements of our traditional Native ways. It is a source of pride, I think, that we can claim all the elements of our diverse heritage and honor each one separately.

A very strong element of our traditional attitudes about death is our always-present consciousness of the unborn who will follow us. We have a soul connection not only with the children, grandchildren, and great-grandchildren we know, but also with those unknown generations who will follow. Just as we have a soul connection with our parents, grandparents, great-grandparents, and all those who came before.

I still don't know what to think about my own death. I don't know what happens to our souls when we die, and I don't believe anyone else does either. I've read a lot about other people's ideas and experiences. Ideas about an after-life, or about re-incarnation, stories from people who died and were revived. None of them are convincing to me. All of them seem only to follow the patterns suggested by the culture of the narrator. Combinations of cultural conditioning and wishful thinking.

People who have met death, in close encounters for themselves or in the passing of others close to them, are much more happy and welcoming of their own end when it comes than those who avoid however they can the thought and experience of death.

From conception and birth life has provided many challenges and many rewards, and looking back I am grateful for it all. The hard times, the lonely times, the confusions, frustrations, the gifts of others, and the victories by my own efforts. It has all been good, every moment had value. Since it has been good so far, I must believe that whatever happens next must also be good.

If I die tonight I will die content. I have done my best, brought more love to people than I had been given and had it returned to me in overwhelming measure, by my beloved, by my family, by my friends, by the prisoners and all the people in all the circles I have convened, by the dear members of my tribal band and other indigenous people I have met throughout the world, by people who have only read my writings and have written or called and even visited just to thank me and tell me how much my reaching out has meant to them.

But it is another morning now. So far so good. I made it through the night, and here is my beloved by my side. Another day now to add to the story, another challenge to meet. As my favorite line in Wavy Gravy's song "Basic Human Needs" goes, "Thank goodness for something to do."

When I die do not mourn for me, rather celebrate. Celebrate that you are still alive, that we made a connection that was important to me, that we were and are still one, and that I and all Creation are waiting one day to greet you again.

Until then – Wuniish – Go in Beauty.

Eaglefeather

13

Suppositions of the Spirit World

"You assist an evil system most effectively by obeying its orders and decrees. An evil system never deserves such allegiance. Allegiance to it means partaking of the evil. A good person will resist an evil system with his or her whole soul."

— Gandhi

The Lost Six

A Yuwipi (Spirit Calling) was conducted by Chief Eagle Feather at the University of South Dakota while I was in law school. Down through three decades, the powerful ceremony stands out vividly in my memory. Off and on, I have constantly thought about this revealing calling and it has galvanized or catalyzed itself to become the major reason why I have decided to make this undertaking. This ceremony has repeatedly nudged me to address its power, to investigate more than its assumed role or call, way back then. The following recall is told in detail in several of my writings, but for the sake of the issue I'm probing here, an attempt at a wholesome repetition of the details is very important for the issue of this work.

This particular ceremony, in my opinion, has provided for me the most clues as to our major quest in this writing. What lies beyond in the Spirit World? It has assured me, for myself, at least, that a Spirit World does exist. Secondly, I have also been reassured that powers, or abilities by some, extend far beyond the powers we humans are limited to. These Spirits, I have discovered, are not all-knowing at the beginning. For what that discovery is worth, I have a few questions that I could ask quantum physicists, cosmologists, astronomers and related scholars. I became more curious about this fascinating happening which I was so privileged to become exposed to by my two mentors Fools Crow and Eagle Feather. Most folks are simply awed with respect for such a powerful happening, as was Celinda Kaelin when she viewed her experience. I did not venture too far regarding major suppositions that began to build until investigating other supportive Spirit callings and then began to summarize the evidence. It may be difficult for some to co-relate the ceremony's role from the finding of six college student crash victims which was the issue of this ceremony - the Lost Six - and onward to suppositions of the Spirit World, but we must not lose sight of the fact that we are dealing with a Spirit in this happening. Let me back up a bit, more precisely; it was five college students, a Speech Team from a South Dakota college, and the Speech Team coach who was also the pilot of the airplane which crashed fatally for all aboard. Grey Weasel was the name of the Spirit who was called upon. Indian names are seldom made for the movies but that simply was his name. Some Indian names can be highly deceiving, however. Grey Weasel and Good Road, the Spirit in Fools Crow's earlier protective ceremony for Vietnam, were both very powerful and accurately predictive entities.

Were it not for their accuracy and veracity, I never would have ventured to speak of my experiences. Bear in mind always: If it happened, then it most certainly was ordained by the Ultimate Power of the All Truth, as was the Lone Cloud Sun Dance happening. Creator alone, controls the Force; is my belief. It will be impossible for many, however, despite what happens in some Native ceremony, to admit that such supernatural force can happen; especially when it occurs outside of their particular belief system. It is actually quite odd that so many modern humans are so sheep-like, programmed by mere man that they will believe otherwise.

The environmental change is just around the corner, however. By then, in its aftermath, ignorant human, once so smugly all-knowing, will possibly begin to believe in great panic that Creator alone, indeed controls all Forces upon Its realm!

I received a call from my boss, the Director of Indian Studies in regard to the crashed airplane about a month after the tragedy. I was told to contact either Bill Eagle Feather or Chief Fools Crow for a Spirit Ceremony in conjunction with what we had termed, the 'Lost Six;' the five speech team students and their pilot/professor who crashed somewhere in the remote, snow-covered region called the Nebraska Sand Hills. They were returning from Denver to Sioux Falls, South Dakota, and encountered a blizzard. The pilot developed vertigo and it was presumed the plane had crashed on the windswept prairie and was covered by snow. An all-out search began - even the National Guard was used - but after a while it was too expensive and futile to continue. The search was called off. At that point the University of South Dakota Indian Studies program, where I worked during law school, had connections with Sioux holy men. Therefore, they were called upon by the University President.

It is a bit complicated but for the sake of verification, which this dissertation will surely provoke; the students were from a Christian Protestant College, Augustana College in Sioux Falls. The president of that school of higher learning was at his wit's end, and had called on the University of South Dakota president for possible help to relieve him of his dilemma. Even though the search had been called off by the National Guard, he was besieged by grieving parents as to what other efforts he was committing his position. The University president decided to offer him the service of the Indian Studies program, which the college president knew had close connections with the state's reservation holy men, namely, Chiefs Fools Crow and Eagle Feather. Their reputation had even reached into Dominant Society by then. There is an old saying that a drowning man will reach for a stone thrown to him. Maybe this was the case of the college president wanting to relieve himself from the constant concern of the understandably emotional parents. Whatever, when the holy men were mentioned to him and that a possible Spirit Calling ceremony could be in the offing, the distraught president readily agreed. Rumor has it that his remark was, "Maybe I don't have to believe in what they are doing but I am at my wit's end and at least I can state that I was willing to try anything!" The University president's wife was becoming a close friend of mine while I was in law school, particularly due to my position of Asst. Director of Indian Studies, and she was a strong supporter of the Native Studies program. At many of our meetings and Indian Students club she was often in attendance which we welcomed.

Fools Crow was unavailable so I called the Rosebud Tribe's police station. Bill was a typical medicine person for those times; most usually did not have telephones. If one needed to contact a holy man or a medicine woman, you simply called the police station. If the police deemed your call as 'official' they would dispatch a squad car out to get the person sought and bring them to the station telephone. Within an hour, Bill was on the line. "Nephew, I understand, you are looking for me," were his first words. Without waiting for my reply, he added, "You want me to find those bodies, don't you?" Having by now, finding myself getting used to the gifted man's psychic abilities, I was not startled. "That's right," I added, rather business - as - usual like.

"I have a singer ready to drive me and he has good tires." Bill went on. "I have my bag packed and was waiting to hear from you." In those days it seemed almost customary that the medicine men all had those tin suitcases that have now long since disappeared. "Last night I did an Inipi (Sweat lodge). Your buddy, Grey Weasel, said you'd be calling." Eagle Feather had a sense of humor, as was the case with many Sioux holy men. Chief Fools Crow was far more somber. Chief Eagle Feather would tease occasionally, including into his teasing, his major Spirit helper, Grey Weasel. "Grey Weasel says, he will teach you a thing or two about flying and steal that pretty blond pilot friend you fly with." Maybe Grey Weasel had the humor as well. Bill was referring to another University pilot whom I worked with and occasionally flew with, even out to the reservation occasionally where Bill was located. We would fly in a professor who would teach a class for several hours and wait for him by visiting Bill if he was available. She, my pilot friend, held a commercial flying license and was an undergraduate student and happened to also be a very skillful aviator. The two of us flew a Cessna 180, a tail wheel model with oversized tires to land on the rougher reservation roads and hay fields occasionally, instead of the usual paved runways. We also flew a Mooney 21 which we used for normal runways and smoother landing fields only. The flying helped defray college costs considerably.

"We will have two rooms waiting for you at the Coyote Motel," I answered, ignoring his humor.

After a night's sleep, the Rosebud holy man paid a morning visit to the University museum where the ceremony would be held that evening. My pilot friend, Carol, and I were with him when we went downstairs to inspect the room where the ceremony would be conducted. Several members of the Yankton tribe were with us. One was a woman who would make up 405 tobacco offerings individually connected by a long string which would mark the boundaries where Eagle Feather would be separated from the audience. Carol suggested that a rug should be placed in the middle of the room over the hard floor, where Eagle Feather would be laying face down.

Eagle Feather became curious about an adjacent room. We opened the door of the smaller room and turned a light on. Across the room were many wooden ammunition boxes on tables and some were spread across the floor. These sturdy, reinforced boxes are often used by anthropologists in particular to carry or store fossils and bones. They even have convenient handles made of rope on the ends for two-man carrying ease. Some of the boxes were open and various human bones could be viewed. Bill walked up to one box and lifted out a human skull. 'Mandan woman' was written in ink on the skull and the coordinates of where it was found were also written on the head in tiny figures. Many of the other bones bore similar markings. I looked closely at a skull with 'Arikara male' written on it. It too, bore coordinates. Bill held the woman's skull thoughtfully. It was cupped by his huge hand and the eye sockets seemed to look up at the holy man. It was one of those images one holds for a long time; even to this day I see the large Sichangu, standing like some over-sized Greek philosopher gazing deeply. I picture the scene, including myself and Carol, as two on-looking students, while the ponderous holy man seemed to offer compassion to the skull which looked up to him. After a long silence, he nodded to Carol and spoke to me. "Hmmmmm Nephew. This is not good!" was his sober remark as he gently placed the skull back down. * *See note at end of chapter – Remains.*

We left the room and departed from the museum to Carol's sorority house where the holy man wanted to look at some aerial charts for the route between Denver and Sioux Falls. I can still see Eagle Feather and the pretty, shapely pilot bent over a large table in the sitting room of the sorority house, both seriously studying the map and busily making commentary as to its route and the placement of the deadly storm that downed the Cherokee Six bearing the students. A line was drawn from Denver to Sioux Falls, upon the aerial map. Later, we would return to the museum for the ceremony to find the Lost Six.

That evening, in the late 60's, many so-called "credible" people from the white man's viewpoint attended. These were university professors with graduate degrees. I will name a few that were in attendance. It has been some years now and no doubt, I am missing a few.

Major General Lloyd Moses, U.S. Army Ret. And University Indian Studies Director

Dr. James Howard, Museum Curator

Dr. Joe Cash, University History Professor

Lula Red Cloud, Great-great-grand daughter of Chief Red Cloud. She would hold Eagle Feather's Green Jade Pipe during the ceremony. I erroneously stated that a Yankton woman held the pipe in an earlier writing and was corrected by Miss Red Cloud.

Dr. John Bryde, Psychology Professor and Author of *Modern Indians*.

Mrs. Constance Bowen, the wife of the President of the University.

Carol Draeger, University Pilot who would later fly with me the day after.

Adelbert Zephier, Yankton Sioux and Artist. I possess a recording of Adelbert and myself doing an interview in regard to this happening.

Walt Thornton, Yankton Sioux and his wife.

Gene Roubideaux, WWII Veteran and Purple Heart Recipient, Yankton Sioux

The audience was primarily made up of non-Indians, mostly professors. Indian Upward Bound graduates were sprinkled among them, mostly in their freshman and sophomore under- graduate years. One professor, a shy full-blooded Sioux who was in the Art Department was missing from the audience. I personally invited him and thought he would attend as he did not tell me he wouldn't. Rumor had it that his dominant wahshichu wife opposed his attendance. His attractive daughter, who was a University sorority sister, was half Lakota, yet never joined our University Indian club and avoided us. I was fairly well-known on campus and she went out of her way to avoid me, going so far as to walk across to the opposite sidewalk several times rather than pass by me and did so likewise to other Indian students. It never bothered me or the rest of the Indian 'Skins' as we referred to ourselves among each other. As good Indians we never made any harm for her and simply let her be. I must admit that we did enjoy a chuckle among ourselves, now and then, out of her paranoid antics. The Indian professor, her timid father, was a gifted artist depicting our culture however and became quite famous.

After the crowd was ushered into the basement of the museum, a rectangle a foot or so longer than a tall man and a bit narrower in width was laid out with the 405 tobacco offerings provided by the Yankton woman. These offerings were draped around four, pound-sized coffee cans which contained prairie dog or mole dirt and each bore a distinctive flag rising from the enclosed earth. Each flag was either red, yellow, black or white and stood for the four directions. Eagle Feather had earlier poured a bucket of dirt taken from several prairie dog mounds just outside the tobacco offering boundary and just in front of where the pipe-bearing woman, Lula Red Cloud, would sit facing where he would soon be lying prone. Eagle Feather took his pipe from the woman and briefly conducted a pipe ceremony to the Six Powers and ended with the seventh offering up to the Great Spirit whom he mostly referred to as 'Taunkahshilah - Grand Father'.

He returned the pipe to the young woman who then sat behind the mound. Eagle Feather crossed over the tobacco offerings and flattened down the dirt with his palm and drew several symbols upon the earth with the quill of an eagle or possibly a hawk's feather. From having traveled with the holy man, I knew that four symbols were inscribed on Eagle Feather's pipe stem. These two symbols on the dirt altar were also reflected upon his pipe. The crowd sat silent while the holy man went about his preparations. I sat down beside Carol and on my right side was Connie Bowen, the University President's wife. Connie was an exceptionally beautiful woman, close to my age. I had flown her to several interstate functions. She was genuinely concerned about Indian people, even the return of our own Way. Passengers in light airplanes often cover many subjects. At the Sun Dance a year later, I could not help but look straight into her piercing blue eyes when I was standing in the arena. Not many, if any, university president's wives attend Sioux Sun Dances.

Eagle Feather returned to the rectangle and removed all but his khaki trousers. Walt Thornton and I stood by with a tying rope and Eagle Feather's Yuwipi blanket. Eagle Feather's Sun Dance scars were numerous upon his chest. He placed his hands behind his back and Walt began to tie his hands and wrists. I helped Walt drape the blanket over the Sichangu's large frame. We carefully positioned it so that the eagle feather sewed to its top, hung backward, dangling down to the nape of his neck. Strange symbols were sewn on to the blanket, Moon, stars, planets and the blue of the outer world, for it would be that outer world Eagle Feather would be contacting. Another rope, longer, was handed to us by the singer and Walt made a noose, looping it over Eagle Feather's neck. Six more times Walt wrapped downward upon the holy man with the rope, tying at his backside and ending with a loop around Eagle Feather's ankles where the rope was knotted. Once Eagle Feather was covered and bound, we lowered the huge man face first to the rug. Dr. Howard had to help us. I returned to my position between the two blonde ladies, Connie and Carol, and the lights were turned off. The ceremony began.

The singer boomed out the calling song. At the end of the song there was silence. Bill grunted some words in Lakota and the singer sang the same song again. Again there was silence. Eagle Feather offered a muffled grunt through the blackness and then began to chastise Professor Joe Cash, (who was not popular with the University Indian students) for not joining in with the spirit of the ceremony. He pointed out the startled professor's paternalistic thoughts and even his body movements - in the pitch-black dark, telling him he would have to leave if his attitude toward Indian ceremony did not change. Cash nervously admitted his guilt and asked to remain. Connie Bowen pulled me closer and whispered a disappointed remark at the professor.

After admonishing the university historian to project a more cooperative attitude, the calling song was again begun. The drum boomed to a steady beat and the singer's high wailing song. A pair of rattles banged about but always within the rectangle of tobacco offerings although the room or the rectangle now seemed so much larger. This time, within a few minutes, the Spirit People entered in the form of whirling, diving, ascending blue-green lights streaming in front of us like a school of tiny, shiny, exceptionally maneuverable fish. It was like a miniature Fourth of July or a dazzling toy air show. The calling song to the spirits finished with a flourish. The pair of buckskin rattles stilled. A purring sound filled the room. The patter of small feet was accompanied by the excited chattering of a weasel. Eagle Feather introduced his Spirit Guide to the crowd. We all unabashedly greeted the creature or the Spirit. "Hello Grey Weasel," we yelled in unison and unrehearsed, including the University President's wife sitting close to me. Bill began to talk in Sioux to the animal, and the visitor chattered and purred as the holy man spoke. It seemed that Bill was informing Grey Weasel because the non-Indian words, 'airplane' and 'Denver' and 'Sioux Falls' entered the conversation. The Sioux word, 'wahshichu' was spoken several times. Wahshichu means white man, or white people in general, which we know by now. The conversation ended. Eagle Feather informed his singer to strike up a song. The lights reappeared. The electrical-appearing lights whirled for a few orbits and exited through the wall. The Spirit had left us was my conclusion - right through the museum wall. Eagle Feather called for the song of Chief Gall of the Hunkpapas. The singer sang out. It was a longer song and at his conclusion, Grey Weasel came forth once again.

This time the animal or Spirit seemed to do the most explaining or sound making. They continued to converse in what seemed a long period until finally the animal no longer chattered but purred slowly. Time seems not to exist when one enters a Yuwipi.

Then Eagle Feather called for the same song, and as the song began, the audience heard a woman singing at the top of the wall separating us from the adjacent room: 'the room of the skulls', as Carol and I had by now referred to it. A glowing, ice-colored image appeared, super-imposed on the wall, roughly the size of a woman's head. The woman sang in a high wail before the image disappeared. It was such a startling scene that Connie reached for my hand and held it tightly. It was so startling for me as well, that I cupped her hand between both of mine. When her song finished, a loud crack came from the center of the floor and something slid toward the keeper of the pipe.

I felt it stop at my feet and quickly let go of Connie's hand. I remained motionless, expecting the object to move.

Once the song ended, Eagle Feather called out: "Ho, Grey Weasel has made six predictions! In the background, Grey Weasel could be heard scratching the floor and purring, his purrs broken by an occasional excited chatter.

Bill spoke: (The following is a basic recollection of what he conveyed.)

1. The airplane crashed in a storm not far from a town that has two creeks with almost the same name. We should send an airplane out to look for it. A man and woman will fly that airplane.
2. The animals will point to where we should go.
3. If we fly where the animals point and head past the town beyond two creeks, other animals will point for you. You will fly over the plane, but it is pretty well covered with snow.
4. The plane sent out will have to land but everyone will walk away from it. You will be forced to the ground but do not worry; the pilots will be smiling as they look back.
5. In the next day or two some people who are not looking for the plane will be led to it by an animal.
6. After you do these things, only five will be found. One of the six will be missing. She landed away from the others, but she will not be too far away. Her face will be upon an ice-colored rock. She has a Chinese (pageboy) hairdo and wore big glasses. The animals will have been eating on all of them.

"Those are the six predictions. Now also, a rock that looks like ice has entered the room. It will have these signs I spoke of and one more prediction upon it."

I was relieved that Chief Eagle Feather called the object a rock and it did come scraping across the hard floor, rather heavily to bump into my outstretched leg. I thought of a snapping turtle at the moment and jumped up and to my right - into the University President's wife's lap. My fear of a presumed snapping turtle was such that I actually stayed where I landed, even though I have to truthfully admit that I had enjoyed holding her hand previously. I thought that this was some sort of punishment for letting my mind wander, now I was in her lap. Connie asked me what had happened. Before Eagle Feather had explained to us, I had no idea what the object was. Connie had heard it coming toward us as well and knew something had hit me. "What is it?" she whispered.

"I don't know." I replied, reluctant to mention my suspicion and the word –'snapping turtle.' I wasn't about to move out of her lap at that moment for doing so would have put me closer to the possible 'snapping turtle'.

Eagle Feather heard our commotion and admonished me in the complete darkness. "Eagle Man, get out of that woman's lap!" I was somewhat embarrassed and slowly slid out of the beautiful woman's lap. The University students twittered joyously. I am sure there were a few twitters coming from the older crowd as well, but I was too embarrassed and perplexed to pay much attention. Eagle Feather continued in the pitch black room. "Reach down and pick up what came into the room." He commanded strongly. "You are of the Rock clan, and should not be afraid of your rock brother. Go on and pick it up."

Despite the assurance of a powerful holy man, I reached down with sheepish hesitation and gingerly picked up the object still thinking of snapping turtles. Had I imagined any movement on its part, I would have surely dropped it on purpose and out of sheer fear. Connie reached over to touch it and instinctively, I gave it to her despite Eagle Feather's order.

Before the final song and the lights going back on, Eagle Feather said "The two who fly like the winged ones shall leave tomorrow," meaning Carol and I would fly to seek the crashed plane, using the stone as a map. Eagle Feather asked for the stone and exclaimed with amazement unusual for the big man. "Look here," he held forth the stone about the size of a cantaloupe. "It has a picture of the girl. The one with the big glasses and the Chinese haircut (page boy hair cut)." A coyote looking back was on the stone, including two men walking and on the opposite side of the coyote, two intersecting lines, and even a grouping of miniature objects suggesting dwellings complete with what could be interpreted as a water tower was etched somewhat naturally in the stone. Deer were in quite a few places on the stone. Bill let out an excited gasp. "Look here!" He pointed to a place where a tiny airplane tail (the rudder and elevators) could be discerned above the coyote. As I mentioned before, it was a grey semi-translucent stone much in the appearance of Black Hills rose quartz except that this stone was a dull light grey which resembled ice.

As it turned out, we followed the deer after take off the following day from the University town's airport near the Missouri River. The deer, which were visible on the stone, came out of their shelter and pointed us downstream. At a creek entering the Missouri, deer pointed us upstream and we crossed over into Nebraska. It seemed to be a very short trip across the vast midland of Nebraska as though we were enjoying a substantial tail wind. We flew on until we came to the two Loup creeks bearing the same name and eventually passed over the small town. Even a water tower was on the stone, past two deepened lines which crossed. The lines obviously represented Loup and Middle Loup Creeks. After passing the town, several deer standing next to each other, were pulling tufts of hay from a hay stack. Close by were a few cattle standing shoulder to shoulder on the same side of a caking trough and also facing the same direction as the two deer. Ranchers often provide their cattle in winter with a supplemental feed made mostly of soy and called soy cake. It is spread in a feeding trough. We banked toward where the cattle faced. We figured out that the cloudy, unclear sign on the stone represented fog, as we were starting to notice the clouds getting lower to the ground. Was this the 7th prediction? Or was it the girl's face on the stone?

After a little while, we circled a few times and searched below us believing we were near or over the crash site. Seeing nothing, we had to reverse course back to our base and land. When we reached the Missouri, the clouds were almost at the top of the river breaks. It was an eerie feeling trying to outrun that encircling fog but again it seemed we had some help from a tail wind that had reversed itself. After we landed and taxied to our hangar, the fog settled to the runway. Indeed, we did smile in thanksgiving when we placed the airplane in the hangar. We headed straight for a bar in the college town to settle ourselves due primarily to our encounter with the fog. There was no homing beacon back at that tiny airport we came from. Flying on instruments in light aircraft, especially civilian light aircraft, was never a task that I looked forward to without a degree of fearful respect. It is simply, too dangerous. In those days, the military had much more reliable instrument flying equipment.

The next day, close to the Nebraska town and where we had reversed our plane's course, two coyote hunters followed the tracks of a coyote. The animal's tracks led them to the wreckage of the Cherokee Six airplane. The tail of the doomed plane was exposed due to the rising temperature from the fog. They reported the position and soon rescue vehicles converged on the scene. All of Eagle Feather's (actually Grey Weasel's) predictions proved true.

Well, there you have a ceremony that the preachers, popes, frenzy manipulators, cardinals, and mullahs can never do. While other religions have their own ceremonies, there are a hundred clues as to the beyond in a powerful ceremony based from Nature. We will explore these clues. Nature's Path, Nature's Way is truly the world's most powerful religion if prediction and communication is the standard. It is also the result of the sheer truth, focus and dedication of the intercessor and, of course, the sincerity of the audience that allows or makes a pleasing atmosphere for the spirits to come in or want to come in. Various tribes had this ceremony as well but called it different names. I imagine the preparation and sincerity of the old Celtic bards produced similar ceremony. I highly doubt if a universal making Creator allows this gift to one chosen tribe.

Without harmony and undiluted truth, however, nothing will happen. I have to add; a degree of respectful obedience as well. Based on what I have observed from the Spirits in such ceremony, it is comfortable to believe that the Spirit World will truly be a truthful and sincere place where earthly lies and manipulation will not in the slightest be allowed or condoned. Superstitious ignorance will be absent as well. Nothing but pure truth will be the total mental (or thought-wise) atmosphere. This is a primary clue for me that Truth is the major reality of the Spirit World. Makes one wonder why we long to stay here!

Is the Spirit World a pleasant place? I believe that it is…for some. Both Grey Weasel and Big Road gave the impression that they were somewhat in a bit of a hurry to get back to where they came from. They did not stay around and linger, that is for sure. After the "business", the main reason for the ceremony was initially discussed; the Spirit's application toward the major purpose was responded to; the Spirit would soon leave. In several cases the Spirit left abruptly after the main conclusion. Never had I heard a Spirit hysterically beg to stay longer, which would have been an indication to me that the Spirit World was not such a great abode after all. A bit of common sense indicates to me that the Beyond can be a fairly pleasant place - for some, as I mentioned earlier. Yes, for some only. We will delve a bit deeper into this area in the next chapter.

It, no doubt, will be considered an impossible ceremony by many, especially by the over-zealous and narrow-minded and even harvest more than a few accusations. Such is the mind-set of modern society that I can hardly object to such reaction. All that I can offer for verification is that many such ceremonies are held, and have been held, down through time at least by members of my tribe and other tribes who hold a basic commonality of beliefs. I cannot change history to satisfy what seems to be a growing multitude.

*Dr. Wm. K. Powers, a noted anthropologist has even written several books on the subject. I am not into convincing anyone, however, but I **do not** shy away from actual observation and real life experience. Doubters and skeptics are free to look me up in the Spirit World. By now, I think that most readers will be convinced that I actually think one exists. Again, I **do not** insist that you necessarily have to believe as I do. Like the 'Lone Cloud' which mysteriously came over our Sun Dance, this happening was another of my mystery-projecting experiences and was certainly observed with a host of other interested people. The participants in this particular situation, and the following, were all University related with some sporting some rather high academic degrees, along with accomplished track records, from an academic point of view. Dr. Bryde still lives as of this writing and he will certainly verify as to this happening as will Lula Red Cloud, the great-great-granddaughter of Chief Red Cloud. Without further distraction let us continue. [1]

Dissection of a Ceremony

What clues do we have from this experience that pertains to the Spirit World beyond?

We are dealing with the Spirit World, are we not? Isn't that the Beyond where Grey Weasel came from? He was here before as a two-legged, therefore he has been in the Spirit World like all who pass on. (I think we should assume.) Or would the childish ones who are loaded with superstition presume that Grey Weasel lurks or takes his residence at some forbidden cave specifically designed by the set shop artists who also designed Harry Potter's landscapes?

Big Road, Fools Crow's Spirit helper, was a known medicine man who was one of Chief Fools Crow's mentors. Maybe there exists a special place where these 'advanced spirits' must reside, but basically I believe it is safe to proclaim or at least harvest the thought that Grey Weasel abides in some form of the Spirit World, as does Big Road. If Grey Weasel exists and we believe in an all-powerful Creator who controls all that exists, then it would make fairly common sense to assume that Grey Weasel does have the blessing, or at least the allowance, of the Supreme Creator to possess such extraordinary power as to go back into time and discover or learn what actually took place that fateful day the plane crashed. He also learned where the event took place. Aside from the actual facts and evidence of the happening, some force informed him as to what the predictions (which all came true) would be! He also entered and exited right through the museum's walls!

For those that think some bad or 'evil' power is responsible for Grey Weasel's appearance, slyly disguising himself as a Spirit Helper then those types who so believe may as well quit turning these pages after coming this far. Go back to wherever you came from and try to put yourself away…as much as you can…from what knowledge you may think rubbed off on you. Take a break and watch a few Harry Potter runs or the trilogy - *Lord of the Rings*. I felt both were highly entertaining (for entertainment's sake). Odd, that so many non-Indian detractors and some Indian ones as well will sincerely believe that the above innocent beseechment, the Yuwipi, intended to bring closure for the bereaved families, which was a direct observation, and even generously intended to help their own kind; this response will be considered preposterous and thus they will have to invoke some sort of 'Evil' to it! Not long ago we would have all been drawn and quartered or burned at a stake for simply wanting to find the six victims. Thankfully, we now have the protection of the clause: Separation of Church and State.

For the sake of some manner of progress for those who are serious about the Beyond let us probe more clues from our contact via the Spirit, Grey Weasel.

1. The airplane crashed in a storm not far from a town that has two creeks with almost the same name. We should send an airplane out to look for it. A man and woman will fly that airplane.

   Man and woman, hmmm; I discover an indication of balance in this prediction. Is not Nature created in balanced form? No doubt Creator had a practical reason; so that Nature can keep on reproducing the numerous progeny of the numerous species of flora and fauna. It seems as though the Spirit Forces that made these predictions wanted a balanced approach toward fulfilling the call made by a much higher spiritual authority than we limited humans. The two pilots would be the direct observers.

   Balance, indeed, deserves its respect, at least upon our present realm. Possibly the Spirit World could be genderless if there is no need for reproduction. This situation would seem to make human's promises of extra wives or 70 some waiting virgins appear quite fruitless; would it not? These promises appear to me as slick marketing tools, more so than promises 'coming from God'.

2. The animals will point to where we should go.
   Animals are utilized to direct us two-legged. These particular animals - the deer in this case, did come out of their normal seclusion and take up their positions to all point westerly. In the morning, one sees few deer compared to their usual habits of exposing themselves more in the evening hours when they usually graze. I live in a town where the deer population comes out in the evenings and at night are grazing on the lawns, some of which are just off main street, but never in the A.M., when they are usually hiding and secluded. The creek emptying into the Missouri would find more deer that had somehow got the message as well, as they resumed the Wamaskaskan (Animal World) beacon; this animal guidance system empowered by you-know-who! A mysterious guidance system for the sake of the fulfillment of the Spirit Force's deliberation was created a bit contrary to the animals ordained habits. Yet they complied. Even domestic cattle got involved. Maybe the same counteraction can be ascribed to the Lone Cloud moving in a no wind situation. At this point, I would think by now, we should be assuming that some powerful force was behind this simple appearing ceremony, especially the acting out of the predictions for the balanced pair of pilots to review and come back to relate to the Holy Man, Eagle Feather.

   Mitakuye Oyasin - are the Spirit Forces and the innocent Wamaskaskan all related as well? I guess that might be just a bit much of a mystery for us to even begin to contemplate.

3. If we fly where the animals point and head past the town beyond two creeks, other animals will point for you. You will fly over the (crashed) plane, but it is pretty well covered with snow.

   We mentioned before how the domestic cattle were also affected if we consider that they too were pointed in the same direction as the deer that were beside the hay stack. Cattle normally eat on both sides of a feeding trough.

4. The plane sent out will have to land but everyone will walk away from it. You will fly over the airplane but you will be forced to the ground. Do not worry; the pilots will be smiling as they look back.

Element of Danger

Were we brave enough to go through with this flight? "The plane will have to land. You will be forced to the ground." Those words echoed within both of us, yet we never mentioned it as we pulled our Cessna 180 out of the hangar at the local airport down by the Missouri River. Carol had plenty of time to say something but she didn't. I felt much more confident and up for the challenge with her presence. Maybe she felt the same about me. We were two fighter pilots off on another mission. It had to be done and that is a warrior's determination and attitude. Bravery and courage were two prime virtues of the Sioux. Were we being tested? What would have been the outcome had we been afraid to go? "You will be forced to the ground," weighed in my mind and surely weighed in Carol's. The exodus burdened Sioux, giving up their comfortable Carolina piedmont to obey a spiritual warning had to be brave and courageous as well.

5. In the next day or two some people who are not looking for the plane will be led to it by an animal.

It does seem incredible that a particular animal, the Wamaskaskan again, would lead two non-interested hunters to the crash site. This specific happening, the major event called for by the bereaved families in the first place... finding the crash site, would bring the episode to the sought-for closure.

6. After you do these things, only five will be found. One of the six will be missing. She landed away from the others, but she will not be too far away. Her face will be upon an ice colored rock. She has a Chinese (pageboy) hairdo and wore big glasses. The animals will have been eating on all of them.

It is obvious that the spirit is able to go back into time and discern what took place. The girl who was thrown out of the plane had her seat belt come unsnapped, no doubt by flying debris or from a high G force, spinning airplane. No doubt some object such as a coke bottle or some other weighted article, maybe a mechanics tool, possibly, perhaps such an item could have been under a seat and during the terrific spin of the airplane could have flown out and hit the seat belt latch and sprung it. The weight of the girl would have been magnified significantly enough to send her crashing through the fuselage. Another scenario is simply: maybe a weak seat belt or a latch could not hold her magnified weight due to the high G force, (gravitational force) or centrifugal force of the fatally spinning airplane. Whatever, the physical cause, the Spirit, accurately stated that she would not be with the others when the aircraft was found.

Extreme centrifugal force ejected her through the plane casting her out away from the others. This prediction would be impossible to conjure. The spirit guide obviously has the ability to revisit this happening back in time to be able to report specifically (truthfully) as to the findings. "One of the six will be missing. She landed away from the others." I find that statement impossible to conjure unless one had 'non-earthly' help. There is no way that a detractor can truthfully claim Bill Eagle Feather schemed up that prediction. It would be impossible to scheme.

This prediction, which even described the girl, assured me that these Spirit Forces were definitely real and spiritually Truthful as I would expect or hope an all-knowing Creator to be. I gained considerable confidence in the

Way by this particular prediction even though it was a tragedy for all aboard and their bereaved families. Here again I find another indication. The Spirit World must have a degree of consideration if it would come forward to respond to the call of bereaved families which initially started in motion all that took place. Bear in mind; all the students were non-Indian. I have personally experienced violent G forces when involved in some violent spins in the Phantom F4 fighter and also when aerial dog fighting in the Grumman F9. You can barely move your arms on your controls when the high G forces become more violent. Eventually you black out and that is why the pilot wears the precautionary G-Suit. At the top of a loop if you pull the controls a bit tight you do pass out momentarily while into the top and come to or revive as you start through the maneuver on your way back down. This is a common event in aerial dog fighting even with the G-suit. On a close air support bombing attack when you have to pull up tightly or abruptly due to mountainous terrain or obstacles, you do experience a blood draining G force as well. This becomes fairly fatiguing when you make pass after pass.

Carolina Influence

This ceremony, in my mind, could quite possibly have influenced the Carolina Dakota as to what danger was about to cross over the Atlantic. It is my mere supposition but if this were the case, then we would have Spirit Forces actually influencing a tribe's safety to get them to get up and move from forthcoming danger. Their surprising and abrupt move could well be a strong indication of spiritual involvement to save one particular tribe. Maybe all tribes were warned but only the Dakota/Lakota responded accordingly. As stated earlier, most all eastern tribes had the spirit calling ceremony.

An interesting thought: If my tribe was literally saved for at least two-hundred years from possible extermination or a 'Trail of Tears' westward march because of their early exodus, than why couldn't others in this day and age experience the same?

But…if the above supposition regarding the Sioux Nation being spiritually warned and no doubt helped along the way in their Exodus, again I have to equate to the present environmental plight we all are facing…then the Christian claim that 'God will take care of us,' could have a high degree of credibility. I cannot completely disavow their claim. I must add that the Sioux took positive action however and did reap at least several more centuries of freedom before they were swallowed up, almost, by Dominant Society. They certainly did not ignore Creator's warnings. As long as we maintain our belief system we do stubbornly claim to be a remaining nation - which we are. Creator is definitely warning all in this land through its Nature but unfortunately this warning remains unheeded by the masses. Al Gore has projected some incredible information in his work, *An Inconvenient*

Truth, which is supported by numerous environmental scientists and their conference declarations, yet both camps suffer appalling ridicule. No positive action to a significant degree is being taken regarding planetary heating, overpopulation and depleted water and resources. Like those eastern tribes that ignored the offered warning, this nation, America, can wind up in tragedy. Will Creator appear for them if they continue to ignore what Creator Itself is showing them through Creator's Nature? We Sioux responded as a nation. Our leaders responded. This nation, America, is not responding as a whole. I suggest strongly that they start observing. In the white man's older Bible, those tribes who ignored spiritual warnings or neglected to communicate spiritually; those tribes were not offered spiritual warning or saving direction like I suspect strongly that my tribe surely received. Evidently the Jewish tribe listened and responded accordingly. The evidence of the Sioux Exodus does lend a high degree of credibility to this premise. Like the Lone Cloud Sun Dance: it happened!

America has yet a few centuries to go on in its freedom but like the Sioux, it will become increasingly difficult as the environmental depreciation journey begins.

Evil Influence

What about the alleged power or manipulation of the white man's 'Devil' or 'Satan?' Well, first, the Traditional Sioux do not believe in such things. They (Man conceived Devils, Satans, Spooky Goblins, Incubi, Werewolves etc.) do seem fairly preposterous. (*Malleus Maleficarum* - Pope Innocent VIII, declares it heresy to deny the existence of Werewolves.) Recently, shortly before his death, Pope John Paul II sanctioned classes on the clergy to perfect their means to exorcise this white man's devil. It was all on the internet news showing many young priests attending classes on the subject. For them, Satan abounds and must be dealt with. Traditional-respecting Sioux reasoning is that a Benevolent Creator has no need to allow such things, nor would they (Spooky Devils included) be in the 'so-called mind' of such a powerful Force. **Where… in God-given Nature is there such evidence?** We Sioux have never seen or observed such things and do not expect to. If you have such an entity, why is it we can never observe it?

Hypothetical vs. Real Observance

A Spirit Calling ceremony and its results are real observance. You see and hear within the ceremony and await the Spirit predictions. The white man however, can only present Hypothetical Suppositions which are never observable and if any predictions are proclaimed they never bear fruit, yet he adamantly proclaims how 'Right' and God-ordained are his fruitless disclosures. He also just as vehemently discredits the real observances of any revelations carried forth from people not of his particular belief sect. He immediately brands any and all such communication as under the command of his Devil or a Satanic Force.

Did the "Devil' control the pointing deer, the finding coyote or even the domestic cattle observed in the 'Lost Six' happening? Does this 'Satan' also control Creator's wind and weather as in the Lone Cloud Sun Dance? I find it impossible to believe that an obvious benevolent and all-powerful Creator would allow any such man-contrived entity to be allowed so to intrude into its supreme domain. Yet, many devious detractors, especially those who fear losing their control and influence over their followers will readily clamor contrariwise. From a traditional Indian viewpoint, it appears heretical, actually, for such folk to have such little faith or respect to believe All-Powerful Creator would allow such interference.

I found it rather comical that a highly touted Christian woman from Georgia made a court case out of the innocent and entertaining Harry Potter series alleging that the production promoted witchcraft and therefore should be banned from public libraries. Her case was thrown out in December of 2006. What about all this literature that abounds in public libraries proclaiming that these 'spooky' religious sanctioned forces are an integral part of our society? As mentioned, we can never see or observe such contrived forces. Hmmm…can I wonder why we Siouxs seem to be immune to their supposed happenings?

I think I hear a possible Contrary at work in my mind or am I simply making one up? I will explain these Indian Contraries but first let us listen for a second or two.

"So Eagle Man, you saw Harry Potter on the movie screen, did you not?" I do not want to give the Contrary any further credence by mentioning his name. "Well, this Devil or Satan guy has appeared a few times also, via Hollywood, of course." He remarked rather smugly with a tutorial English accent.

"Yes but… those projections are all man-made." I remarked and added. "Including Harry Potter."

So far I have kept Sioux Contraries out of this work which is difficult to do for a Sioux writer. I have admitted that it is a bit difficult to swallow - the Little People - so to speak which Celinda Kaelin mentioned in her contribution. We all have our limitations, mine included. I have to admit that my Mother would laugh and tell me how I used to be at solitary play and would speak to my little imaginary friends when I was a young pre-school child. Maybe they do exist and maybe the "Lord' will appear in the sky and banish all planetary heating and somehow take care of the over-population and the related space, food, water, and habitat demands. More folks are lined up on those two sides than are with me; I must admit. It would be a simple solution if the last one, God taking care of it all, would actually happen. It sure would be nice but I do find this also a bit to swallow. Bear in mind, I do admit that I sincerely hope that the group 3 folks mentioned back in my Introduction, do have their expectations fulfilled regarding planetary salvation. Maybe, some of them could take heart in reading Celinda Kaelin's Yuwipi experience.

A Contrary would no doubt be whispering to me about now, "No way would they read what Celinda has to say. Hey, it isn't the planet they are considering. It is only their bunch that will get to go on to this Spirit World you are writing about."

Another Contrary would be chiming in. (They operate in pairs often. Mine do at least.) "They get to go to the 'Better' side of course." He raised his voice with a slight inflection when he pronounced, 'Better'. "I think you might be left out, Eagle Man," he added in a demeaning tone.

"You are really upsetting their 'apple carts', Eagle Man." The first contrary warned.

These Contraries were allowed to roam a bit in *Natures Way- Native Wisdom for Living in Balance with the Earth*. I think I can keep them in check for this work however. My last philosophical work, *Nature's Way*, has its set of Contraries who actually proved quite valuable, my opinion, to get across to the readers some difficult material. They seemed to work out quite well. We call them Iktomis, or some relate to them as Heyokahs. These are our own little mythological creations spawned somewhere back in our history but we readily admit they are just that: **Mythology**, pure and simple. Our Iktomis and Heyokahs are simply mischief makers, tricksters, and are material for humorous antics and stories which entertained many a long winter night. I could inject Sioux humor, and utilize one of my contraries (self-created of course) to clamor that this Satan guy is prejudiced, since he obviously prefers to spook white folks only and ignores us. "We'll have to turn him over to that Civil Rights board," would be typical Iktomi advice since Contraries are always loaded with questionable/humorous 'knowledge'.

Maybe these mythological Contraries are what these 'Little People' have evolved into for some. Celinda and I are close friends and will always remain so. Humans have different experiences which formulate differing perspectives in certain areas. We respect each other's right to disagree. I will always have a high degree of respect for Celinda and am thankful she is a contributor.

Even the Academic Indians are often believers in them (the Little People) as they are also rather 'Chic' in their circles. You can avoid pledging the grueling Sun Dance or enduring a humbling Vision Quest and yet maintain some sort of effective, snobbery credibility if you project or act rather 'Chic' in the Indian academic circles. Well, so much for Contraries which I remain bound and determined to keep out of this work.

Academics

I have criticized the academic world, primarily for their lack of truthful recording from their study of the Indigenous people. Not one book, including those by academic based Indian authors, informs us of the Canton Insane Asylum. The University of South Dakota and all its professors is but a few miles away. When I was in college they were loathe to admit or investigate the damage the boarding schools were doing to Indian education. A simple yellow school bus that runs 5 days a week has solved that problem. I have no regrets regarding my condemnation. They, like our political leaders today need a healthy brew of Introspection.

No one has done more damage to the Indian than the academics, including Indian academics, who, through their cowardly biased University presses, concealed from the public what was so obvious. I recall one cover of the University of Oklahoma Press Quarterly, that displays a chic ranch woman standing resolutely with a Winchester and it is titled; "In a land of Savages!" The worst part of this depiction is that an Indian academic, a national author, a registered member of the Chippewa (Anishinanabe), White Earth Tribe, was a consultant Re: Indians, for the university press. That cover and its title, must have never bothered him.

Connie Bowen

Now, some years long after the Lost Six ceremony, my good friend Connie Bowen became closer to me, or rather we became closer to each other, and after she became single. I last saw her after she returned from her homeland - Sweden, for one last visit. She had terminal cancer and asked me to conduct a ceremony to keep her healthy while she returned to her relatives. I conducted a sweat lodge held in the summer on an island connected with an arched bridge at Carleton College; just her and me. The entering Spirits complied with her wish. Afterwards she departed to Europe and upon her return her bright blue eyes sparkled when she related she was indeed quite healthy for the whole of her trip. Those lovely eyes always conveyed such energy and expression. She died not long afterwards. To me, she was as beautiful then as the years when we were at the University together and the closer time afterwards. She was one of those rare Spirits that seems to intentionally come into one's life to administer needed guidance or a special blend of it to possibly accomplish a mission you would otherwise never think of challenging. I may have been a warrior once and aside from Fools Crow's help (Big Road, as well) I feel I did accomplish those mere episodes when compared to the Spiritual. They were man things, now as I look back. Maybe warriors, some of them, maybe they need to be honed in the areas of bravery and courage before they advance onward. Those are considered major values to the Sioux. But in the much higher realm of the Spiritual, I believe I needed a balancing blend, for that is so obvious in Nature - balance! Was Connie my helper in those formative years? I hope to see her in the Spirit World.

Remains*

The bones mentioned within the University museum were buried out near the Missouri after a meeting held by Eagle Feather and Dr. Howard, the following summer.

14

The Code

"Life is but a mere shadow on the wall compared to the complete reality that lies beyond."

Plato, Athenian, B.C

Advancement

Do we advance onward within that Spirit realm according to the degree of Truth we bring with us? That is a very, very interesting supposition. Truth - it is what Creator is, is it not? The entire Universe operates on very 'Truthful' principles. Are we not a part of that Universe? When we choose not to be in harmony with what Creator demonstrates to us daily, are we then counter or not in 'sync' with our planetary realm? Why wouldn't the real award for our memories in the beyond realm or non-reward as well, be according to how much Truth we have accumulated or neglected to bring in? Is seeking of knowledge or related observation an integral part of that Truth, as well? Bringing natural knowledge into ourselves is bringing in God…in a very big sense, is my opinion. Does bravery and courage also fit in there as well?

What proof do we have that a 'Way' is '*The* Way' which one should attempt to follow?

Look at a people's 'Track Record'. Was Sitting Bull a Truthful Being? Was Fools Crow? Was Eagle Feather? Is this the real heart of the Code - the Holy Grail, so to speak, which most who utilize their God given minds, seek? Their deep spirituality based on their complete acceptance of Truth was the strength of their greatness. What sort of leaders has your Way produced for you? Shall we compare Red Cloud, Crazy Horse, Sitting Bull, Black Elk, Fools Crow, Eagle Feather with Clinton, Bush I, Bush II, Cheney, Falwell, Pat Robertson, Pius Pacelli, Congress or the latest Pope? Strange, indeed; it surrounds us, this God-made Truth, Nature, Creator's Creation and all truthful activity spawning from it, yet, egotistical man chooses to wander away in his own chosen ignorance. How Truthful are the leaders a Way produces? We have studied in depth some exemplary lives that were not all that uncommon back when unaltered and un-abused Nature was so much more abundant and available. If anyone deserves to occupy a high plateau in the Beyond, they surely do. The Natural Way has vividly demonstrated the type of leadership, spiritual and political which can arise from it. Compare those leaders to those we find today!

Creator is all Truth as we have expressed down through the chapters. Not even the most atheistic academic can reliably claim that the Universe operates on untruthful principles, laws, motions, physics, quantum physics and what have you. Let us include 'Time' as well. Ever thought of: 'When time begins? When does it end? Where does space begin? Where does it end? All of these are a bit unfathomable…are they not?

Mother Theresa had a humanitarian 'Track Record' yet she expressed doubts about God in her letters. Do you harbor doubt about your Creator?

Absolutely not! My Creator is all around me and is so evident by its infinite intricate Creations and appearing in a variety of mediums let alone the utter vastness of space where we cannot penetrate. I am very content believing that Creator does exist and as I have expressed: It is also very benevolent. On the other hand I have serious doubt as to the existence of the two Dominant world religion's claim that their Devil, Satan, Evil Spirit exists.

I do respect Mother Theresa however and admire her for expressing her doubts. Possibly if she would have had access to the Natural Way perspective she would have found some solace.

Four Spirit Callings

By now, Dear Reader, you have been exposed to four Spirit Calling ceremonies along with other so-called 'super natural' influences. One depiction occurred long before all of us were born and conducted by a tribal 'Shaman', as some like to name such communicators. I prefer holy man or holy person.

Why is it that the mullahs, ministers or priests cannot perform or initiate such communication? Why can't the shouting, all-knowing electronic evangelists, some bordering on rock band extravaganza; why can't they bring forth such accurate spiritually influenced happenings? Why is it that they cannot admit it? Instead they will have to rant that what we experienced didn't happen. 'If it did somehow occur, then it could not have been with the blessings of God, well…because God just doesn't do things that way and certainly would not allow it!'- will be their devious and untruthful defense. 'Period. The matter is no longer up for discussion.' They will frantically conclude.

One spiritual calling is from a woman's perspective. One was for a warrior going off to battle. One was to find six non-Indians. The first spirit calling ceremony within this work dates back several centuries. Such powerful connection did not recently originate, obviously. Hopefully, due mainly to such accurate predictions made, most of you will begin to cultivate insight that such spiritual communication does happen. I realize that for many it might be a bit startling to one's deeply rooted beliefs. I am at a loss as to what I can do about such a situation I may have caused. I am bound to the truth of my observations however, which I innocently and sincerely believe ultimately came from Creator, or at least were sanctioned by what I sincerely believe is the – All Power. The Lone Cloud happened! The Lost Six Happened! What am I supposed to do; cocoon your brain and keep your mind in a vacuum? All I can say is that I will see you in the Spirit World some day and we can possibly flash back into that allowable time it seems and take a look for ourselves. That is all the evidence I can offer.

Protective Spirits

My close bouts with death and rescuing from such by protective Spirits happened. It did not happen only in the skies of Vietnam either. I crashed more than one airplane or helicopter and walked away from them all.

Once I had two blown nose tires at lift off speed (over 200 knots) in full after burners. Nothing but bare rims were beneath me and some serious rumbling was happening. Those powerful J-79 afterburners were not giving me much time to make my decision. Lifting airborne would have been fatal, for F.O.D. (Foreign Object Damage). Portions of the tires were later found in the engines through the large air intakes which could have proven fatal and definitely an ejection had I elected to lift to momentary safety of the sky, but most likely the engines would have blown. I saved the machine by staying on the ground. It was a very quick decision. I pulled back the throttles and banged my tail hook down as I speeded toward the arresting cables at the end of the runway. I hit it so hard that it jerked me backwards after the huge arrest bungees wound the cable back. When they began to pull the cable back, the smoking nose rims cocked and the huge fighter bomber was also pulled backwards for the cable was still attached to the tail hook cleat. The plane turned in a semi circle from the pull. It was odd facing backwards and watching the fire trucks roaring down to put out the fire from the dripping hydraulic fluid onto the hot tire rims. I froze momentarily and took my time getting out. When I did step down the pilot ladder I made a stupid remark. I looked back at the cockpit and said to the safety officer, a major who drove up. "Damn, Major. I made a mistake. I left the key on." Fighter aircraft have no need for keys.

He looked at me oddly and took me to the base dispensary (Sick Bay). Most of us are not John Waynes after such a startling episode. I was a bit out-of-sorts, so to speak. Anyway, the flight surgeon offered me a stiff shot of medical alcohol cut with orange juice, interviewed me, offered me one more delicious drink and I was back up flying that afternoon.

Another incident was plowing into the ground at night from an emergency ducking of another helicopter to avoid a low altitude head-on crash. His lights were coming right at me and I had no choice. I did a 360 degree rotation and the ground was coming up at me.

"Lights, Lights," I yelled at my co-pilot mid-way through the downward rotation. He sat frozen, and I remember reaching quickly and slapping the landing lights switch despite having both hands full of collective (throttle) and cyclic (control stick). I pulled my cyclic and wrapped on full power to break my fall. I landed hard but suffered only slight damage to my tail section. I stopped bouncing in front of a bright electric billboard advertising, 'Dawson's Motel'. The whirling main rotor was only a few feet away from the billboard. I shut the machine down, looked over at my shaken co-pilot and unhooked my seat belt and shoulder harness. "Lieutenant. You didn't hurt her too bad, just the tail section," came calmly over the intercom from the crew chief. I walked into the motel office in my harness and helmet and asked the somewhat startled motel operator to call the squadron. I should explain that I flew H-34 Marine helicopters before I moved on into fighter/bomber jets. Aircraft crashes do get one's attention, may be an understatement.

No doubt the most dangerous incidents came from the many repeated passes at low level back into the battle zones where you were constantly exposed to small arms fire and some anti-aircraft fire. You never knew what was coming at you, yet obviously they missed. Once in a while you barely got back with low fuel, as sometimes you 'stretched' a mission due to serious need of your ordnance services down below. An engine shutting down while on the taxiway is cutting it close. Marine infantry had it much tougher than I ever did was always my contention, and I was there for a reason. Night-time bombing under flares and cloud cover was just plain scary as hell. After one such mission at night, wherein we took some occasional fire, my R.I.O. (Radar Intercept Officer) who rode the backseat, turned in his wings, complaining that I made just too many passes that night. He would start screaming when I would come in to make a bombing run and I had to turn off his intercom to do my job. I had a wotai stone from Fools Crow's cabin and he didn't.

Bird flu didn't happen! At least the oft-predicted world-wide bird flu epidemic we constantly were warned of did not evolve. Just the simple little lights that have appeared in my mere sweat lodges have happened, and I am a long way from ever being a medicine man, which I never intended to be. These same happenings also happened in much more vivid form in

Chief Eagle Feather's sweat lodges, at least in the many I attended under his direction.

How can I deny what I truthfully observed with my own God-given, God-functioning and God-designed eyes to obsequiously please the vast majority of mere mortals? Too many obsequious Indians of the past are guilty of that conduct while our staunch and loyal medicine people were confined forever to the sheer horrors that awaited them at Canton Insane Asylum: A self-righteous church-sanctioned horror chamber which operated for nearly a half century. It must be much more horrendous to be confined in such a place when you are not one degree mentally deficient. In medieval days when the clergy were totally in charge of most European countries I would have been hauled before a tribunal and commanded to recant: thousands were. I refuse to be unfaithful to Direct Observation, however, which I consider ultimate Truth!

Reflect upon Plato's meaning in his "Allegory of the Cave." What we experience here, and observe here can, and no doubt will, be reflected to a related degree in the Beyond and no doubt, in a much higher form.

Popular Discount Stores

If you don't use your mind, to put it bluntly, you will pay a helluva price. Just walk into one of those popular discount stores and see!

Oooh, that is not a very politically correct statement, is it? Maybe I will have do as President Jimmy Carter had to do with his apartheid statement for his book, Palestine: *Peace Not Apartheid.* The 'politics' of the world made him make an attempt to 'unwind' a 'Truth' that he had declared. I should temper the above by downgrading my statement a bit, I guess. At least I did not name the particular stores, assuming my readership would know. I will not unwind it beyond that however. I try not to be egotistically exact and therefore avoid declarations such as 'you will' or 'this is exactly this' or related macho dominant terminology. I prefer the supposition approach in regard to the spiritual since so much is mystery!' So instead of 'you will pay,' I should retreat and become a bit more explanatory and state, 'In the Spirit World, one could pay a serious price for not using one's mind while here in our mortal state.' Ahhh, that is a bit more mellow which literary society demands but my first proposal, the discount store one, was, however, rewardingly startling wasn't it? (No unwinding!)

Eagle Feather's Teepee (tipi)

Once I sat beside a bay of Lake Oahe with Chief Eagle Feather. A teepee was behind us and we saw its reflection in the water in front of us. That evening he would conduct several sweat lodges for a workshop of Hunkpapa Lakota anxious for the old way to come back. We had just built the lodge and were taking a few minutes of well-earned rest. He pointed to the water and exclaimed. "Nephew, now there is a teaching." This was his customary way of beginning something that he felt was important for a person to know.

"That teepee reflecting in the water, it is telling us something the Almighty wants us to know." He pointed back at the tall canvas structure supported by lodge poles and then pointed out to the water. The reflected teepee stood out clearly in the Missouri River backwater before us. "If you go dive into that water, Nephew, you will not find that teepee." He would always start out with something that was so basically simple and obvious. "If you walk over there and look in the water, you will see yourself." He paused and asked, "Now what does that tell you, Nephew?"

Knowing that I did not know the answer, he continued. "That teepee in the water tells us first there is a world beyond. Some say Spirit World. Next, it tells us that we have a home in the Spirit World. But if you want to jump in the water now, you will not find it." He stood up and motioned for me to follow to the water's edge. When we looked down in the water, we saw both our reflections.

He pointed at my shadow as the sun was starting its downward trail to the West. "*Ho wana* (Now), what is that?"

"My shadow," I answered

"Oh huh," he grunted and pointed to the water. "When you die, you will no longer have a shadow. Your shadow will then go into the teepee's reflection through the teepee's door and you will have found your home!"

I followed him back to the teepee and we sat back down in front of it. "All these things are simple, Nephew, yet they are way beyond the *wah shi chu*." (Although he used the Lakota Sioux term for "white men," it can easily be understood as "Dominant Society," from his perspective.) He paused and looked sourly. "Creator did not need to make reflections or shadows, for they seem to be of no use for us." His look brightened. "You will come to learn that every little thing, no matter how unimportant it seems, what the Creator makes, has a teaching. Some have powerful teachings like I just told you." A pair of horses in a corral nickered above us beside an old abandoned missionary church with a broken-down steeple resembling now; a fallen dunce hat. Its cross now leaning against Mother Earth. Maybe that scene alone symbolized that we would go back to our old Natural Way…at least some of us. As we looked toward the four-legged, he added. "That church up there could never convince the Indians there was a Beyond Life for all of us." He added, "Not like our own way can do it!"

"So when I die, Uncle. My shadow will go into the teepee door and I will be in the Spirit World?"

"Oh huh," he echoed with a brief laugh. "That won't be for a while yet. When you look at some of our peace pipe bundles, those buckskin coverings, you will see the two teepees beaded on them. The teepees have doors. One is for when we come into this world. The other is for when we go into the Spirit World: One reflecting the other. A holy man gets you ready for the Spirit World. At least he lets you know that there is one because he believes that." He grunted harshly. "Some damn fools think no such thing exists."

I remembered many Sioux peace pipe bags that bore that same symbol even though artists had severely altered the various designs through beading or drawing. "Artistic license," I thought. Yet there was a commonality. The pair of teepees on the medicine bundles were always opposite. One reflecting the other.

"A life here. The teepee represents our home. Life beyond. The reflection in the water tells us we have a home beyond and someday we will all go there," I offered.

Chief Eagle Feather seemed pleased with my reply. He smiled broadly, before speaking with authority." You are learning, Nephew. Tomorrow night we will do a *Yuwipi*. After these *Inipis* (sweat lodges) tonight and the Yuwipi, you'll be pretty well convinced there is a Spirit World!"

Another Path Beyond

Eagle Feather suggested that the path from one teepee to another, that we call life, is just a part of our life path experience. It has another path Beyond. What goes on in either teepee is mystery. Mystery just might play its role in our own lives, more so than we can imagine. I firmly believe that mystery (the Spirits, so to speak) just may have protected me on more than one occasion and which I never knew about or was predicted. Once my hunting dog Rex, led me out of a blizzard back to my car. The Spirits were certainly working with him. If our journey continues into the Spirit World, it seems highly probable to me that the earth process of seeking and finding justice is reflected and will carry over into the next realm. If we are allowed to take with us our memories, we will be free forever in the Spirit World to chastise all who wronged us; and conversely, you will be chastised by those whom you have wronged. Certainly we will be able to honor those who helped us, wouldn't one think? Wouldn't one seek out the person who jumped into a raging current to successfully save one's helpless daughter and lost their own life in the attempt? Such honor a mother would bestow once she found that brave person in the Spirit World. Traditional Indians – those who believed in the old ways – feared no divine judgment. They lived with only the certainty that they would leave their body behind at death and be left with their memories.

The Big Calculator Above

Does God sit above with an electronic calculator and tap down all the wrong that one does? All the wrongs that are going on in this 7 billion populated world at this very moment? Wouldn't it be a bit simpler if God gave us all memories? Each of us would remember what happened to us once we 'hit' that Spirit World? If we receive the mobility that Grey Weasel displayed, then it looks probable that we might be able to get around up there or whatever, quite efficiently, wouldn't you think? Is it possible that we will be able to corner our own transgressors and at least chastise them for the wrongful transgressions not in league with Creator's Truths proscribed for us? Wouldn't a victim want to confront the victimizer especially when she or he had no means to do so while here? I mean the victims who have not been lulled into a forgiveness stupor by repeated trips to the psychiatric couches which they have paid dearly for. The way it is now for Dominant Society is that the victimizers can receive their 'forgiveness' by simply issuing certain verses while here, according to white man rules: Seems to be a bit contrary to the word Truth. Does a pedophile who caused a lifetime grief smugly say to his victim in the Spirit World, "Uhhh, I've been forgiven. Forget it!" Is forgiveness, thus a means that states what really happened...well...uhhh... it really didn't happen after all, now did it? Let us all just forget it, should we not? Are we not attempting to erase Truth again? The major obstacle to this way of thinking and/or believing is that the victim just cannot forget what the hell really did happen to them. All the mullahs, priests, ministers, sky pilots and psychiatrists just can't make the lifetime despair and mental pain truthfully go away. The mind that Creator gifted us with just doesn't operate or function accordingly. It seems that most victims clamor rightfully that they want the victimizer to pay some degree of punishment for their transgressions, either here or there. Some times, injecting a bit of common sense into religion gets all sorts of folks into a dither, however.

Conscience and Consequences

The old-time Indian did not have this sugar coated pill of 'forgiveness.' One could not cover up what one wrongfully did to others. Depending upon the severity of the offense, the victimizer could be put to death or banned from the community, which was almost a death sentence, as enemies could easily dispatch a lone individual. Living your life with an awareness of consequences both here and in the Spirit World is one of the greatest of all medicines according to the old-time traditional. I cannot and will not change or alter the historical viewpoints of a people who held to such a workable and earth conscious life style just to placate a certain majority within a reading audience. This is what too many Academics, both Indian and non-Indian have been guilty of. One does not cover up what one does to others; I repeat. You sometimes refer to it as conscience.

Direct Observation Again

It is so obvious. The teepee reflecting in Lake Oahe is a very good example of Nature teaching us again and again. When we look in a mirror we have a similar teaching. This time we could equate ourselves as staring at each other's souls or spirits. The reflection, whether mirror or from a pond or lake, covers the total picture. Nothing is left out or covered up. Such is the all encompassing difference of Nature than from what man contrives. Have you ever thought of it that way? That entity looking back at you exists exactly as you are. Creator could have easily designed a world in which there are no reflections. 'What use are they anyway?'- the know-it-all detractors will claim. A reflection has no meaning for them, as it is. Their stunted minds simply do not have the intellect to perceive the depth of thoughts which can emanate from serious study of all that Creator allows or creates.

A Common Sense Solution

The Oahe is a man created Missouri River lake that once held excellent fishing waters which have diminished considerably. As of this writing, billions of dollars has been spent on the Bush/Halliburton/Cheney war. Maybe it is more appropriate to call it the Cheney/Halliburton/Bush War, (CHB War). That expenditure will be regretted someday when the Southwest begins to run out of water. It could have built pipelines/canals to carry the Mississippi or Missouri floodwaters westward. The Red River in North Dakota annually floods and almost annually, inundates several towns. These floodwaters, at least can be diverted to the Missouri River whose dams within the Corps of Engineers system beginning at Ft. Peck, Montana down to the Yankton Dam in southern South Dakota have suffered severe drought ever since the turn of the century. Of course, this is too much common sense thinking despite saving thousands of farms and ranches. That forthcoming loss really bothers me. Instead the Great Lakes citizens have been put on notice that their waters are being scrutinized for future consumption in the Southwest. Practically speaking, the Missouri and Mississippi are a bit closer. Along the way, the vast, sparsely settled Badlands, which had been an ancient inland sea, could become the new 'Great Lakes' and would create rain for the drought suffering farms and ranchers. (Besides settling and purifying the silt laden run off flood waters.) One way or another, all those folks will need water. Every spring, billions of gallons go out to the sea. Non-availability of water is not the problem. Common sense and the resources to do it is.

Too often, writers parrot complaints but are reluctant or lack the creative ability to offer at least some attempt at a solution. Mine may seem a bit far fetched but it is at least an attempt and sooner or later what may seem extreme nowadays may become the only practical one available. Time will certainly tell. It certainly is not as far fetched as the Great Lakes idea or spending billions of dollars and over 4,000 American lives and tens of thousands Iraqi lives (At the time of this writing.) with nothing but disaster to show for it. What if all that expenditure had been spent instead on a vast inland lake, a very large one? Not only our farms and ranchers would be saved from drought but the whole nation would have benefited. Leaders have to avoid always thinking war as their solution.

Plato's Allegory

Plato's Allegory conveys a deeply rooted message. Several thousand years ago it was issued and it still survives through its many reiterations by leading scholars. "Life is but a mere shadow on the wall compared to the complete reality that lies beyond."

Briefly, Plato explained his allegory. He imagined several slaves having no freedom. They were to be chained and immobilized to face a tall wall within a dimly lit cave. Behind the slaves, a road would course into and out of the cave entrance and beyond the portion of the road coursing under the cave ceiling would be built a fire significant enough to cast the traveler's shadows upon the wall and therefore this on-going activity would be viewed by the slaves who we must remember as always facing the wall. The traveler's shadows would bespeak considerable variety. Lone, quiet travelers, boisterous travelers in groups, occasional horse riders or chariots with loud rumbling; all, of course casting much different shadows and each emitting differing sounds or none at all. This would be the entire known world the slaves would be able to understand; to so-called see and register into their minds, their thoughts. This would be the totality of the slave's mind or knowledge.

I almost want to compare the slave's situation and equate it with those who do nothing to advance themselves, academically, adventure-wise, world-view wise, spiritually or environmentally, in this knowledge/

wisdom abundant modern world with all its communicative tools. Those who do not and will not observe Nature with all its creations; I have to add. These are the Soap Opera Sarahs or the Couch Potato Charlies which make up a too huge a majority of Dominant Society. We see them every day, work with them and some are even our close relatives. This category also encompasses those who will foolishly allow themselves to be led religiously or spiritually like blind, baah, baahing sheep, never questioning and rarely utilizing the potentials of a God-given, God-designed mind.

Finally after staring at nothing but reflections, the slaves will be freed and taken to the mouth of the cave which over looks a teeming metropolis. They would be in awe. Life would have very little resemblance to what they had constantly viewed in the cave and which formulated their earlier concepts.

"Life is but a mere shadow on the wall compared to the complete reality that lies beyond." So can this allegory be a reflection when we enter the world beyond? The Spirits we have viewed or been exposed to in ceremony have mobility far in excess and capability than any human. Did not Grey Weasel leave through a museum wall and return with information pertinent to the calling? A human body cannot do what he did. Grey Weasel went back into time obviously to find the information that he brought back to the ceremony. He viewed or somehow learned of the happenings on a swirling blizzard night, quickly, almost immediately, somewhat of the speed of an informational quest on the internet. Then the Spirit with the misleading name came back. Will we have that same capability when we enter that mysterious world? Rather should I say, will some of us, hopefully those who used their gifts while they were here, will they reap that capability? Obviously some have.

An internet communication can travel the world in a flash. It too can come and go through a 'museum wall' like Grey Weasel. Creator is showing us that certain 'miracles' are allowed right before us. A book, 100,000 words can be copied in a heartbeat. Every period, comma, bold space, italics, pictures and indentation will be exactly as the copied folder. A half-century ago this was unthinkable. Do not take this marvel for granted, however. It is Creator's way of letting you know how vastly powerful It really is. This minor miracle happening right before you could not happen had not the Higher Power already 'ordained' it, so to speak. All such happenings are not 'inventions' of mere man. They are simply 'allowances' already 'invented' for our usage. Obviously, the Ultimate wants us to communicate more efficiently and has now given us the means to do so.

A Benevolent Creator

You seem to have little fear of your concept of God, Eagle Man. What proof would you offer that your Creator concept is benevolent?

Let us look at some simple proofs. Do we not heal from most of our injuries? Creator has engineered our bodies to repair themselves to a great extent and even provides us with a warning system, a degree of pain so we will refrain from using an injured limb, for example. The pain will go away once it is repaired or healed. On a more intense scale, we often will faint when we incur severe pain and hence be temporarily removed from pain. An injured appendage will often become numb almost instantly. The Creator did not have to provide us with such reactions. This indicates to me that Creator indeed cares for us and the animal creations as well.

Does not the Creator design and create the numerous varieties of pleasant flowers? Hold up a bouquet of flowers and think about the entity that created them. I always think that Creator is truly benevolent and pleasing when I do so.

Why is it that organized religion's "holy men" so to speak, cannot are do not have the 'power' to call in a helpful 'Spirit'.

Because they do not have the necessary focus. Therefore they have to scream to 'High Heaven' that anyone that does have such communication is readily branded with a litany of detractive names. Practically all that I have encountered, the accusing clergy, have two main detractions which severely limits their focus - money and control. Ego and a false sense of superiority play as well. Name me one 'white man sky pilot' that does not want to build a church or temple reaching to the sky or have some religious based college or university named after him. A true holy man has a goodly degree of humility which I find missing in organized religion's leaders who are far more attuned to pageantry, pomp and regal ceremony and thus far removed from what their own Christ or Moses displayed. Spirits are like people in one sense. If you are not focused upon them when you call them in and of course what the Ultimate Creator has created for us in this world, then they have no intention or desire to work with you as a religious leader. Fairly simple to understand despite what the white man's religious leaders will deny or claim. Simply observe for yourself every Sunday on TV. The truly devout holy man can call in the helpful Spirits (Wanagi) and these others cannot. I have never observed a Sioux holy man rant and rave either like I can watch every Sunday morning on television.

Who do we associate with in the Spirit World? (Assuming by now, it exists.)

Hopefully if we have maintained a positive image we will associate with our own kind as mentioned above. Life is a mere shadow. The teepee in the water reflects exactly. The mirror image of you resembles yourself exactly suggesting that what we are goes on. What our mind is, its associations carry onward as well. All influences and associated desires no doubt travel onward. Do we not attempt to associate with our own kind while here upon this world? Yes, we strive to surround ourselves with similar thinkers (or non-thinkers). If you like to bowl, you go bowling and do not mind socially knowing those who enjoy that sport and the camaraderie that goes with it. Often a beer or two with those folks and a hamburger or pizza makes the crowd more enjoyable. If you play golf, usually you abhor the idea of a brother-in-law or some relative inviting you along on an evening's bowling outing. Likewise he may not feel comfortable on the golf course or hobnobbing with the golf-loving crowd you associate with. Avid tennis players usually do not play much golf and vice versa. The retiring snowbirds bound for Phoenix, scurry about to find those others with similar tastes and views. The arch-right certainly do not plan socials with the arch-left. Albert Einstein probably preferred a session or two with others of like scientific mind or a chess player rather than the bowling or golfing crowd or 'heaven forbid – the right wing extremists. I reiterate: We choose our own kind to be with if we have the choice. Why should it be any different in the Spirit World?

Jerry Falwell, now deceased and Pat Robertson seemed to prefer each other's homophobic rant and even blamed the 9/11 destruction on the homosexual communities in their immediate media commentary following the destruction. Maybe God can do most folks a favor and give those two their own separate cloud way off in space. If a homosexual person exists; would it not have been created by Creator in that particular way or leaning? There are millions of innocent homosexual originated folks in the Spirit World waiting to chastise the homophobic extremists according to my theory. Falwell and Robertson, among many, will not have a pleasant reception.

This could be the real 'Heaven or Hell' most of us wonder or ponder about, if we are at all truthful and of course; observant. It does seem a bit more practical and reflective of what we experience while here.

Hopefully, there exists a Spirit World in which we can be with our own kind. That categorization, also hopefully, will not be a separation by race or worldly accomplishment, but one of how well we utilized our mind while here upon this journey. How much did we place into this greatest of gifts which Benevolent Creator has designed specifically just for us! Courage, bravery, generosity and sharing - the four cardinal virtues of the Sioux may also have their importance toward our final destination. This could be the real 'Heaven or Hell' most of us wonder or ponder about, if we are at all truthful. It does seem a bit more practical and reflective of what we experience while here.

What would merit punishment?

Human's negative or harmful acts would be the basis for punishment, should they not? Why? Because basically, they are untruthful to Creator's Code. Are we not repulsed somewhat by these types of selfish and non-harmonic folks who cross into our lives? They are contrary to the harmony we find throughout Nature. Possibly the neglect of exhibiting critical bravery or courage when direly needed could be a factor if one could have fulfilled such a role. Abandoning one's offspring is considered a very capital offense against God's Nature which tribal people who are traditional valued respect. The animals rarely remove their young from provision and protection except for those certain species that will still continue without parenting. We have a direct observation to base this holding on. Simply study the many species. I also believe that failure to exhibit sincere appreciation or thanksgiving could no doubt merit a degree of punishment or, at least, chastisement. Maybe the possibilities for advancement in the Beyond will not be as readily available for those who have developed a mind-set of taking Creator's gifts for granted.

The Earth Mother, Creator's creation for us to live upon is in serious danger. I don't mean that you have to hug every tree you see or expect punishment for not stopping your car and picking up every beer can or Coke bottle. Do not worry about stepping on an ant or two, either. What of those who refuse to stand up for her especially when we have been made aware of the specific detrimental causes? The coal company CEO who chastised and falsely accused Al Gore for his environmental courage will no doubt have to eat his words in the Spirit World. Will not the future generations offer some severe chastisement based on the environment they were forced to inherit when they enter the Spirit World?

What punishment should we expect?

The white man is loaded with punishment. It is a perfect 'fear' item, loaded - to control; a wide variety of explicit forms of dire punishment, mostly eternal are forewarned. He '**knows**' that a fiery hell awaits any and all who disagree with his religious view-points.

Most traditional Indians do not see it that way. Quite possibly the Beyond is a place where we may go with our own kind, and that coupled with an incapable mind that will no longer progress, could well be our major punishment and not some form of fiery hell which sounds quite medieval. Excess appetites or detrimental habits that repeatedly dull the mind-process and also occasion severe human suffering for others could or may bring a form of punishment that does not appear very pleasant if we consider a revelation of one particular holy person.

Peter Catches, Sioux holy man, once journeyed down into the Spirit World in his sun dance vision. "Drunks were there. They were reaching out for a dancing bottle before them. Women who had abandoned their children were wailing. The lonely cries of their children could be heard." It would seem that these who cared little for their offspring are now with their own kind and it does not seem a particularly refreshing place to be.

"Go back and tell them what we suffer," he was instructed.

All of you Archie-Bunker types go over there. All Ku Klux Klan members, hate groups, child molesters, and women beaters, go way over there! All of you religious fanatics whose egos told you that you knew everything, yet did not observe what was in front of you, go over there! All you harmful ones who had many victims: Those whom you made suffer; they are waiting for you over there because they have not forgotten their sufferings. They can chastise you for an eternity if they so desire. A traditional raised woman friend states that she was taught that such will have to come back here to the Earth, having no rest in the Spirit World, as the victims of people like they were. If/when they repent, then they can progress to a rest in the Spirit World.

If I am not a murderer, a pedophile, a thief or one of those who constantly spreads lies and hatred: Will I have to associate with those kinds?

Hopefully, and which common sense seems to point out; it would seem that those kind are not followers or upholders of Creator's Truths which are quite obvious here on this world we start from. It would seem that those who hate and those who did not seek harmony would not find much truthful compatibility would they? More harmony would be promoted if both groups, the good and the bad, would remain quite separated. Will young boys cling to pedophiles? Will rape victims seek the company of rapists? I hardly think so. I also believe that such ilk, the victimizers will no longer have the advantage of size, or power, or stealth and deceit to be able to harm more victims as they did while on earth. The hell these folks will experience is to have to be with their own kind, and one which does not appear very pleasant. These types constantly avoided Creator's truths while here and created serious harm toward all around them. Their ability to carry on with their lustful appetites will be severely curtailed in the Beyond, if Truth reigns. Creator shows us every day that Nature all around us reveals constant truth and constant harmony. This is the way Creator wants it! The Spirit World should be certainly reflective and wherein incoming human will not have any powers to disrupt such truth. Makes comforting sense to me.

What reward should one expect?

Your mind is your greatest reward. It is up to you to use it, however. We have all been given various freedoms to utilize this great gift, at least in this land we have. Yes, and we have all been allowed our distinct Individualism! Do we not all have our own distinct face (identical twins-the exception), our own readily recognizable voice, our own finger prints and even our own smell? Since our own distinct mind is the Ultimate gift, and with unlimited capabilities, why would it not be rewarded with to the degree as to how well it was utilized? Do we go on seeking knowledge? I think that may well be the profound pleasure that is the so-called 'heaven.' But, one must prepare one's mind while here and we obviously are given the choice. Most do not, however, and will be entering that Spirit World with a blank disk and little to build upon. Their choice, however. Most are too carried away with control and seeking of material possessions: Again, their choice.

Creator is all truth, all knowledge; is it not? The more knowledge one accumulates, the more one becomes closer to the Great Knowledgeable One. It could become a pleasurable endeavor. Do not the creative folks or those who are project oriented find great bliss while busy at their task? I have visited with many a once hard-working, retired South Dakota farmer or rancher who always speak glowingly of the lifetime efforts they projected daily to bring their lands to fruition. It was a hard time for most but they all spoke with a deep pride in their efforts. Their mind as well as their physical being was constantly at use. Maybe in the Beyond we may feel the same. Makes sense to me: Makes more sense than floating on some cloud and strumming a harp.

Maybe the blank disk folks will have plenty of Wal-Marts to endlessly keep themselves occupied. Maybe there are plenty of meaningless soap operas and couch potato events. Eternity could be for a while.

What, of the deceased, goes with him or her into the Spirit World?

Ancient Egyptians even buried wives with their pharaohs in their tombs along with boats, weapons, gold and living utensils. Tribes worldwide did similar burials most often, excepting the accompanying wives or offspring. Many Mormons expect several wives in the beyond. Jihad warriors expect 70 some waiting virgins. Women had, and have, very little to say in these religions. It appears that men's ideas, not women's, get preference. Hmmm, could that be because it is men who have invented these ideas and hence successfully passed them on as God-ordained?

What doesn't?

If one were to examine an exhumed human corpse, I doubt if one will find any body parts missing. Somehow, those of the Mormon and the Islamic faith must believe that the Beyond abounds in sexual activity and somehow certain body parts go along with the mind or the soul on the journey. I will admit that this subject can become quite a selling point for prospective members. If you can have sex in heaven, why go without?

What would a traditional espousing Indian have to say?

I believe most Indians would simply shrug and indicate by their body language and expressions. 'Ahh, the Wahshichu, he has to bring sex into everything!' Most of the Natural Way believe that the Spirit World is upon a much differing plane in regard to Sex which probably remains where it has its God-designed role upon this habitat. If sex portrayed a painful and revolting experience on each occurrence, there would not be much procreation, would there? This could be accused as not a very romantic response but it is at least a bit practical. I must re-mention that most of what we take exception to is because it is men who have invented these ideas and hence successfully passed them on as God-ordained.

"You are going to ruffle the Macho world's feathers when you make such a statement!" A Contrary would warn. "Remember Eagle Man, keep in mind the number of book sales."

"In case you don't know, Eagle Man," the other Contrary would also chime in. "The formula is: The less of the Two-legged, as you Siouxs prefer to call them, and of course the ones that read of course, the fewer of those you 'ruffle," this Contrary paused, and I must mention that he also had a scholarly English accent as well. "Well, old chap, you just do not ruffle too many feathers in the literary world," the Contrary added with a bit of firmness. I may as well admit that their names are Finkley and Finchley. How in the world can an Indian and an Oglala Sioux, former combat warrior, have English contraries? Well, first they are what they are called. They are totally opposite, well almost, of what you think they should be. I have made a few trips to England, quite a few actually. Maybe they hitched a ride back with me. They were allowed in one of my books by a fairly prestigious publisher who obviously could have rejected them through the famous firm's considerable editing. Their actions and advice you just cannot make out sometimes, but be wary, often they are quite accurate.

I must move on and keep these two, Finkley and Finchley at bay. Maybe this is all a ploy of theirs to get you, Dear Reader to purchase the book where they were allowed to have their roles. One just cannot accurately predict a Contrary, is all I have to say. Yes, a bit of Sioux humor can indeed be a comforting respite for such a heavy dissertation.

What we have observed in the Spirit ceremony with the Spirits in command has proven to be quite 'contrary', so to speak at least in comparison to what Dominant Society has offered to its flocks and what it projects in regard to the separation of the sexes. In Mother Nature, balance is shown and practiced throughout. I hope that we have progressed enough to recognize that Creator is behind all. Direct observation speaks for itself. I do not believe man's egotistical ideas and selfish preferences will command much allowance in that abode beyond.

Wannabees and New Age

Won't I be considered a Want to be Indian if I partake in a sweat lodge or start to follow the principles of Black Elk's Vision?

Why did Black Elk issue his powerful vision out to the world through John Neihardt, the writer laureate of Nebraska? Chief Fools Crow, my mentor stated, "These ways are not ours alone. They are meant to be shared." My other mentor, the powerful medicine man, Bill Eagle Feather echoed Chief Fools Crow's words. With the environmental situation the planet is facing, all races cannot afford not to listen to the North American Indian, primarily those who have the philosophy and religious base common to the Northeastern tribes from which the Sioux came from. Detractors who think otherwise will have some tall explaining when they face Black Elk, Fools Crow and Eagle Feather in the Spirit World once they enter. I would not want to be in their shoes in the Spirit World especially with the disastrous happenings erupting in this world. They will be chastised severely.

Odd how the cowards want to pick on the mostly innocent New Age folks. To me, a New Ager is someone who has the brain power to stand up and say, "I'm not going to take this superstitious, all male, dominating, controlling Mumbo Jumbo anymore! I am going to spend my religious/spiritual journey seeking and studying other avenues." I may not be an adherent or follower of numerology, taro or horoscopes but our sweat lodge may not be of interest to them. Most speak highly of the Dalai Lama and I have to admit that I do as well. We are all so different from one another because of our varied experiences. It is the way Creator made us.

Native Americans who condemn New Agers should stop and seriously consider that:

1. It was not the New Agers that banned our religion and prohibited our language from being spoken.
2. No N. A. ever lobbied Congress to successfully have a Federal Insane Asylum erected to confine our holy men. The two hundred bodies (mostly innocent Sioux and Chippewa holy men) buried between the 5th and 6th fairways on the Canton, SD golf course have no connection to the New Age. Nor did they erect confining Boarding Schools upon reservation land, and had our children forced to attend where they received a pitiful education but plenty of Dominant Society's religion. It was a one way bus trip for the Indian students that separated them from their parents for nine months of the year. A six yr old must have felt very lonely, as well as the other ages also.
3. I have never seen or heard of a New Age (or Jewish) missionary or proselytizer. (I never met a New Age who demanded, passed out

literature or offered that I should join or take up his/her particular religious beliefs or convictions.)

4. In South and Central America it was not the N. A. that enslaved the Indian people to spend a life time of slavery in the silver and gold mines and which much of their mining product wound up in Portugal and Spain to gild the church altars and interiors.

5. Chief Crazy Horse spoke of cowards who condemn and blame the wrong people just before he died. I echo him. In my opinion you are a genuine, lowly coward to condemn the innocent and neglect to take a real look at what really happened! I will look forward to meeting any and all in the Spirit World who want to disagree!

6. I have a friend who wants me to add these comments. ….there are those culture vultures and spiritual pirates that will totally bastardize the Way just to make it accommodate their self centered foolish little lives…so that they can brag and be cool to their friends…both White and Indian…that's all that I meant by 'New Agers'. I should've called them the Culture Vultures rather than New Agers….my fault, but you know who I mean….You can tell those with an honest heart…but there are a lot that don't – they're all about the show.

Meeting God

'Eagle Man. Don't you believe you will meet God, in the Spirit World?'

Sorry folks, but I am a Teton Lakota. The old traditional Indian was loathe to issue out false promises, especially in the realm of the Spiritual. He/she had too much respect for Truth. When they did not know something for sure, they were not about to spew a bunch of sugar coated promises. How in the world would I know if we meet Creator or sit at Its side? Anyone that declares we do, is far less credible than the innocent person who declares they do not know for sure, my opinion.

I definitely believe a Spiritual Beyond exists and it is a 'home' so to speak. Creator takes care of us 'here' and obviously Creator takes care of us 'there' from what I have learned from my experiences in the Spirit Callings. I have such confidence and trust in the Ultimate Power that I do not fill my mind with what I consider foolish thoughts. I am quite content to be able to discover from my own culture that a Spirit Realm does exist. It gives me great confidence while I walk upon this present realm and reminds me daily to prepare myself for that Beyond Realm. My Creator is 'here' and It talks to me daily through all that it creates. I have a good feeling that It will continue to talk to me and have its presence all around me in that Beyond.

By honing my mind 'here' in respect to the ethics, morality, bravery, generosity and true respect, It wants all of us to exemplify; I firmly believe that in that Beyond, I can somehow become closer with the Ultimate Power - the Great Mystery - Wakan Tanka to we Sioux.

Beware the Marketers

Why would we want God to come down and greet each billion of us? What do we say? "Hi, God?" Do we end our conversation with, "Have a good day, God?" Of course the marketers are telling you all kinds of flowery and sweetened promises. It brings ecstasy to the enraptured audiences. Rock concerts do the same although a bit on the higher volume scale. You will be told that you will have a direct audience with thee Higher Power and even sit in or at 'His' right hand. Afterwards, all will become ultimate bliss for you. Most folks seem quite pleased with this conception and I expect few to adjust to my direction. Rock concerts offer no promises and are not scheduled weekly however, and therefore charge a higher fee for each performance. Both relieve the cheering sheep from their purses and mental drudgery. Eventually two-leggeds outgrow the rock concerts thankfully wherein most serious followers will commendably, seek interpretations of the Beyond based mostly on what men of millennia past have written and little if any from Direct Observation. At least, they will seek. One should be commended for seeking.

Suppositions of the Spirit World

I do not expect the world, at least members of a differing belief set to readily change from the way they have been raised. At least, not yet. Mother Earth is about to bear down severely however, and then tremendous attitude change will begin, obviously. The 'Great Awakening' is now in its beginning stages. I can only hope that modern man and woman start to use their own God-given, God-created minds now- to think more for themselves. I was once told, yes, told repeatedly that I was privy to *The* one 'True' religion. All through my childhood I believed fervently what I was told. I would have never believed that once I would leave college, soon I would have more open experiences and in my case it was my culture which would change my way of looking at a Spirituality which was here in my own backyard. The 'Way' of my ancestors, I would reach into, regardless if it was federally banned at the time. Had there been no Fools Crow or Bill Eagle Feather, or a Ben Black Elk, or maybe even the book of Ben Black Elk's father, I may have never changed. The old Sioux blood was one which could – adapt; adapt to what they considered was better. I changed for what I believed was better for me once I became more aware I was a Sioux. Not all Siouxs have adapted back to the way of our ancestors but each summer, according to the blossoming Sun Dances, the numbers increase significantly. For myself, I have absolutely no regrets.

Leaders (The Good Ones)

What changed me? Leaders did it for me; at least they thrust a questioning mind into motion. These leaders were not mere 'Saint's pictures on a wall'. They were living real. I had enough of the 'Saints on a wall' always with somber stares heavenward. They were unrelated Ghosts who had to have done a church's bidding to be thus elevated. Martin Luther, who turned the course of a corrupt church and tacked his defiance on a church door is not on those walls. Gandhi or Martin Luther King were not canonized. George Washington who refused to become a dictator, which he easily could have or Abraham Lincoln who freed the slaves are not there either. Ummh, this is the same Abraham Lincoln, however, who signed the order to hang 38 of my Dakota relatives the same week he signed the 'emancipation' proclamation. My DNA or whatever mystery it is from, bloodline maybe, refused to have or allow me to identify with such myth. Those gruesome, cold, unhappy appearing pictures on colored windows simply could not spiritually move me. Elevation is relevant on whom or who does the elevating; sort of like who writes the history of a people, the conquered or the conquerors. Two unlike versions result. The white man's church was too full of unpleasantness. To this day I abhor unpleasantness in a relationship be it social, personal or spiritual and rapidly walk away from such. My thoughts of Creator is one of Benevolence. It is not a wrathful or extreme punisher; although It does allow us to create our own unpleasantness in the Beyond should we choose untruthfulness and non-harmonic lifestyles. Providing Nature (Creator's Creation) is much more pleasant than it is unpleasant.

Humor…Yes, even humor!

I never met a missionary who could laugh like my people did! They had no funny Spider Iktomi stories or Heyoka clowns doing funny antics at pow wows. Bill Eagle Feather made me laugh many times. Everything of the missionaries seemed to condone suffering, control and fear. They even had Devils who could mystically fly around everywhere and mostly at night. They lurked behind doors, in closets, down in darkened basements and behind trees if you dared to go outside at night, waiting to pounce on you. Yet, I never physically met up with one let alone being 'pounced' upon. And no one I ever knew who claimed to support such things could ever show me or take me to one. I seriously believe that even the Pope of Rome, who claims to exorcize 'possessed' individuals, cannot convince me that such an exorcism-needy individual is indeed 'possessed'. People who do not believe in a Devil or Satan never need to be exorcized, do they? Hmmm...doesn't that tell you something? People who do not believe in a 'Sasquatch" have no fear of the woods unless they reasonably respect rare grizzly bears if they happen to be in the same area. My Creator has indicated too much evidence to prove that only Its supernatural power exists upon this planet. How insulting to Creator to think otherwise!

Superstition

As I said earlier and it is well worth repeating; *Superstition is like Drugs. If you never let it in. It can never harm you!* But there exist millions, No! Billions of superstitious sheep exist upon this planet. People love superstition! Despite the availability of knowledge-spawning modern communication they will continue to 'Baah, Baah' behind their Pied Pipers of control. Simply turn on your television on Sunday morning. You can watch the Extremes who are unconcerned about what is happening to the environment, world wide: Their loss; but unfortunately our planetary loss as well. I wonder how they will feel when they enter the Spirit World where I am surely hoping all Truth resides and hopefully will be revealed.

Does Superstition exist in Creator's created Nature or even out in space? If one relies on direct observation the answer is clearly; No! If Creator demonstrates to us that it is non-existent why is that so many fools proclaim the many forms and myriads of superstition? Well, likewise, gamblers believe in such a force as 'Luck' or often called- 'Lady Luck'. They deny the sheer mathematical odds that Creator has in effect and which the casinos rely faithfully upon. The gamblers lose and the casinos win.

The God-Given Mind

In my mind, I have now, greater insight, and can use my mind so much more and definitely have received so many more spiritual experiences. For some of you, your spiritual or religious experience is to go to church every Sunday, shake hands with your minister afterwards, feel pleasant and 'good': then do the same thing week after week until you die. Some may go to mass, attend or volunteer to go to confession occasionally and worry that you have a mortal sin here and there for breaking various church propagated rules. Too many of these folks are totally unconcerned about the ongoing reality of God's Creation - Nature. Yet the communicative news speaks of it daily! Basically, I see it this way. White Man wants fallible human to tell him who God is. The Indian will go out on his own and find

Creator by himself by studying what Creator shows him. This is the major difference between the two ways.

Denial

Some have even committed heinous tragedies against other individuals and their victims are out there suffering dearly from their perpetration, yet somehow, they comfortably look forward to meeting the Maker because they somehow have managed to be 'forgiven' at least by the words of some supporting, mere earthlings down here. Most people, obviously in this great land we abide in are quite satisfied with their religious insulation; thus performing their lives under prescribed protections or related forms of religious manner. Tom DeLay, the former Congressman from Texas is a not too shining example. From an insect exterminator he made millions in his reign through shady lobbyist contributions and connections. He adamantly portrayed his church affiliation and staunch beliefs when he came under serious investigation and finally was forced to resign from his powerful office. Most, and here I will single out for example; most pious Catholics simply cannot or/and refuse to condemn reported blatant atrocities committed by their hierarchy whether it was occasioned repeatedly in the past or is ongoing today, for example; the pedophile revelations. 'My Church, right or wrong' or 'It is all a planned conspiracy from the outside to destroy my Church.' These chants become litanies despite blatant evidence that the hierarchy constantly shifted repeated perpetrators to new parishes full of new victims with the same results. Instead of defrocking Cardinal Bernard Law of Boston, who covered up for the most dangerous priest, Rome came to his rescue. Willfully abetting a repeated victimizer molesting innocent youth is a criminal offense. Such barriers the powerful ego of the world's largest church can erect to hide Truth. A celibate priesthood is unnatural. It is contrary to Creator's Nature. Change! - and the Catholic Church will have fewer problems and far less lawsuits. At least with our memory concept, victims may receive their justice in the Spirit World while the truly honorable and often unheralded will receive their due honor.

Introspection

If we look at the white man's track record and especially in regard to their dealings with the American Indian, they have left out Creator's Truth in their character, reputation and yes… even in their religion.

For those who remain obstinate and stubborn to truthful introspection; "Have at it," is all I can say. I personally find that excuses that avoid introspection are dangerous to one's spirit. That is my choice however and theirs is their choice and I can understand why they would absolutely want no part of my spiritual attempts, interests or practice. They 'know' that I am on the errant path and 'know' I will meet my just' punishment while they can look on smugly with, 'I told you so!' I only 'know' that they shun placing new knowledge upon their 'Disks of Life' and their memory banks will have some extreme vacancies when they pass on.

Leadership, Superstition, Denial, Introspection: they can all lead you toward Truth or away from it. To embrace the Code; you must move toward it. Common sense is often the result of how Nature would do it and generally avoids foolish complication. False, errant, ego-driven and chosen ignorance merely projects man for himself with little rewarding wisdom as the outcome. His own kind suffer as a result but worse; it is Mother Earth that suffers as well. She, however, is now signaling a severe backlash. She will defeat his Untruth in the end.

Spiritual Leaders

I look at my old ways as a child, as what a child could believe in. As a warrior, a man, I have gone on so much further than the play of a child who was dependent upon adult provision, teaching and leadership. Except for my old spiritual leaders, who are all gone now, I just cannot get too enthralled about any particular religious leader at the present except of course brave, introspective, intelligent examples such as the Episcopal Bishop Spong or a Father Stolzman exhibits. I have to back up here and admit that I do find many an influential spiritual person every now and then, but most of those have no particular titles. Celinda Kaelin is one. Now, mostly, I lead myself with the wisdom of a Bishop Spong interceding at times or simply drawing tremendous strength in watching a young holy man conducting a Sun Dance and Creator happens by to move the cloud shapes in such a rewarding fashion or maybe viewing just a pair of 'real life' eagles hovering overhead at a very particular moment. I doubt if some detractor's claim, that imaginary 'evil spirits' can adjust the movement of a particular cloud or tell eagles where to fly. A bit more class than a Central Park Concert, I must say.

I refresh my spirit when I read or re-read what Sitting Bull or Crazy Horse did with their relatively short lives… or Gandhi or Martin Luther or Martin Luther King. The wisdom of Jack Weatherford's *Indian Givers* research proves to me that the Red People in America were remarkable individuals, enough so that Creator was no doubt, well pleased with them. Maybe an old book by James Corbett comes back, when the magnificent Bengal Tiger was truly free or Thor Heyerdahl teaching me again about Motane Island. I do combine the wisdom and knowledge of so many I have met upon my trail of life right along with what God's Nature is telling and revealing directly.

Over Population - The most serious environmental, planetary disaster which, of course, should be our utmost concern.

Creator designed and implemented Math and beyond ordinary Math, Creator also designed error-less exponential Math. Yet human ignores that which is before him. The Church ignores both Maths. Why? Because, "the Church is the Bride of Christ and she can do no wrong!" Such is the dogma of hierarchal men who deem themselves far above and removed from Creator's ultimate knowledge and wisdom. They ignore what the Ultimate Power reveals to all. Fortunately there are those who have avoided the foolish egoism and false superiority of Church leaders and their sheep followers in regard to serious environmental warning. Leading scientists and ordinary laymen of practical and respecting common sense are extremely concerned regarding human's utter ignorance regarding the over-population doom which human will not be able to walk away from in a very short time to come.

For those who have touted their Bible as the Ultimate answer to all of the world's problems...oddly...nothing within bespeaks of the environmental consequences starting now to besiege our planet earth!

Summary

So what do these thoughts and stories do for you, Dear Reader? You are not of a tribe; at least most of you and so very few of you are not from any tribal connection actually. No one has access to a Fools Crow or an Eagle Feather anymore, yet my nephew has discovered his spiritual leader and my daughter is in contact with several good spiritual leaders. My son conducts a sweat lodge on the lake shore behind him while his brother tends fire. You are now even barred from some Traditional Sioux ceremonies by some of our own leaders who seem to have brought 'politics' into our way, but then again that line needed to be drawn because of too many who could not conquer their egos and could not learn patience and true respect. We must mention that a long list of major Sioux holy men did not desire that such a proclamation should be so strongly worded. Time will rule out, is my belief. The Spirits will set the true course eventually which may borrow from both factions. Behind it all...Mother Earth (Creator's Creation) shall deliver the ultimate Remedy!

I have no answers or even much in the way of responses to these men-created dilemmas. I would like to see more harmony and understanding, yet can realize that somewhere a line in the sand needed to be drawn. Our beautiful, rewarding Nature approach toward the spiritual has survived its

Holocaust and now seems to be coursing onward is what is important. Hiawatha, Canton Insane Asylum; it is torn down, every single brick. All evidence meticulously covered.

Hopefully, many of you can now Think in a differing manner from what knowledge may have been gleaned from the experiences put forth here and hopefully to be coupled with your adventures out into Great Spirit's created Nature with possibly a more powerful vision. If so, then you are approaching the Code. I do have faith in the Spirits and find it hard to believe that a Spirit will reject you if you call upon them. If there is a sincere call and a need, I do not think that the Spirits will abandon your requests. Ask! A Spirit Guide is a very effective entity toward your progression. The Great Spirit does not favor one tribe only, is my firm belief. It certainly gives us adequate evidence that it has no intention of so doing. I think the Great Spirit may appreciate those who discover its values and the depth of its creations, however. Remember what the author, Stanley Vestal had to say about Chief Sitting Bull: "A man who . . .was devoutly religious, whose prayers were strong, and who generally got what he prayed for."

With this new insight as to the spiritual, it surely should be of such information that a newer outlook may have spawned within your own spirit. The projection of this information, happening or observation is by no means an intention to somehow 'save' any one or 'own' anyone. There will be no dues requested or sign up sheet offered. No religious organization of any sort will be spawned. I do hope, at least, that affected readers will become stronger environmentalists, however. Begin with reading Al Gore's works or seeing his film production. Go from there but do become involved and caring. Such true concern and care for Mother Earth could enhance one's status or standing in the beyond world. I also believe that the anti-environmentalists, the anti-Mothers, so to speak, are on shaky grounds, very rumbling grounds, actually, in regard to their reception into the afterlife. I am not one to hurl spiritual threats but maybe such a declaration in this danger becoming time could open the eyes of some few, at least.

Stand up for we Indigenous as well. We are not witchcraft or the degrading terms, heathens and pagans, which Dominant Society, especially their religious leaders ignorantly hurl at us. You may have to stand forth and educate a few, but also be prepared to walk away politely from the many who refuse to alter their false and hurtful views about us. Say to yourself: 'Mitakuye Oyasin.' (We are all related.)

You can remind them how patriotic we are; we tribal people in America who have the highest volunteer ratio in the armed services, especially in time of war. Not even allowed citizenship in WW I, yet Oglala Sioux volunteered and went to France. We prefer the Airborne, Rangers, Special Forces or the Marine Corps. Senator Inouye- D-Hawaii study, proves this claim. We also honor our returning warriors as occurred in the Vietnam Honoring related in the Participation chapter.

The Sioux are not as CNN and Dee Brown's lamenting book, *Bury My Heart at Wounded Knee* would like to depict us. 'Lo Behold the poor Indian!' We are a proud nation and have a track record to be absolutely proud of.

1. We kept our language. Most of the other tribes lost theirs. (Through little fault of their own, however.)
2. We kept our culture, customs, songs, and dance. At the pow wows across the nation, it is the Plains Indian that the dancers copy.
3. We kept our history and lineage.
4. Most importantly; we kept our religion (spirituality)! Our annual Sun Dance is held annually throughout our reservations in the summer. Our young men and women are deeply influenced and will carry it onward along with our sweat lodges and the confidence building Vision Quest.

Lastly, your insight into the Beyond! I trust that you will walk with a new confidence because you can realize new knowledge based on true observation and utilizing common sense is indeed reassuring. I rarely make predictions as I recognize I am not so thus gifted, but, Dominant Society, I presume, will now endeavor to distort this new knowledge which has been conveyed to you. Stand your ground! What happened within the pages of these writings you have just explored is all that the old leaders can leave you with, not me. A writer only conveys. The leader is what the writer relates from. Without the leaders, there would be nothing to relate. You may as well watch soap operas or read those silly romance novels that are meaningless to real knowledge. When we reach the Spirit World, you will be able to verify for yourself. I guess I have to add that you will be able to check on those with the ego-driven accusations also and mainly their motives for so doing. Creator's Truth, I do firmly believe is the total atmosphere of that entity beyond. Untruth is not a product or an ingredient of the Natural from what we can observe here on this realm. The Beyond, I would presume, will be purely pristine and unblemished. If it isn't, then many of us will be in for some sheer disappointment. Something tells me not to worry about it.

It seems from our observations and explorations, there does exist a Code. Some ceremonies seem to require a certain protocol in the manner of certain seeking, but as long as one acts sincerely from the heart and seeks in a truthful manner, I would expect a confidence-building connection eventually. We have now vicariously experienced the spiritual communication the Code allows. The so-called protocol, we have observed, was never a fine, given line after all, was it? Focus was required but who we are or were has no bearing, as long as we have the sincere, non-ego heart. Truth, unblemished, uncoated truth, is your connection to the Code. It is a challenging path to follow, is what I will leave you with.

Notes

Chapter 1
1. George Catlin, *Episodes From Life Among the Indians* (Norman: University of Oklahoma Press, 1959), p. xxv.
2. Ed McGaa, *Native Wisdom, Perceptions of the Natural Wa*y, (Tulsa, OK, Council Oak Books, 1995).

Chapter 3
1. Joseph Bruchac, *American Indian Museum* (New York: National Geographic Volume 206, no.3, September, 2004), Supplement.
2. Dr. Bea Medicine, *Learning to be an Anthropologist and Remaining "Native,"* (Urbana and Chicago: University of Chicago Press, 2001), p. 188.

Chapter 4
1. M. I. McCreight, *Chief Flying Hawk Memoirs*, (Pasadena, Trail's End Publishing Co., Inc., 1947), p. 117.

Chapter 5
1. Larry McMurtry, *Crazy Horse* (New York: Penguin, Inc., 1999), p. 12.
2. Ibid., p. 13.
3. 10. Ibid., pp. 7, 8.
4. Ibid., p. 8.
5. Ibid., p. 9.
6. Ibid., p.10.
7. Robb DeWall, *Crazy Horse and Korczak - The story of an epic mountain carving.* (Korczaks Heritage, Inc., Crazy Horse, SD, 1982), pp. 49-56, with some abbreviation.
8. Eli S. Ricker. Edited by Richard E. Jensen, *The Indian Interviews of Eli Ricker, 1903 – 1909* (University of Nebraska Press, Lincoln & London, 2005) p. 251.

Chapter 7
1. Time Editors, *War for the Plains* (Time-Life Books, Richmond, VA, 1994), p. 150.
2. M. I. McCreight, *Chief Flying Hawk Memoirs,* (Pasadena, Trail's End Publishing Co., Inc., 1947), pp. 111 – 115.

Chapter 8
1. Thor Heyerdahl, *Fatu-Hiva, Back to Nature* (New York: Doubleday and Company, 1974), pp. 198-202.
2. Bill Moyers, *Global Environmental Citizen Award speech (Boston: Center for Health and the Global Environment at H*arvard Medical School, 2004).
3. www.hiawatha.historicasylums.com
4. Dr. Dale Stover, *Eurocentrism and Native Americans: Review of Clyde Holler's Sun Dance Books and related commentary on other writers.* (www.aril.org/booksf97.htm).

Chapter 9
1. John Bryde, *Modern Indians* (Vermillion, SD: University of South Dakota Press, 1971).
2. Ibid.
3. M. I. McCreight, *Chief Flying Hawk Memoirs*, (Pasadena,Trail's End Publishing Co., Inc., 1947), p. 121.
4. Ibid., p. 118.

Chapter 10
1. Mikkel Aaland, *Sweat* (Santa Barbara: Capra Press, 1978).
2. Bruchac, Joseph, *The Native American Sweat Lodge: History & Legends* (Crossing Press, 1999).

Chapter 13
1. Powers - *Oglala Religion and Yuwipi* (Lincoln, NE: University of Nebraska Press, 1977 & 1982).

Other Books written by Ed McGaa

Mother Earth Spirituality:
Healing Ourselves and Our World

Rainbow Tribe:
Ordinary People Journeying on the Red Road

Native Wisdom:
Perceptions of the Natural Way

Eagle Vision:
A Sioux Novel of a Tribe's Return

Nature's Way:
Native Wisdom for Living in Balance with the Earth

Crazy Horse and Chief Red Cloud

These titles are available at www.edmcgaa.com and at most Barnes and Nobel and Borders book stores, or Amazon.com.

To order copies please go to www.edmcgaa.com
(Price: $15.00 + $3.00 S/H).

For Mail Orders please send a check or money order in
U.S. Funds to:
Four Directions, 188 Moreland Ave. E., W. St. Paul, MN 55118

Correspondence: eagleman4@aol.com or order@edmcgaa.com

I am often asked where one should send their donations regarding the Sioux. There are two main recommendations:

Crazy Horse Memorial
Avenue of the Chiefs
Crazy Horse, SD 57730-9506
A fascinating project with the
best Indian Museum in the
nation, in my opinion.

St. Joseph's Indian School
PO Box 89
Chamberlain, SD 57325
This school is a home for orphan
and foster care Indian children.